Citizenship and Disadvantaged Groups in Chile

Citizenship and Disadvantaged Groups in Chile

Pablo Marshall

LEXINGTON BOOKS
Lanham • Boulder • New York • London

Published by Lexington Books
An imprint of The Rowman & Littlefield Publishing Group, Inc.
4501 Forbes Boulevard, Suite 200, Lanham, Maryland 20706
www.rowman.com

6 Tinworth Street, London SE11 5AL, United Kingdom

British Library Cataloguing in Publication Information Available

Library of Congress Cataloging-in-Publication Data Available

ISBN 978-1-4985-6314-7 (cloth : alk. paper)
ISBN 978-1-4985-6316-1 (pbk. : alk. paper)
ISBN 978-1-4985-6315-4 (electronic)

∞™ The paper used in this publication meets the minimum requirements of American National Standard for Information Sciences Permanence of Paper for Printed Library Materials, ANSI/NISO Z39.48-1992.

Printed in the United States of America

Contents

Introduction

This volume studies the challenges, developments, and perspectives that various disadvantaged groups face in terms of their citizenship in Chile, adopting a heterogeneous array of theoretical premises and methodological perspectives. After setting the table through a brief overview of the constitutional framework that has characterized Chile in the last three decades and a brief discussion of the concept of citizenship, this introduction will offer an overview of the chapters of this book.

THE CHILEAN CONSTITUTIONAL ORDER: A COMPROMISE WITH AUTHORITARIANISM AND NEOLIBERALISM

The contemporary Chilean constitutional framework is the direct result of the compromises and consensuses forged by the leaders of the center-left parties and the elites of the civic-military dictatorship headed by General Augusto Pinochet—an arrangement supposedly oriented to achieve a peaceful transition to civilian rule and the progressive democratization of the constitutional order, but one that ultimately led to the permanence of the Constitution enacted by the Military Junta and, through it, of the political-economic neoliberal order that it symbolizes and entrenches.

The existing Constitution began to be drafted in October 1973, right after a military coup overthrew Socialist President Salvador Allende on September 11 of that year. The anticommunism that animated that seizure of power, and that led it to brutally repress the left and the unions, soon coalesced into the embrace of the neoliberal program promoted by a group of Chicago-trained economists, a truly revolutionary project that promised to disarticulate the social bases of the popular movement and to increase the wealth of the propertied classes. Jaime Guzmán, a young right-wing organizer and a law professor at the Catholic University, played a leading role in the process of drafting a new Constitution, enacted in 1980 after a plebiscite held during a state of siege and denounced as fraudulent by the opposition forces and international observers.

The coming into force of the Constitution in 1981 represented a significant change in the ideological foundations of the Chilean institutional order. Its bill of rights strongly reinforced property rights and economic freedoms, the very ideals that had animated the coup against Allende. They also articulated the normative foundations of the process of deregulation of social services that began that year with new legislation that allowed private individuals to open and own universities and that would continue with the privatization of social security and of health insurance. Labor legislation had already been revamped in 1979, creating a system of free dismissals, denying unions the right to strike, and reducing radically the scope of collective bargaining, changes that were also ratified in the text of the Constitution.

In terms of the structure of government, the Constitution established a period of 8 years in which the legislative and the executive power—the latter, including ample extraordinary powers to restrict public freedoms and individual rights—would be exercised respectively by the Junta and by Pinochet. The Constitution determined that, after this period, a plebiscite would either ratify or reject a presidential candidate proposed by the Junta; and that, after that event, elections would be held to elect a Congress whose powers had been reduced to give the President control of the legislative agenda. The possibility that this power could be used to transform the institutional order created by the Junta, however, was considerably reduced through three veritable *locks* on future legislative change: the electoral laws, instituting the so-called *binominal* system, which tended to create two coalitions with practically the same amount of seats in Congress; the requirement of a congressional supermajority for changing several laws that were not part of the Constitution; and the creation of a Constitutional Court in charge of controlling the compatibility of future legislation with the existing constitutional text and entrusted with ample powers to invalidate laws. In sum, in addition to entrench neoliberalism and authoritarianism, the Constitution protected these ideological programs against future democratic majorities.

The presidential candidate of the Junta turned out to be none other than Pinochet himself; who, to the surprise of many, including himself, lost the 1988 ballot. In securing this outcome, an important role was played by a new center-left coalition, the Concertación de Partidos por la Democracia, which included the Christian Democratic and the Socialist parties, whom before the coup had been strong rivals. The Concertación leaders sought to channel their opposition through the existing institutional means. Unsurprisingly, their decision to call people to participate in the 1988 plebiscite was criticized by more radical actors as a form of instilling legitimacy in the institutional processes of the Pinochet regime. The immediate success of their strategy, however, rewarded the center-left parties with considerable political gains, securing for their spokesperson, Patricio Aylwin, the key to the Presidential Palace La Moneda in the 1989 general elections.

Considering the historical circumstances, it would have been logical to expect the Concertación governments to maintain social mobilization in order to support democratizing reforms and redistributive policies; instead, what was delivered was social demobilization and ideological moderation. Several circumstances explain this outcome. Within the Concertación, the hegemonic position was held from the beginning by the more conservative faction of the Christian Democratic party, embodied in Aylwin, who in 1984 called the opposition to accept the validity of the existing Constitution and its transitional mechanisms in order to negotiate a peaceful transfer of power from the Junta to civilians. The economic advisors of the Concertación leaders, on their part, quickly experienced a convergence with their predecessors. And, for the left that joined the Concertación, the real and perceived failures of the Allende presidency, coupled with the ideological crises that both the Soviet world and the Western left began to experience at the time when Chilean socialists were living their exiles in Europe, triggered a process known as the *renovación socialista* (socialist renewal) that brought them closer to the kind of moderate politics promoted by Aylwin and the Christian Democrats.

Aylwin's approach to the constitutional problem created the opportunity for negotiating with the Junta some constitutional amendments in 1989. These amendments repealed a constitutional ban on communist ideas and decreased some of the powers that the Presidency had to control the legislative activity of Congress; but it preserved the existence of a significant portion of unelected senators, among whom four had to be former military. Another set of constitutional amendments in 2005 got rid of unelected senators and increased the sway of civilian over military authorities. The electoral laws were modified only in 2015. But the bill of rights, which creates powerful judicial remedies for the protection of private property and entrepreneurial freedom, and deprives social rights of any meaningful bite, has remained almost intact since 1990. And many other checks on majoritarian politics persist until today, including the existence of supermajoritarian requirements for modifying certain laws, and a Constitutional Court that most of the time serves as a *third chamber* that blocks legislation according to the political preferences of the right.

As a result of the existing constitutional constraints and the consensual political culture of the Concertación, the almost three decades of civilian rule since 1990 have witnessed very slow progress in fields related to political democratization and social equalization and saw practically no significant distributive policies beyond the neoliberal logic of targeting social spending to the poorest members of society. These conditions account for many of the shortcomings that the chapters of this book will study.

THE QUESTION OF CITIZENSHIP

What do we mean when we speak of citizenship? And what does that lofty ideal mean to disadvantaged groups? The first term, citizenship, undoubtedly presents a significant challenge to whomever tries to elaborate it conceptually. Fundamental concepts of political discourse, rightly characterized as essentially contested, are characteristically hard to pin down. The concept of citizenship is, to be sure, no exception.

Bearing that in mind, our objective in this section is not to set, once and for all, a definite and authoritative definition of the concept of citizenship, but rather to explore forms of understanding this notion, in such a way to render visible the theoretical agenda that brings together the essays that make up this volume. We suggest that the notion of citizenship can be understood in two different but largely complementary ways: i.e., as the active membership in a republican polity, and as the full enjoyment of the protections provided by an institutional order. We call these paradigms political citizenship and substantive citizenship.

The classical reference to understand political citizenship, in the sense that we understand it here, is undoubtedly Jean-Jacques Rousseau. While we do not aim to offer an examination of Rousseau's position within the history of ideas, it is worth noting that in *The Social Contract* (1762) he managed to radically transform the ideological orientation of contractarianism, which explains the emergence of political authority as the result of the collective surrender of individual prepolitical liberties to a central nexus. If Thomas Hobbes first developed it in *Leviathan* (1651) to justify complete obedience to the monarch, and if John Locke revamped it in the *Second Treatise of Government* (1689) to justify the elevation of the protection of property rights into the ultimate justification for the existence of the state, Rousseau reorganized this philosophical construct in order to cement a politically republican and economically egalitarian theory, one that would provide the intellectual seeds for revolutionary action and radical thought in the modern era.

Rousseau's understanding of citizenship is, indeed, and above all, republican in its nature. It expresses the status of a full member of the republican political community, one who can take initiative and summon others to collective action through public discourse and, in that way, enable collective self-government, the ultimate aim of the republican political project. The status of citizen is, in consequence, the cornerstone of a legitimate form of government. In Rousseau's terms, "[t]he constant will of all the members of the State is the general will; it is through it that they are citizens and free" (Rousseau 1997, p. 124). Only through the existence of citizens who take active part in the dealings of government can one attain freedom through government. Rousseau believed, prefiguring themes later on taken by deliberative democracy theorists, that this practice of government was the only way to reconcile self-interest and right, the utility of the majority and the imperatives of justice.

The Rousseauian paradigm of citizenship is also strongly linked to the idea that citizenship not only provides its holder with rights to voice and participation, but also with duties towards the political community anchored in the idea of civic virtue. As Rousseau himself put it, "[b]orn a citizen of a free State, and a member of the sovereign, the right to vote in it is enough to impose on me the duty to learn about public affairs, regardless of how weak might be the influence of my voice on them" (Rousseau 1997, p. 41). Rousseauian citizenship is, in consequence, not only an entitlement that confers the right to participate; it lays on the shoulders of its bearers the responsibility, even the duty sometimes, to take part in public life.

The political paradigm of citizenship seems to coincide reasonably with the commonsensical understanding of citizenship. In that sense, it could seem difficult at first hand to find another contribution that truly enlightens the notion from a different perspective. The merit goes to T. H. Marshall, whose contribution to contemporary reflection sought to underline, as the title of his most cited work suggests, the relation between citizenship and social class. In doing that, he not only offered a more dynamic idea of what the focus of citizenship is, but also emphasized that the notion of citizenship must be understood in relation to what it provides to the lives of its holders. It is in that sense that we refer to this complementary paradigm as substantive citizenship.

The historical context in which Marshall wrote, when the expansion of the welfare state in Britain had just reached its culmination with the creation in 1948 of the National Health Service, explains the progressive—and, from the present vantage point, almost naïve—confidence that he displayed in elaborating an almost teleological notion of citizenship that coincided with the institutional developments of his time. In that sense, Marshall could perhaps be described as the Hegel of the British welfare state. For Marshall, citizenship was a notion that had been constructed through the historical expansion of the sphere of substantive interests protected through state legality: first, civil citizenship had been built around the protection of individualistic interests, e.g., freedom of movement, freedom of speech, and private property; then, it had been expanded in the form of political citizenship through the creation of egalitarian institutions and processes of representation; and then, in the 20th century, social citizenship had been established through the creation of labor legislation and social services.

In Marshall's view, the institutions of the welfare state sought to redeem the promises of republican citizenship in the context of the industrial society, seeking to enable people of all social classes to nurture the ethos of civic virtue and to exercise their participatory freedoms. In that sense, we could see substantive citizenship as an artifact designed to make political citizenship a living reality. That substantive citizenship can present itself as a veritable condition of possibility of political citizenship results from the fact that the former covers or protects a wider array of substantive interests; i.e., not only negative freedoms and political participation, but also access to various primary goods (education, healthcare) presented conceptually as social rights. Their aim is not merely, as Marshall himself put it, "to abate the obvious nuisance of destitution in the lowest ranks of society," but it assumed the guise of "action modifying the whole pattern of social inequality" (Marshall 1950, p. 47). Where political citizenship is quite specific in terms of the link that it establishes between the individual and the institutional order, substantive citizenship is ampler: it can protect interests that are not strictly political in nature, such as the interest of having access to social security. It does so, nonetheless, for *political* reasons: the aim is to decrease patterns of social inequality in order to create space for a truly egalitarian republican politics.

OVERVIEW OF THE BOOK

As the reader will see, both the authoritarian and neoliberal legacy of the Pinochet dictatorship, on the one hand, and the diversity of manifestations of the idea of citizenship, on the other, are present in most of the chapters of this volume.

In chapter 1, Fernando Muñoz examines problems affecting gay, lesbian, and trans citizens. He introduces the concept of sexually diverse citizenship and analyses three episodes of the struggle for recognition of sexually diverse members of the community: lesbian parenting, discrimination for reason of sexual orientation and gender identity. Drawing on these case studies, he then argues that the protection of the interests of lesbian, gay, and trans people has exhibited a series of developments in the last decade that can be summarized succinctly as evidencing slow legal and institutional change in a context of steady cultural change.

The following four chapters address problems affecting women. Abortion, political participation, domestic violence, and sex work are considered in turn. In chapter 2, Lieta Vivaldi sketches a brief history of the feminist fight for abortion. The recent and quite limited legalization of abortion in cases in which woman's life is at risk, in cases of rape, and in cases of fetal anomalies incompatible with life can be understood only against a backdrop of a long-standing prohibition of abortion under any circumstances. Being one of the few countries that did not permit abortion situated Chile as a theater for feminist strategies that generated novel ways of resistance and agency on the margins of the law.

Chapter 3 also analyzes one of the main feminist issues of our time: the political participation of women. Yanira Zúñiga thoroughly describes and interprets the history of the struggle of women to access politics in post-dictatorship Chile. Her piece uses the concept of women's citizenship to highlight the democratic debate about the scarce presence of women in decision-making positions. The global debate on normative proposals to subvert the existing systems for distributing power in order to provide for more female participation is described as a dispute between provisional incentives to the political participation of women (*quotas*) and the structurally transformative principle of democratic parity. Using this theoretical framework, she explores the normative expansion and failure of those discourses in generating a transformative process of the Chilean political system. Her focus in the leadership of Michelle Bachelet provides some elements that confirm the advantages associated with the presence of women in politics, but also raises questions about the true impact of female leaders in the deconstruction of gender patterns.

In chapter 4, Paula Hollstein makes an interesting contribution to the Chilean debate on domestic violence trough a reinterpretation of the violation of human rights during Pinochet's dictatorship from a gender perspective. Her comparison between torture and domestic violence rests, on the one hand, on a detailed review of the literature in both concepts and, on the other hand, on a careful reading of stories of the victims of Pinochet's state terrorism and contemporary records of victims of domestic violence. She found dilemma, instrumentalization and pervasive psychological effects as the common elements among these two different phenomena, while the kind of relationship that mediates between victims and perpetrators remains the main point of difference among them. This difference permits Hollstein to suggest an approach based in a politics of care, promoting women's autonomy to deal with domestic violence while preferring a punitive approach to deal with terrorist torture.

Concluding the contributions focused on women's issues, chapter 5 observes the recent development in the mobilizations of sex workers for a demand for respect. In this chapter, Paula Nuño and Ximena Valencia focus on the absence of a regulation that promotes and protects the life and well-being of people engaged in sex work. Such absence permits violence and abusive identity controls by the police, as well as marginalization from the rest of society not only by being prevented to have access to housing, social security and health, but also by being unable to change jobs due to the social stigma. Feminist abolitionist and prohibitionist political discourses are duly discussed by the authors prior to formulating a proposal for decriminalization of sex work based on its recognition as work for all its legal purposes but also on the protection of sexual and reproductive rights of women who work in the provision of sexual services.

In chapter 6, Luis Villavicencio presents a case where issues of women's rights intersect with the problems that affect the Mapuche people, the main ethnic minority living in contemporary Chile. Addressing the main literature on the problem of multiculturalism, Villavicencio use the case of a minority within a minority to consider the main challenges that Chile must address to complete its transit to be a multicultural jurisdiction. Pluralist legal theory constitutes a field of negotiations to address to challenge of building mechanisms that support respect for the construction of an identity of self in the context of shared identities, while in practical terms intercultural jurisdictions may contribute to protect women's right to dissent within their communities. The Mapuche people are also considered by Matías Meza-Lopehandia in chapter 7, although in a less optimistic way. He considers the neoliberal policies implemented during the last 25 years by the Chilean government to tackle the demands of Mapuche people for recognition and redistribution in a critical light.

Cultural pluralism in Chile has become a more complex issue in the last twenty years. In addition to the revitalization of Mapuche demands, Chile has consolidated as one of the favorite destinations for those who look for social and economic opportunities in Latin-America. A synopsis of the various legal and social problems that the migratory process has been experiencing since the increase of mass immigration towards Chile is presented in chapter 8. Jaime Bassa and Fernanda Torres, some of the few scholars that have dealt with immigration from the legal perspective, analyze the current debate on Chilean immigration law. They focus on how the legal framework has an impact on the recognition and protection of the fundamental rights of immigrants, showing the existence of a significant gap between the international standards and the law that is applicable in the country.

In chapter 9, Paz Irarrázabal argues that there is a historical correlation between the politics of public order and consolidation of experiences of inequality in public space. Drawing on the concepts of oppression and discrimination, she analyses the power relations instantiated by the preventive power of Chilean police to ask for identification and search people in the streets. The control of the dangerous population is found as a trigger of this kind of strategy, which take advantage of the criminalization of petty offences to extend the use of police violence. This critical framework is used by Irarrázabal to illuminate the daily experiences of people controlled by the police through data collected from interviews addressing discrimination and police abuse, humiliating experiences, urban segregation and the lack of protection by the police of vulnerable groups.

There is a continuum of politics of exclusion that affects the underprivileged groups. While the focus of chapter 9 is the public intervention of the police in the street, chapter 10 focuses on the consolidation of a politics of exclusion that is perfected with mass incarceration and deprivations of several citizenship rights to those deprived of liberty. Pablo Marshall and Carla Moscoso trace connections between the concept of citizenship and the Chilean prison reality. They find that the most common prison practices and their understanding by the people subjected to them contribute to affirm that prisoners are not full members of the political community and that there is a productive breach that is exploited by prison and government authorities. The practices of degradation and arbitrary treatment are only compatible with a regime that overlap punitive, disciplinary and exclusionary rationalities.

In chapter 11, Jose Luis Ugarte, a leading labor law scholar, describes the model of labor relations prevailing in Chile, one that disempowers workers by making collective bargaining with employers difficult. This issue has profound importance to characterizing citizenship in contemporary Chile due to the social and symbolic impact that the neoliberal labor relations system has had in configuring the political subject of post-dictatorship Chile.

REFERENCES

Marshall, T. H. 1950. *Citizenship and Social Class, and Other Essays*. Cambridge: Cambridge University Press.

Rousseau, Jean-Jacques. 1997. *The Social Contract and Other Later Political Writings*. Cambridge: Cambridge University Press.

Chapter One

The Institutional Response to Sexually Diverse Citizenship

Readaptation and Resistance

Fernando Muñoz

INTRODUCTION: SEXUALLY DIVERSE CITIZENSHIP

Homophobia and transphobia, rooted in heteronormativity and cisnormativity, have been important sociocultural forces in contemporary Chile, the last country in South America to date to abolish its general ban on sexual intercourse among consenting adults of the same sex.[1] A substantial part of Chileans of all social classes and geographical regions have always considered it socially acceptable to display in public extremely derogatory attitudes towards gay, lesbian, trans, and other types of sexually diverse people; many TV shows displayed gay characters in stereotypical and demeaning ways; and acts of homophobic and transphobic violence were underprosecuted and went mostly ignored by the media and the public. However, in the last two decades, significant changes have taken place both in the terms of public conversations, from soap operas to political talk shows, and in the orientation of legislative and institutional action. Increasing segments of Chilean society are recognizing the legitimacy of sexual orientations and gender identities that, until quite recently, were dismissed as abnormal and morally corrupted; and sexual diversity is becoming an object of institutional protection. Quick cultural change, expressed in a rapid reversal of majoritarian beliefs about sexual orientation and gender identity, is triggering institutional change, expressed in the readaptation of legal and institutional apparatuses in order to protect sexually diverse people against lingering prejudice. And while the temporal sequence of events allows us to be optimistic about the increase in the public freedom and personal autonomy of sexually diverse people, a careful analysis of the circumstances that surround the changes in institutional attitudes towards them makes visible the hardships that sexually diverse individuals still face, even from the institutions that should be protecting them.

This chapter seeks to conceptualize and illustrate the institutional readaptation involved in providing protection to sexually diverse people against the threats that affect their lives. The premise of this analysis is that the transformations of the last two decades in the field of sexual diversity are contributing to establish in Chile what we could call sexually diverse citizenship , i.e., an institutionally protected status that seeks to guarantee gay, lesbian, trans, and other types of sexually diverse citizens the enjoyment of their fundamental rights. Sexually diverse citizenship is materialized through a normative repudiation of the specific forms of harm that affect those goods, written into constitutional clauses and landmark legislation, and through institutional designs and actions aimed at giving efficacy to that repudiation. Sexually diverse citizenship, in that sense, consists in the recognition and protection afforded by the legal system and the institutional order to the interests that define sexually diverse people collectively, expressed in its most abstract form as the interest to live lives that are in no way harmed or hindered as a consequence of their sexual orientation, their gender identity, or their free and consenting sexual conduct.

It could be argued that sexually diverse citizenship is the natural consequence of victory in the struggle for recognition of sexual difference. Thinking in these terms allows us to draw parallels with previous historical episodes of collective struggles for recognition. Once the collective interest of a certain group of people—think of the bourgeoisie, the working class, ethnic minorities, or women—gains moral and political recognition from the constituted powers within a political community, the natural political consequence is a readaptation and perhaps even a reordering of the concrete institutional order of that community. A victorious social struggle for political recognition should trigger dynamics of institutional readaptation to give shape and content to a new form of citizenship.

Nevertheless, sexually diverse citizenship faces significant threats, as heteronormativity and cisnormativity continue to make their effects felt in society and in its institutions even after political institutions have officially granted them recognition. This creates important questions: how effective are the protections offered by sexually diverse citizenship? To what extent do they achieve their objective? Answering them is vital in order to adequately ground our moral and political judgments about the true significance of the constitutional state for its sexually diverse citizens. We should remember Marx's lament about the 1848 French Constitution: "so long as the name of freedom was respected and only its actual realization prevented, of course in a legal way, the constitutional existence of liberty remained intact, inviolate, however mortal the blows dealt to its existence in actual life" (Marx 1963, 31). Sexually diverse citizenship, in light of this warning, reveals itself to be only as good as the constitutional principles, the legal rules, and the administrative actions that give it shape and content. In that sense, sexually diverse citizenship is no different from other forms of citizenship, such as political citizenship or social citizenship (Marshall 1950), whose substance depends on the institutional arrangements that materialize it.

It is necessary to recognize that the degree of citizenship afforded to a particular collective demand is a function of the intensity of the political recognition gained by its bearers, which often is in its turn a function of the collective power of that particular group. It is in this sense that the state apparatus can be described, as Poulantzas (1980) suggested, as an institutional condensation of relations of power and the complex and contradictory struggles to subvert them. Thus, although it is convenient to define citizenship as a status, we must keep in mind that this particular status is intrinsically relational and therefore dynamic, because what defines it is the effective relation that its holder has—or can have if necessary—with the institutions whose actions materialize the protections the status affords. In the case of groups whose victory in the social struggle for moral recognition is not complete and that lack political resources such as donors and lobbyists to mobilize institutional action, the dynamics of institutional readaptation will often be countered with dynamics of resistance and obstruction from the very institutions in charge of implementing the new form of citizenship.

In sum, the quality of sexually diverse citizenship depends on the variety and intensity of the protections effectively afforded by the institutional order to sexually diverse people. In order to assess its current state in Chile, I will here discuss a few cases that involve legislative and judicial action aimed at the institutional definition of the rights of sexually diverse citizens. These episodes give us a good sense of the recent debates that have shaped Chilean sexually diverse citizenship during its formative years. The 1999 legislative amendment that erased from the Penal Code the crime of sodomy, which sanctioned sex among consenting male adults, could be considered as the foundational moment of sexually diverse citizenship in Chile. It expressed a growing social and political consensus about the moral legitimacy of diverse sexual orientations that has provided historical impetus for a wave of further changes with respect to the institutional treatment of sexual diversity; since then, dynamics of institutional readaptation through legislative action began that made possible the legislative enactment of an Antidiscrimination Statute (2011) and of a Civil Partnership Agreement (2015).

The abolition of the crime of sodomy, to be sure, faced vehement opposition from conservative lawmakers; particularly from the right-wing congressmen of Unión Demócrata Independiente (UDI), the party that in postdictatorial Chilean politics assumed the defense of the legacy of the Pinochet dictatorship. Their congressional opposition to the decriminalization of sodomy forecasted the dynamics of institutional resistance to sexually diverse citizenship that ensued. Many of the fears and caricatures marshaled by UDI congressmen in opposition to the decriminalization of sexual relations among consenting male adults—including the belief that sexually diverse people all can transmit sexual diseases and are prone to pedophilia—reappear in the episodes that we will review. The cases in question involve the treatment given by the higher courts in the country to a lesbian mother who fought for keeping the tuition of her daughters and to a gay couple who petitioned the recognition on constitutional bases of their right to be married; the legislative debate around the creation of a judicial remedy against discrimination on the basis of, among other causes, sexual orientation and gender identity; and the response of lower courts to petitions filed by trans people who, in the face of legislative delay in the discussion of a statute recognizing the right to gender identity, demanded to have their gender identity recognized. Concluding remarks put an end to the chapter.

RESISTING SEXUALLY DIVERSE FAMILIES AT THE HIGHER COURTS: THE *ATALA* AND *PERALTA* CASES

Sexually diverse citizenship emphatically demands the recognition of sexually diverse families. Since creating a family is a fundamental and universal expression of personal autonomy, restricting the right to marry or the right to raise children to only some of the members of the society has always been interpreted as the creation of a second-class status. Sexually diverse families, however, represent a significant readaptation of the traditional family order characteristic of Western societies. It is no wonder that the recognition of marriage and parenting rights for sexually diverse couples and families have become important battlegrounds in the contemporary struggle for sexually diverse citizenship. The stakes of this struggle are even more evident in the case of Chile, whose Constitution, with Catholic undertones, declares family as the "fundamental nucleus of society" (article 1, 2nd paragraph). The argument for the recognition of sexually diverse families rests on the right to equal consideration of sexually diverse citizens; absent strong constitutional objections to their rights to institutional recognition for their marital bond and to raise children as parents, equal consideration demands that we grant those rights, enjoyed by heterosexual and cisgender families, to sexually diverse families.

Nevertheless, homophobic and transphobic beliefs can provide, from the perspective of those who hold them, normative and factual grounds to raise objections to sexually diverse parenting and marriage considered by their proponents as constitutionally compelling. This has been the case in Chile, where judges from the higher courts have couched in doctrinal terms their resistance to sexually diverse families. I will discuss here two examples: the 2004 ruling of the Supreme Court on the Atala case, involving the struggle of lesbian judge Karen Atala to keep custody of her daughters after she came out of the closet; and the 2011 decision of the Constitutional Tribunal on the Peralta case, involving three couples who petitioned the court for recognition of their right to equal marriage.[2]

The Atala case has become well-known because, after being decided by the Chilean Supreme Court, it landed on the Inter-American Court of Human Rights, becoming its first landmark case on sexual diversity rights. I will not discuss here the latter ruling, focusing instead on the lesbophobic arguments that were used to deny her parental rights and, through this, to exclude sexually diverse women from the constitutional definition of what a family is. Many factual circumstances surrounding the *Atala* case resemble the family stories of thousands of Chileans: Karen Atala, a law graduate who soon would become a judge, got married in 1993, had three daughters, born in 1994, 1998, and 1999, and dissolved her marriage in 2002, obtaining the children's custody after an agreement with her ex-husband, also a lawyer.

This is the point where the story diverges from the usual. On January 2003, and after finding out that Atala's lesbian partner had moved in with her, her ex-husband filed a custody lawsuit in the Villarrica Family Court claiming that her ex-wife was "not capable of taking care" of the children because "her new sexual life option and her cohabitation with another woman are producing and will necessarily produce damaging consequences to the minors' development." Among other lesbophobic (and far-fetched) arguments, the plaintiff pointed out that the mother's sexual practices exposed their daughters to the risk of contracting sexually transmitted diseases, such as herpes and AIDS. After a preliminary judgment granted custody to the father, a second ruling transferred it to Atala on October 2003, arguing that there was no evidence of "the existence of concrete facts that could damage the wellbeing of the minors due to the presence of the mother's partner at home."

Atala's ex-husband appealed to the Court of Appeals of Temuco on November 2003, which confirmed the lower court's decision on March 2004, leading him to file before the Supreme Court a disciplinary complaint or *recurso de queja* against the Temuco judges. This motion, whose primordial function is to punish judicial abuse or arbitrariness, at the time was often employed to enable the Court to change the content of lower-court decisions. The brief argued that the mother's behavior had caused in the minors "a confusion in sexual roles that interfered and will continue to interfere on the development of a clear, well-defined sexual identity." The complaint was received by the Supreme Court on April 2004, arguments were heard by mid-

May, and the ruling, favorable to the father, was delivered on May 31. To ground its decision, the Court wrote a short opinion where it presented in stark terms the psychosocial dangers created by the family structure provided by the mother and her lesbian partner. Its narrative blamed Atala for neglecting her maternal role in order to follow her sexual desire; in this account, "the father presented his lawsuit to gain his daughters' custody based on the fact that the decision taken by the mother of following her homosexual tendencies damages the full psychological development and the social environment of the three minors." The judges decided to deny Karen Atala custody of her children, arguing that, practically as a matter of definition, a same-sex couple could never provide a proper setting for raising children:

> this cohabitation may cause (detrimental effects) in the wellbeing and the psychological and emotional development of the daughters, considering their ages; the eventual confusion of sexual roles that can be produced in them due to the lack of a male parent at home and his replacement by a female person configures a risk situation for their full development as minors, from which they must be protected.

It was precisely the tone of this decision that made Atala and her lawyers present her case to the Inter-American Commission of Human Rights. It is worth noting that although the 2010 decision by the Inter-American Court of Human Rights instructed the Chilean state to formally acknowledge its blame in the discriminatory act against Karen Atala, one of the judges of the Supreme Court, acting officially as its spokesperson, insisted that their 2004 ruling was "not discriminatory" because it did not focus on the sexual orientation of Atala but rather "on the best interest of the children, on whose basis it concluded that the current situation at the time was one of risk, which is the reason why custody was granted to the father" (*El Mostrador* 2012).

Both the Supreme Court's own decision in the *Atala* case and its reaction to the Inter-American Court ruling evidence that homophobia lingers in Chile among institutions that are entrusted with protecting constitutional values. To some extent, this is to be expected in a country whose Constitution was drafted and enacted during a reactionary dictatorship that claimed to uphold Catholic values. In addition to the constitutional text, the constitutional legacy of the dictatorship is visible in the positions of power held by constitutional scholars and practitioners, often linked to the Universidad Católica de Chile law school, that to this day profess adherence to the constitutional work of the dictatorship, subscribe to a conservative Catholic interpretation of constitutional principles and rights, and articulate their opposition to women's sexual autonomy and to sexual diversity through the discourse of Catholic Natural Law (Muñoz 2014). This is particularly evident in the next case that we will overview: *Peralta con Servicio de Registro Civil*, where a substantial majority of the Constitutional Court ruled that the Chilean Constitution does not guarantee to same-sex couples a constitutional right to marriage.[3]

The Peralta case was fought by gay activists from the Movimiento de Inclusión y Liberación Homosexual (hereinafter, MOVILH) who wanted to trigger a pronouncement from the Constitutional Court on the right to equal marriage, invoking the right to equal protection under the law and the right to the full development of the human personality. In so doing, they challenged the constitutionality of article 102 of the Chilean Civil Code, which defines marriage as "a solemn contract that binds together a man and a woman irrevocably and for life, with the purpose of living together, procreating, and assisting each other." While public opinion on the issue of marriage equality still remains divided, the trend in the last decade shows a consistent increase in its support. In light of this progressive cultural change, the leadership of MOVILH thought that bringing a case before the courts could help to stir public opinion in their favor. This involved a risk from the perspective of sexually diverse citizenship, as the conservatism of many members of the Constitutional Court made it conceivable that a majority of them ruled that the constitutional protection guaranteed to families in article 1 of the Constitution was reserved exclusively to traditional, heterosexual marriage. The risk was deliberately welcomed by MOVILH, however, as this would allow them to try to bring the case under the jurisdiction of the Inter-American Court.

The case began in September 2010, when three same-sex couples were denied a marriage license by the Registry and Identification Service. The three couples, led by plaintiffs César Peralta and his partner Hans Arias and assisted by MOVILH, filed a *recurso de protección*, a suit for the protection of constitutional rights, before the Santiago Court of Appeals on October 2010. Given the constitutional implications of the case, the Court soon referred the matter to the Constitutional Tribunal. After granting certiorari on January 2011, the Court heard the attorney's arguments on July, and issued a decision on November 2011. Nine judges held jointly that the Court lacked jurisdiction on this matter and that it had to defer to the decisions taken within the political and legislative sphere. Only one dissenting judge sided with the plaintiffs, arguing that the Constitution prohibited discrimination based on legitimate personal choices or inclinations and that the clause restricting marriage to heterosexual couples had to be erased from the Civil Code.

The judges that made up the majority, however, added separate concurring opinions to express their substantive positions on the issue. One group, made up of three moderately progressive judges, called the legislator to create a solution for providing legal protections to same-sex couples, hinting that a civil partnership would be enough. The other five judges, however, wrote concurrent opinions arguing that marriage is, by its nature, a union between a man and a woman. Had they managed to gain one more vote, they would most likely have read this conclusion into the Constitution. Raúl Bertelsen, a member of the Opus Dei, wrote in his concurring opinion that "the social significance of marriage" is expressed in "the purposes that article 102 of the Civil Code recognizes, among which it includes procreation;" thus, he argued, "it is congruent that the law reserves the celebration [of marriage] only to people of different sex since *only the carnal union between them is what, naturally, may lead to produce procreation*, and that [the law] excludes persons of the same sex from the celebration [of marriage]." In his view, the reproductive complementarity between biologically different sexes provided sufficient justification for determining that the differential treatment given by the legislator to heterosexual and same-sex couples did not amount to a discriminatory difference under article 19.2 of the Constitution, which guarantees the right not to be discriminated against.

Judge Bertelsen's interpretation of the legal purposes of marriage, I have argued (Muñoz 2013, 18–19), is flawed. Procreation could conceivably be interpreted as a legal purpose of marriage in light of article 4 of the 1884 Civil Marriage Statute, which declared that people afflicted by "perpetual and incurable impotency" were legally barred from marrying. Marriages among impotent couples were, therefore, legally inexistent. But the 2004 law that legalized divorce also abolished that prohibition, legally dissociating marriage from procreation. Nowadays, to say in Chile that procreation is or should be a purpose of marriage can be either a moral, religious, or political statement, but it is certainly not an accurate claim about the law. Nevertheless, the fact that conservative and homophobic judges occupy positions of power that allow them effectively to say what the law is without regard to legal substance represents a significant obstacle to the dynamics of institutional readaptation that should be at work.

A PREJUDICED ANTIDISCRIMINATION STATUTE? HOMOPHOBIA IN CONGRESS DURING THE LEGISLATIVE DISCUSSION OF LAW 20.609

Homophobia and transphobia are not, sadly, characteristics that set Chilean judges apart from the other branches of government. In this section, I take a look at the legislative process that led to the enactment of Law 20.609, the Antidiscrimination Statute that came into force in 2012, in order to show how the delays in its congressional discussion made possible the inclusion of clauses inspired by prejudiced and demeaning fears of homosexual deviance.

The enactment on July 2012 of the Antidiscrimination Statute was meant to be an important milestone in the progress of sexually diverse people's interest in gaining protection against sex and gender discrimination from public and private actors. To be sure, discrimination is a problem that affects various kinds of persons for different kind of reasons; but there are good reasons to link the Antidiscrimination Statute to sexually diverse citizens. In the 1990s, social activists and constitutional scholars became aware that the judicial remedy for the protection of constitutional rights established in the Constitution, the *recurso de protección*, was both designed by the drafters of the Constitution and interpreted by the courts in a way that protected private property, but not the right to equality under the laws (Atria 1997). The effort to overcome this situation came from both civil society and academia. In the early 2000s, MOVILH, the gay rights organization, and professors from the Human Rights Clinic of Universidad Diego Portales (UDP) led a joint effort with other organizations to lobby the center-left government of Ricardo Lagos (2000–2006) for a constitutional amendment that would strengthen the clause that guarantees the right not to be discriminated against. They also drafted a comprehensive legal framework for fighting discrimination and asked the government to sponsor it.

At first, President Lagos accepted the first demand, but only to reverse its position soon. Since then, no constitutional amendment has been passed on the right not to be discriminated against. As to the second proposal, while President Lagos rejected the text drafted by activists and scholars, his legal advisors began working on their own version of an antidiscrimination bill, consisting of a set of declarative principles and the regulation of a judicial procedure for filing antidiscrimination lawsuits before courts of appeals. This bill, sent to Congress in March 2005, was approved in October 2005 by the Lower House, and then in June 2008 by the Senate Committee on Human Rights, only to get stuck in the Senate Committee on Constitutional Affairs and Justice for three years. It did not leave that desk until August 2011, after having its text drastically rewritten by the members of that Committee and their advisors.

Some of the alterations made to the bill sought to make a reality the political objective sought by the right-wing government of Sebastián Piñera (2010–2014) in the legislative process; as the Minister General Secretariat of the Presidency, Cristián Larroulet, put it when addressing the members of the Senate Committee on Constitutional Affairs and Justice, "to avoid that the creation of any judicial remedy that the bill may institute results in an abusive filing of lawsuits before the courts, which, in themselves, also affect other fundamental rights" (Biblioteca del Congreso 2012, 706). In other words, the objective of the Piñera administration was to make antidiscrimination lawsuits less effective in order to protect the honor and the economic interests of potential antidiscrimination defendants. The Senate Committee on Constitutional Affairs and Justice obliged, and in order to discourage litigation, it deprived the judicial remedy of a monetary compensation for the successful litigant, and introduced a penalty fee for the litigant who could not prove his claims. In the words of law professor and advisor to the Minister, Claudio Oliva, "the mere existence of such a norm would serve a dissuasive role" (Biblioteca del Congreso 2012, 707).

The actions of the Senate Committee were detrimental to the quality of the bill, but they were only part of the circumstances that have conspired to render the Antidiscrimination Statue inefficacious. As several scholars have noted, the Statute is plagued by shortcomings. It does not satisfy international standards in human rights protection (Díaz 2013); its wording does not seem to offer protection against discriminatory acts as such but only against discriminatory acts that impinge on another constitutional right (Díaz de Valdés 2013); and it does not create an administrative authority with the adequate powers to enforce it (Coddou y Vial 2013). Perhaps more problematic from the perspective of comparative antidiscrimination standards, it does not instruct judges to shift the onus of proof from the plaintiff to the defendant, and it does not instruct them to examine the arguments of a defendant *prima facie* suspected of discriminatory actions with a stricter level of scrutiny (Muñoz 2015a). All of these shortcomings, it must be noted, were already in place in the text sent by President Ricardo Lagos to Congress. Not only the right-wing, but also the center-left political forces are to blame for the inefficacies of the Statute.

But it was not everything. The Senate Committee on Constitutional Affairs and Justice added other things to the letter of the bill: more specifically, homophobic fears of pedophiles and rapists. This is what lies behind an amendment introduced by Christian Democratic Senators Soledad Alvear and Patricio Walker that declared that the law's protection against discrimination based on, among other things, sexual orientation,

> cannot be invoked to justify, validate, or exonerate conducts that constitute a breach of the laws or public order. Therefore, for example, will not be able to complain for discrimination for sexual orientation the individual who is indicted for sexual acts that are violent, incestuous, or oriented to minors, if they constitute a felony, in the terms of existing laws, or that offend against accepted standards of propriety. (Biblioteca del Congreso 2012, 765)

The legal advisor of the Christian Democratic senators and constitutional scholar, Patricio Zapata, explained during the senatorial meetings that this amendment sought to "prevent absurd or dangerous interpretations," and that the category of sexual orientation "cannot serve to protect or to legitimate the conduct of those individuals whose sexual interest is focused on minors (pedophilia), or that obtain pleasure inflicting pain to others (sadism), nor it comprises evident pathologies consisting in having an erotic fixation in animals (zoophilia) or objects (fetishism)." These explanations only make even more evident the homophobic imaginary that fed the amendment introduced to the bill by the Christian Democrat senators.

The second, explicitly homophobic sentence of the Alvear-Walker amendment was ultimately erased from the bill. But the first, implicitly homophobic sentence became part of the law as enacted. Its strange admonition, which reminds the reader that individuals who often are discriminated against have no right to break the law, reminds nevertheless of its origins, which lie in the belief of the senators Alvear and Walker that homosexual people not only have the tendency to commit sexual aggressions and perversities but also are treacherous enough to try to get rid of any punishment through convoluted legal interpretations.

How effective has the Antidiscrimination Statute been in providing judicial protection to citizens that have experienced discrimination, be it for their sexual orientation, gender identity, or any other grounds? Some news outlets announced that the coming into force of the Antidiscrimination Statute would result in a "deluge of lawsuits" (La Segunda 2012). But that was hardly the case: Oliva seems to have been right about the deterrent effect of the fine. In the first three years of the Antidiscrimination Statute, courts issued only 36 decisions on antidiscrimination lawsuits; only four of those decisions dealt with sexual orientation and gender identity and, among them, only one sided with the plaintiffs (Muñoz 2015b, 188).

The blame for the poor results of the Antidiscrimination Statute should not be attributed exclusively to the executive and to legislators. Judges, through their interpretation, have predominantly given the statute a restrictive reading. This is largely due to the prevalence among them of a formalist understanding of the concept of arbitrary discrimination, which restricts it to "irrational" and "capricious" behavior, "ungoverned by reason" and that lacks any justification whatsoever. This narrow understanding of the constitutional concept of arbitrary discrimination was embraced in the 1990s by the Supreme Court and has been used explicitly by judges to construe the Antidiscrimination Statute (Muñoz 2015a). With this restrictive definition of discrimination, it is not surprising that many judicial opinions declared, without much discussion, that in the case at stake there was no discrimination. Another frequent conclusion reached by many judges was that the plaintiff had not sufficiently proven the alleged facts or their discriminatory character. These decisions, however, show that judges have often employed a strict standard of proof and justification to evaluate the claims of antidiscrimination plaintiffs, instead of using flexible standards of proof and applying a close scrutiny to the evidence and the arguments offered by defendants (Muñoz 2015a). Unsurprisingly, in the very few cases when judges applied a strict scrutiny to the normative and factual allegations of the defendants, the judges tended to side with the plaintiffs. Judges, in sum, also hold considerable responsibility in the shortcomings of the Antidiscrimination Statute.

JUDICIAL RESPONSES IN FACE OF LEGISLATIVE INACTION: JUDICIAL RECOGNITION OF GENDER IDENTITY

In the last section we saw prejudice and indifference towards sexually diverse citizens in both the lawmaking and judicial processes. There are cases, however, where Chilean judges have stepped in, in the face of legislative inaction or delay, to readapt the legal system to the demands and needs of sexually diverse citizens. One of these cases has been the right to gender identity, where lower courts through their case-law have reinterpreted preexisting legislation on name changes in order to recognize the right of transgender citizens to have their social name and their gender identity recognized by state institutions. A recent decision by the Supreme Court not only ratified this jurisprudential trend, but also, recognizing the latest trend in the contemporary progression towards personal autonomy in respect to gender identity, freed the exercise of the right to gender identity from the requirement of a previous gender reassignment surgery.

Chile currently lacks legislation on the right to gender identity. In order to address this problem, some congressmen introduced on May 7, 2013, a bill that recognizes this right and creates a procedure for allowing transgender adults to change their name and gender at the Registry and Identification Service. After more than five years of legislative debate, however, this bill has not succeeded in coming into force, due to the opposition of key conservative members of Congress such as UDI Senator Jacqueline van Rysselberghe. The legislative delay in this matter suggests, nonetheless, that the recognition of the right to gender identity is not a political priority for the Executive and Congress. Still, the absence of a law that explicitly regulates the right of transgender people to have their name and gender officially recognized has not meant that this demand has been completely ignored by Chilean institutions. Judges have embraced through their case law a legal interpretation that has granted some individuals the right to have their name and gender changed. The traditional conservatism of Chilean courts, often staffed by old-fashioned personnel and in general reluctant to be perceived as a progressive actor in the social struggles and moral debates of the day, has been overcome in this matter through a legal strategy devised by the UDP Human Rights Clinic and activist organizations such as the Transgender Organization for the Dignity of Diversity.

This strategy consists in employing the name change procedure instituted by Law 17.344 of 1970 to request that courts instruct the Registry and Identification Service to recognize the name and gender of transgender applicants. This statute establishes that any person "may request, only once, that he be authorized to change his or her names or surnames," a request that may be presented only when they are "ridiculous, laughable, or morally or materially demean him or her" or "when the applicant has been known for more than five years, for plausible reasons, with names or surnames, or both, different from their own." The law also establishes that newborns cannot be given a name that is "equivocal with respect to their sex." Moral impairment, social recognition, and sexual equivocation have been the conceptual resources employed to build jurisprudentially a right to gender identity. Between 2012 and 2014, 86 judicial decisions were issued on applications for name and gender change presented by transgender people (Muñoz 2015c). Of these requests, 69 requests, representing 80.2% of the total, were accepted; 6, representing 7%, were partially accepted, accepting the name change but rejecting the gender change, often for absence of a gender reassignment surgery; and 11, representing 12.8%, were rejected. The overall trend suggested that the judicial construction of the right to gender identity relied on its simultaneous pathologization and surgicalization (Muñoz 2015c). In other words, while judges showed openness to medical narratives that portrayed gender dysphoria as a pathological condition that brings undeserved suffering to individuals, a moving plight that gave judges enough humanitarian impetus to espouse an expansive legal interpretation that left them assuming an activist position in the issue of gender identity, this medical paradigm led them to transform the performance of a gender reassignment surgery on the body of the transgender applicant into a condicio sine qua non for the recognition of gender identity.

The surgicalization of the right to gender identity, however, has been recently questioned by the Supreme Court in the case *Barrera Cea*, decided in May 2018. In this landmark ruling, the Supreme Court ruled that the Chilean legal system must recognize a right to gender identity to transgender citizens unconstrained by the condition of undergoing gender reassignment surgery. The progression of the case through the courts reveals the significance of the jurisprudential shift taken by the Supreme Court. The decision by the judge of first instance, issued on February 22, 2016, argued that, "since there exists no norm that regulates and authorizes the issue, the decision on applications for name and legal sex change of transgender people rests on the personal criterion of the judge hearing the case." In the case at stake, the judge observed that the plaintiff has not presented to the court sufficient evidence to back his application, specially noting the absence of any "medical records that confirm the performance of a sex reassignment surgery." The judge said that the inexistence of legislation for the official recognition of gender identity "is a problem that, in the opinion of the court, must be addressed by all of our society, but specially, in light of the legal, social, and cultural effects that the demand has, by the lawmaking authorities, a role that cannot be replaced by the reasonings that could be offered through a judicial opinion." After being confirmed by the Court of Appeals of Santiago on August 9, 2016, the case arrived to the Supreme Court for the revision of its legal reasoning. Almost two years later, on May 29, 2018, the

Fourth Chamber of the Supreme Court delivered its opinion, correcting the interpretation of the lower courts and reversing their decision not to accept the application of Barrera Cea. The opinion rebuked the thesis of the judge of first instance that in the absence of explicit legislation on the right to gender identity, the decision on applications for name and gender change was left to the personal discretion of the judge; "the interpretation of existing legislation," argued the Court, "must be performed in light of constitutional and legal principles," including in this case "the right to identity" belonging to "all people without discrimination." The Court pointed out that the Chilean state was bound by various human rights treaties that established the right not to be discriminated against, and it endorsed the recommendations and observations put forward by the Inter-American Court on Human Rights through its Advisory Opinion on Gender identity, and equality and non-discrimination with regard to same-sex couples, issued on January, 2018, which declared that member states could not demand gender reassignment surgeries as a precondition for the recognition of gender identity. The Court thus reversed the lower court's decision, condemning it as shaped by "a reductionist vision that would equal the legal definition of sex with only one of its dimensions, in this case, the presence of external male genitalia, neglecting the most important constitutional mandates and legal principles and harming the personal identity of the applicant."

The precedent set by the Fourth Chamber of the Supreme Court has increased the likelihood that individual transgender applicants can expect a favorable answer to their judicial applications for name and gender change. Nevertheless, the possibility that some first instance judges refuse to abide by the Court's ruling still creates some legal uncertainty for transgender citizens; and the delays and expenses involved in interacting with courts reduces the likelihood that members of this particularly vulnerable subset of the population will exercise their rights. At the time of this writing a bill regulating an administrative procedure for the exercise of the right to gender identity still lags in Congress; the question now is whether it will come into force any time soon and whether it can simplify and make more accessible the exercise of the right to gender identity. Only through a positive answer to these two questions could Congress pay its debt to transgender citizens.

CONCLUSION

This chapter has sought to describe the current institutional status of sexually diverse citizens in Chile. The cases we have examined suggest that the last two decades can be summarized succinctly as evidencing a slow and hurdled process of institutional readaptation to sexually diverse citizenship in a context of steady cultural change.

Specifically, with respect to the initial normative questions, two things can be said. Are Chilean institutions responsive to the specific needs required to combat heteronormativity, cisnormativity, homophobia, and transphobia in the specific Chilean context? A positive answer is not, after all, a possibility to be dismissed aprioristically. Several political demands and legal claims heard by various institutions in recent years would have been summarily dismissed one or two decades ago. The fact that some of these demands and claims were finally unmet should not erode the significance of having set the first step in the institutional door. A good example is the same-sex case heard by the Constitutional Court; it is reasonable to suggest that in the early 2000s the Court would have quickly and silently rejected granting certiorari in a case like this. In that sense, the Chilean institutional order should be characterized, as a whole, as more responsive to the needs and problems of its sexually diverse citizens.

However, that reflection should not be interpreted as commendation of the actions of the institutional actors themselves, e.g., legislators or judges, but rather as praise of the resistance of courageous individuals, combative groups, active social networks, and morally or politically committed litigants, that persisted in their struggle for justice against the reluctance of institutions that again and again sought to close their doors in their face. It is their hard work that made those institutions more responsive.

This leads us to the second normative question. Are the existing institutional means for the protection of sexually diverse citizens adequate for their goal? The answer is, sadly, no. In some cases, as with the Constitutional Court, we have institutions whose decisions have consistently sided against the recognition of the dignity of sexually diverse people and against the protection of their interests. At this point in time it is fair to say that never has the Constitutional Court worked as a defender of sexually diverse citizens. When it comes to the lawmaking powers, the Presidency and Congress, the record is certainly more heterogeneous and complex. Both the Presidency and a majority in Congress, in the last decade and a half, have shown a certain commitment to legislate in favor of the wellbeing of sexually diverse people. But this commitment has paled and waned when faced with the most polemically charged and thus consequential discussions, such as that of same-sex marriage. Interestingly, at the time of this writing, a bill to guarantee same-sex adoption has been announced, but still no same-sex marriage bill gains a foothold in the political arena. And in those cases where the lawmakers have produced a result, although with considerable delay, as in the case of the Antidiscrimination Statute, they have failed to come up with effective judicial remedies and administrative institutions endowed with the capacity to put an end to discrimination and to persecute and punish homophobia and transphobia. Judges, also, have failed to protect sexually diverse citizens against discrimination; their formalist view of key concepts and their passive understanding of their role set them as hurdles rather than allies of the antidiscrimination project. A few exceptions, and a few situations in which transformations begin to be apparent, restore our hope in the future.

There is a last inhabitant of the sociolegal ecosystem that these concluding remarks have not discussed so far: the academics, their participation in the production of new discourses and in the elaboration or implementation of new legislative or judicial strategies. That topic in itself would merit a whole research project in itself. How can legal scholars contribute, through their teaching duties, their disciplinary research, and their public involvement, to sustaining theoretically and technically the strategies for counterhegemonic social change that better fit the situation at stake, its institutional constraints and the correlation of forces that surrounds it? How have they tried so far to do it in contemporary Chile? I will finish here, leaving these questions open for consideration.

NOTES

1. This article forms part of Project FONDECYT 1180895, "Discriminación y Trabajo."

As a colony of Revolutionary France, French Guiana was the first South American territory to decriminalize same-sex intercourse among consenting adults through the 1791 Penal Code. Argentina, Bolivia, Brazil, Paraguay, Peru, and Suriname all decriminalized it in the 19th century. Uruguay (1934), Colombia (1981), Ecuador (1997), Falkland Islands (1989), Venezuela (1997), and Chile (1999) did so in the 20th century. Guyana still criminalizes same-sex sexual activity.

2. This section draws from (Muñoz 2013).
3. I argued this case before the Constitutional Court as co-counsel.

REFERENCES

Atria, Fernando. 1997. *Los Peligros de la Constitución: La Idea de Igualdad en la Jurisprudencia Nacional*. Santiago, Chile: Universidad Diego Portales.

Biblioteca del Congreso. 2012. "Historia de la Ley N° 20.609."

Coddou, Alberto, y Tomás Vial. 2013. "Estándares y criterios para la creación de un órgano antidiscriminación en Chile: desafíos pendientes y opciones institucionales." *Anuario de Derecho Público* 4: 216–33.

Díaz de Valdés, José Manuel. 2013. "¿Es la Ley Zamudio Verdaderamente una Ley General Antidiscriminación?" *Actualidad Jurídica* 28: 279–97.

Díaz, Iván. 2013. "Ley chilena contra la discriminación: una evaluación desde los derechos internacional y constitucional." *Revista chilena de derecho* 40 (2): 635–68.

El Mostrador. 2012. "La Suprema defiende polémico fallo contra Karen Atala que llevó a la CIDH a condenar al Estado de Chile." Online newspaper. 21 de marzo de 2012. http://www.elmostrador.cl/noticias/pais/2012/03/21/la-suprema-defiende-polemico-fallo-contra-karen-atala-que-llevo-a-la-cidh-a-condenar-al-estado-de-chile/.

La Segunda. 2012. "Discriminacion en Chile: La 'avalancha' de casos que podrán llegar a tribunales con la nueva ley." Online newspaper. 26 de mayo de 2012. http://www.lasegunda.com/Noticias/Nacional/2012/05/749578/discriminacion-en-chile-la-avalancha-de-casos-que-podran-llegar-a-tribunales-con-la-nueva-ley.

Marshall, T. H. 1950. *Citizenship and Social Class, and Other Essays.* Cambridge: Cambridge University Press.

Marx, Karl. 1963. *The 18th Brumaire of Louis Bonaparte*. New York: International Publishers.
Muñoz, Fernando. 2013. "El núcleo fundamental de la sociedad': Los argumentos contra la crianza homoparental en los casos Atala y Peralta." *Ius et Praxis* 19 (1): 7–33.
———. 2014. "Morning-After Decisions: Legal Mobilization Against Emergency Contraception in Chile." *Michigan Journal of Gender and Law* 21 (1): 123–76.
———. 2015a. "Estándares conceptuales y cargas procesales en el litigio antidiscriminación. Análisis crítico de la jurisprudencia sobre Ley Zamudio entre 2012 y 2015." *Revista de derecho (Valdivia)* 28: 145–67.
———. 2015b. "La Ley Zamudio en acción: sentencias de primera instancia sobre acción antidiscriminación emitidas entre diciembre de 2012 y marzo de 2015." *Anuario de Derecho Público* 6: 172–91.
———. 2015c. "El reconocimiento legal de la transexualidad en Chile mediante el procedimiento judicial de cambio de nombre: Un caso de complementariedad epistemológica entre medicina y derecho." *Revista médica de Chile* 143 (8): 1015–19.
———. 2016. "Cisnormatividad y transnormatividad como ideologías que articulan el tratamiento jurídico de la condición trans." *Revista Austral de Ciencias Sociales* 30: 161–81.
Poulantzas, Nicos. 1980. *State, Power, Socialism*. London: Verso.

Chapter Two

Autonomy, Vulnerability, and Resistance

Brief History of the Feminist Fight for Abortion

Lieta Vivaldi

INTRODUCTION

Until September 2017 Chile was one of the few countries in the world in which abortion was forbidden in any circumstances. Even if the life of the woman was at risk or if the pregnancy was a product of rape, women could not choose to have an abortion, leaving them to seek the procedure clandestinely. This was not always the case. From 1932 to 1989, the Health Code in Chile permitted therapeutic abortions. However, one of Pinochet's last acts in office was to make abortion completely forbidden. Feminists never imagined that once democracy was restored the prohibition would last for more than 25 years. From 1989, various bills to legalise abortion have been presented to the Senate and the Chamber of Deputies. Most were not even discussed, and the last attempt was defeated in the Senate in 2012. However, in 2015 President Bachelet introduced a bill in order to allow abortion in three circumstances: when a woman's life is in danger, when there are foetal anomalies incompatible with life, and in the case of rape. Since January 2015 until 1 August 2017 this bill was extensively discussed, finally approved, and then published the 23rd of September as the Law 21030, Regula la despenalización de la interrupción voluntaria del embarazo en tres causales (regulates the decriminalisation of the voluntary interruption of pregnancy on three grounds). A group of Senators and Deputies then filed two constitutional challenges before the law could be enacted. A strong opposition from conservatives delayed its approval and some aspects of the original bill were changed in order to limit the access to abortion. The law allows abortion only in limited cases, so women will continue to seek abortions clandestinely. There is still much work to do to fully recognize women's reproductive autonomy.

In this chapter I will first analyse the history of feminist formation and struggles regarding abortion in Chile, especially in terms of the impact of Pinochet's regime and neoliberal rationality. Following Foucault's lectures on governmentality, we can understand that even though the economy is perceived as an autonomous realm of reality, with its own laws and regularities, the rationality of markets expands to other spheres of life. Secondly, I will explore the use of Misoprostol, or medical abortion, which is a method that has decreased the risks associated with abortion dramatically. The case exemplifies how certain feminist circles have developed novel ways of communication and social awareness that may be interpreted as resistance in a Foucauldian sense.

BEING A POLITICAL WOMAN IN CHILE: FEMINISM, SOCIAL STRUGGLE, AND NEOLIBERALISM

In this section I will outline some features of the progressive formation of feminist activism and the fight for reproductive rights in Chile. At the beginning of the twentieth century, women started to organise themselves in clubs, groups, centres and meetings (Kirkwood 1982, 13–25). Not all of them were necessarily *feminist*, but they all claimed recognition in different aspects: cultural, economic, social, political and so on. Additionally, Chilean women engaged in international events, supported international women's organisations, and obtained support from them, especially the suffragette movement.

Furthermore, working-class women created their own organisations in which they began to analyse their position as women. Different publications with a feminist profile started to appear, for instance *La Alborada* (1905–1907), and later on, *La Palanca: publicación feminista de propaganda emancipatoria* (1908). Then, in 1913, Belén de Sárraga, Spanish anarchist, feminist, and anti-clerical activist, visited Chile and gave a series of talks on secularism and free thought. She denounced the role of the Church in the subordination of women (Maira et al. 2008, 19). The Chilean workers' feminist organisations incorporated these new ideas and formed well-organised women's centres expanding throughout the whole country (Observatorio 2009). Women declared themselves secular and freethinking; they encouraged education, spoke of free love and rejected marriage. From 1915 onwards, women from the middle and upper classes created their own ladies' clubs and reading groups (Baldez 2002, 13; Kirkwood 1982, 17). In 1919 the first Women's National Congress was founded, as a first project to obtain political and civil rights.

With regard to healthcare, in the first decades of the twentieth century, child mortality in Chile was among the highest in the world (Salazar, 1985). Poverty, social injustices and the lack of health care programmes concerned with reproductive rights prompted women to abort in order to control their fertility, with highly risky consequences. In Santiago alone, it is estimated that there were 7,000 abortions in 1923 (Del Campo 2008, 138).

In 1931, article 226 of the Public Health Code legalised abortion *for therapeutic purposes*, permitted if the life or health of the woman or foetus was in danger, for which the authorisation of three doctors was required. In 1967 the Public Health Code was modified by Decree with Force Law number 725, which established in its article 119 that the opinion of two doctors was required. The main impetus behind the regulation was to lower the high maternal mortality rate (cf. Bascuñan 2004; Del Campo 2008). However, what constituted "therapeutic purposes" was left ambiguous; from its legalisation in 1931 up until Pinochet's period in power, the interpretation of article 226 (later 119) changed throughout different governments. These shifts occurred due to diverse factors, such as the development of the public health system, women joining the workforce with unequal conditions, the suffragette movement, the urbanisation of the country and other cultural transformations that prompted the adaptation of public health policies (Matamala & Vivaldi 2014, 8). Del Campo states that for certain women it was simpler to get an abortion. For instance, the medical discourse was more lenient towards single women, as it was often assumed they were abandoned by a man, and therefore would face inevitable social condemnation for having fatherless children (2008, 143).

Despite the new regulation, the situation did not improve substantially, provoking a reaction from doctors. In 1935, the head of the San Borja Maternity Hospital, Victor Manuel Gacitua, wrote a report denouncing the catastrophic consequences that clandestine abortion had on women's lives (Eguiguren & Ferrer 2014, 24). In 1936, at the Convención de la Asociación Médica de Chile (AMECH), doctors agreed to propose so-called *scientific abortion* for social and economic reasons, as a solution to the high rates of maternal mortality (Del Campo 2008). Del Campo draws attention to the fact that it was the first time in Chile that doctors addressed reproductive rights. In fact, according to the participants of the abovementioned convention, it was necessary to prioritise women's lives over the embryo because "the existence of their offspring, who are already inhabiting this Earth, also depends on them" (Del Campo 2008, 163). Even though gender roles were reinforced in this declaration, which omitted the father and held women responsible for reproduction, it is interesting to note that the "conflict" between the woman and the foetus was resolved in favour of the former (Matamala & Vivaldi 2014, 9). Up until today, this "competition" between the foetus and the mother continues to be very significant in public debates, as I will analyse further on in the investigation. As I will discuss below, despite the progress made, the medical proposal to liberalise the abortion legislation did not succeed and therapeutic abortion continued to be the only kind of abortion accepted in Chile until 1989, when, as one of Pinochet's last acts in office, it was prohibited.

It was in the 1930s when women's movements started to articulate their demands regarding the regulation of reproductive rights, especially the possibility of having legal abortions. In 1935 a group of Chilean feminists founded the Movimiento Pro-Emancipación de la Mujer Chilena (Movement for the Emancipation of Chilean Women, MEMCH as per its initials in Spanish). This group was particularly interesting because it gathered women from different social classes, backgrounds and ages (Rosemblatt in Baldez 2002, 25). The MEMCH's statutes established that it was "a female organisation that aimed to attain the comprehensive emancipation of women, especially economic, legal, biological and political" (MEMCH 1938). The MEMCH was the first movement that clearly addressed fertility regulation as a women's issue (Jiles & Rojas 1992, 104). According to Jiles and Rojas, different reasons could have influenced the incorporation of these issues to the feminist demands: the family planning movement in Europe and the United States; the economic crisis that impacted the life quality of the population; and also awareness of the consequences suffered by women due to abortion and prostitution (Jiles & Rojas 1992, 104). Regarding abortion, they claimed that "with respect to our biological bodies, our actions will not stop until we call the attention of scientific and legal authorities to the distress caused to poor working women who are forced to get pregnant and to give birth repeatedly" (Caffarena 1935). They also pointed out that too often the result of this dire situation was a clandestine abortion, with all the problems that came with it: misery, malnutrition, forced abandonment, etc.

The MEMCH addressed its demands mainly to public health authorities and doctors. For instance, in 1935 it sent a letter to the Health Service Director demanding free contraception pills and treatments, which would enable women to "live as human beings" (cited in Jiles & Rojas 1992, 106). The recognition of reproductive rights was strongly associated with the condition of women as human beings. They also requested free abortion provided by the state for specific cases, such as large families, or those affected by illness or poverty. The MEMCH was against compulsory maternity, and it fought for the rights of working-class women, pre and post-natal care, access to nurseries, the right to breastfeed twice per day and fair wages. It declared that "society cannot ask women to have children if they do not give women means to feed them" (cited in Jiles & Rojas 1992, 107).

It is clear that abortion was an important concern for the feminist movement. At this point, however, it was understood mainly as a class problem: abortion should be permitted for those women who cannot afford to have children in "good conditions." The movement spoke in favour of abortion, but mostly focused on healthcare, poverty, and family planning. This is because the defence of abortion was mainly articulated in terms of working-class women, who suffered the worst consequences of unwanted pregnancies, economically and health-wise (Kirkwood 1990).

In 1946, the Partido Feminista Chileno was founded. In 1947 many women's organisations—religious, political, feminist and economic—came together to form the Federación Chilena de Instituciones Femeninas (FECHIF). Its main goal was to obtain the right to vote, which was gained in 1949. Since then, the women's movement began what Julieta Kirkwood has referred to as "period of silence" (1990). According to her, there were two main reasons for this retreat of women from politics. Firstly, after the suffrage achievement there was apparently no reason strong enough to unite the movement on a bigger scale. Secondly, the first female member of the Parliament, María de la Cruz, was expelled in the middle of a corruption case. She was also the president of the Partido Feminista Chileno. Kirkwood argues that this episode would have created a feeling among women that, as women, they were not prepared for politics. Kirkwood (1982) also analyses the way the Partido Feminista Chileno was attacked by traditional political parties, creating internal divisions and a weakening of the movement. From this moment, women who continued in politics participated in social projects but did not necessarily have a discourse centred on the emancipation of women.

In 1964, a subsidised "family planning programme" was implemented under the government of Eduardo Frei, a Catholic President from the Democracia Cristiana party. The family planning programme was created in order to reduce maternal mortality and unwanted pregnancies, it included the provision of contraceptive and intrauterine devices, and also the creation of the first national programme for sexual education (Brito 2012, 149; McGuire 2010; Jiles 1994). The plan was completely guaranteed by the State, as a matter of fact "Chile became the first Latin American country, outside of Cuba, to inaugurate a publicly subsidized family programme." (Casas & Shepard 2007, 202). It was developed under the leadership of progressive medics and the Asociación Chilena de Protección de la Familia (APROFA), a branch of the International Planned Parenthood Federation (IPPF). It was also a reaction to complications from clandestine abortions. In 1964, it is estimated that there were around 70,000 hospitalisations due to abortion complications (Matamala & Vivaldi 2014, 10).

As with many of the public policies on reproductive issues, the aims and means of the family planning programme were contentious. The family programme faced strong criticism from the Catholic Church and also from some left-wing sectors. The latter were suspicious of the intentions behind population control, because they linked it to the U.S. agenda (Matamala & Vivaldi 2014, 11).

According to Brito et al., in general, the measures related more to medical intervention than to a woman's autonomy over her body (2012, 147–14). It could be said that family planning is a specific site in which the two poles of biopower intersect (the anatomo-politics of the individual body and the biopolitics of the population). Feminist studies have shown how demographic concerns do play a role in reproductive policies, as women are encouraged to have children or dissuaded from doing so, based on health, racial, ethnic or class reasons (cf. Yuval-Davis et al. 1989, Mottier & Gerodetti 2007). This can be seen as a way of disciplining women by means of the "meticulous control of the operations of the body" (Foucault 1977, 137). Through the use of *productive* techniques, women follow a series of instructions in order to organise their sexuality and be able to control their reproduction.

Even though the programme did not embrace a gender or women's-rights perspective, at least women did have some control over their fertility. It improved the practical conditions of many, because the possibility to have access to contraception enabled women to make decisions (Rojas 1994). Brito et al's view (2012) excludes any explicit agency by women, and in this sense aligns with Foucault's concept of docile bodies.

The results this time were as expected; maternal deaths and hospitalisations decreased dramatically (cf. Faundez, Jiles & McGuire). During Allende's government (1970–1973), Frei's programmes were improved and made accessible for all women of reproductive age (Brito et al. 2012, 149). Healthcare policies were strengthened, promoting the distribution of contraceptives and professional attention throughout the entire pregnancy and post-pregnancy periods. Different politicians openly supported abortion on women's request and this was also reflected in the media. (Matamala & Vivaldi 2014, 12–13). Although public policies were still focused on *mothers and families*, the idea of women being able to decide how, when, and whether to have children became a crucial point of discussion for the government. The abortion regulation was more freely interpreted, allowing a factual different implementation of the law. In the Hospital Barros Luco a group of doctors interpreted the law broadly, permitting abortions until the 12th week of pregnancy upon women's request (Pieper 2009; Matamala & Vivaldi 2014).

During this period women participated in political parties, contributing to the different social change programmes that were happening in the country. However, the focus was not on any specific feminist demands.

After the coup d'état, which in 1973 abruptly ended Allende's socialist project, a new system was forcefully instituted. In order to do so, the State used extreme violence and in the period 1973–1990 almost 3,000 people died and at least 400,000 were tortured according to the *Report of the Truth and*

Reconciliation Commission (1991) and the *Report on Political Prisoners and Torture* (2010). Pinochet remained in power until 1990, when Patricio Aylwin, of the Democracia Cristiana party, was democratically elected. One of the last measures taken by Pinochet was the total prohibition of abortion and until as recently as September 2017 this remained unchanged. In fact, since the beginning of the dictatorship the policies promoting population growth were explicit (Jiles & Rojas 1992; Matamala & Vivaldi 2014).

In order to understand the abortion prohibition, we need to consider a more general account of Pinochet's rule, especially the establishment of neoliberalism and the strong influence of Catholicism, and Natural Law, among the supporters of the dictatorial regime and patriarchy. Neoliberalism can be understood as a political rationality in which the principles of the market serve as regulative principles in other areas of social conducts and power strategies (Brown 2005; Gane 2012). The dictatorial period under the government of Pinochet (1973–1989) converted Chile into a laboratory of neoliberalism. This entailed the privatisation of public goods, deregulation and cuts to social spending, and the maximisation of production and consumption. The main ideologues behind these economic transformations were the so-called Chicago Boys, named as such because they closely followed the ideas of Milton Friedman and other economists of the University of Chicago (Dezalay & Garth 2002; Valdés 1995). This was also reflected in the Chilean Constitution (approved by Chilean voters in a controversial plebiscite in 1980), which strongly protects property rights and economic freedoms, and excludes social, political, and economic rights from its scope, giving only the thin protection of equality before the law. Social rights, benefits and services guaranteed by the state were now the responsibility of the individual, whose freedom was the freedom to choose and acquire goods and services. The philosophy of *laissez-faire*, with its economic and individual liberties, most prominently associated with neoliberalism, conceals permanent forms of vigilance, activity, and intervention. (Foucault 2008, 132)

The Chilean Constitution and the main regulations and policies implemented in the country during Pinochet's dictatorship were closely tied to religion, specifically to the influence of Catholic groups (Muñoz 2014, 129). Natural law discourses thus provided a foundation for Chilean regulations and, in a way, the coup itself. Despite the bloody measures adopted by Pinochet, the right to life was for the first time explicitly protected by the Constitution. The right to life is currently justified by scholars through the invocation of God or religious ideologies. Reviewing the works of Catholic constitutional law professors who have written about the right to life, Figueroa observes that most of them "tend to mention God, Christian ethics, or forthrightly Catholic morals' when they explore the constitutional concept of personhood and the foundations of the right to life" (cited in Muñoz 2014, 133) We can see the Natural Law embedded in the Constitution in article 5, which stipulates the following: "The exercise of sovereignty recognises as a limitation the respect for the essential rights originating from human nature."

Additionally, the military regime forcefully attempted to return to "conventional moral values" (Ríos 2003). The sociologist Maria Elena Valenzuela claims that this regime can be understood as the archetypal expression of patriarchy, reinforcing the role of women as mothers and dependants, thus promoting inequality within the family (cited in Ríos 2003). In 1979 the National Development Plan by the Office of National Development (ODEPLAN) exposed the regime's plans to develop the nation, based on a doctrine of authoritarism, Christian values and nationalism. Its ideas of nationhood relied on essentialist ideas of women (ODEPLAN 1979).

A clear example of this conception of women can be found in Pinochet's speech for the anniversary of the National Women's Office, in which he claimed "When a woman becomes a mother she does not look for anything else materially; she seeks and finds in her own child the goal of her life, her only treasure, and the target of all her dreams" (cited in Valdés 1995, 203). A pro-family bioeconomy was therefore implemented and traditional values were reinforced (Harvey 2005, 39) This reinforcement of traditional values was also happening through the work of other institutions, like the Centro de Madres (CEMA) (cf. Valdes et al 1989).

It is hardly necessary to underline the patriarchal and heteronormative overtones of his speech, but I would like to show how this type of discourse had consequences for the rearticulation of the women's movement. As is widely known, the military regime was a period of strong social and political repression: people were disappeared, tortured and murdered as part of State policy. Social movements, strongly present during the Unidad Popular, were suppressed during this terror campaign. However, at the end of the 1970s and the beginning of the 1980s, some groups started to re-emerge, among them women's groups. The government's position towards women in fact made their public political meetings possible. The government did not see women's groups as a political risk to the regime. The role of women was seen as limited to the family and the private sphere, and it was traditional political parties mostly associated with men which were repressed. In this context, women organised around their efforts to find their relatives, but also in relation to the care of children and other daily activities such as cooking (the *ollas comunes*, soup kitchens) and various workshops in poor settlements. In this period, specifically in 1977, the Círculo de Estudios de La Mujer (Women's Studies Circle) was founded, it was the first explicitly feminist organisation at the time. During the 1980s diverse women's organisations appeared, for instance Mujeres por la vida (1983). While discussing democracy, women became more aware about the strong injustices that they faced simply for being women (Gaviola 1994). As Julieta Kirkwood (1990) has shown, the struggle against the authoritarian regime also made evident other forms of authority that women lived under prior to the coup.

The discourse about reproductive rights and the right to choose in the Chilean feminist movement entered the discussion in the 1980s. Women started to talk about reproductive rights and denounced the injustices committed in the patriarchal and neoliberal system regarding the lack of control over their bodies (Kirkwood 1990). They saw the abortion restriction as an issue linked to the state and male control over reproduction (Maira 2008). Specifically, the prohibition was seen as a patriarchal weapon that a democratic country should defeat. This democratic future imagined by feminists did not happen.

In 1989, abortion was prohibited in every circumstance by Statute No 18.826, of the 15th of September of the same year, changing the Public Health Code and establishing that "No action will be performed in which the aim is to provoke an abortion." The Chilean Constitution in its article 19 N°1 establishes "[t]he right to life and to the physical and psychological integrity of the individual," adding that "[t]he law protects the life of those about to be born." This last paragraph was interpreted in contradictory ways: for some scholars it constituted ban on abortion (see, for instance, Cea 2012; Vivanco 2004) and for others it was just a protection mandate (see, for instance, Bascuñán 2004; Figueroa 2007; Gómez 2005)

The transition to democracy was based on agreements and moderation. The first democratically elected government established an institution responsible for women's affairs, the Servicio Nacional de la Mujer (SERNAM); international and national agreements were ratified, and offices and programmes for women multiplied at all levels of public administration (municipalities, ministries, services), as well as in universities, trade unions and political parties.[1] Some significant regulations were approved, such as one that made it possible to get divorced. However, these changes did not challenge gender roles, especially regarding reproductive rights. There were some attempts to legalise abortion, at least in some circumstances, but all of them were unsuccessful (cf. Maturana 2014; Casas & Vivaldi 2013) until 2017. There have also been some specific events since the mid-2000s when the topic of abortion and reproductive rights has been widely discussed, for instance the legal battle regarding the distribution of the emergency contraception pill (see, for instance, Muñoz 2014; Marshall et al. 2008; Jimenez & Marshall 2010), or the case of Belen, a 11-year-old girl who became pregnant in 2013 after being systematically abused by her stepfather, which appeared in the national and international media.

There are two main strategies which have been implemented the last few years in Chile by feminist groups regarding abortion and reproductive rights. On the one hand, the strategy of legal reforms has sought changes from the governments and regulations in laws and public policies. These changes have included the legalisation of abortion at least on certain grounds, and the support and elaboration of different laws not just regarding abortion but reproductive rights in general, as in the year 2000 with the "Norms About Information, Orientation, and Services regarding Regulation of Fertility." More recently different feminists and feminist organizations signed a letter written by the feminist NGO Humanas in March 2016, asking Congress and the President to defend the original bill. As it was said in the introduction, the bill was finally published on September 2017. The other strategy is the cultural and social legalisation of abortion, whereby feminist groups have created spaces for discussion, debate and sensitisation about the common experience of abortion and also to offer actual support to those women who were experiencing an abortion. I will analyse one specific case of this second strategy in the next section.

FEMINISM AND CARE OF THE SELF IN MEDICAL ABORTIONS

In this section I will consider the propagation of misoprostol by the Free Abortion Hotline as an example of strategies on the part of feminist groups to culturally and socially decriminalise abortion, and to help women actually have abortions. I will argue that its social and political significance or interest resides in part in the bio-political implications inherent in the use of a prohibited drug in a power struggle over the control of women's bodies and their reproductive rights, but even more in the fact that it is an instance of feminist political agency. Besides the fact that misoprostol promotes both women's autonomy and vulnerability, this case exemplifies how certain feminist circles have developed novel ways of communication and social awareness that may be interpreted as resistance in a Foucauldian sense. I will proceed by describing the main social aspects of the use of misoprostol for abortions in Chile, and then turn to the role of the Free Abortion Hotline in that context. Finally, I will make a Foucauldian reading of the social function of the Hotline.

AUTONOMY AND VULNERABILITY: THE USE OF MISOPROSTOL

Misoprostol was originally used for gastric ulcers, but it can also be used to end pregnancies because it causes contractions in the uterus, thus interrupting gestation. In 2003 The World Health Organization (WHO) issued specific instructions in order to guarantee a safe abortion using misoprostol. In the past 15 years the use of misoprostol to end pregnancies has increased significantly, lowering the risks associated with other methods, such as rubber probes, scissors, wires, or other riskier methods (Chong et al. 2004). Misoprostol is a scientific dispositive playing a role in this social struggle in which many variables intersect (Ganatra, Guest & Berer 2015; Berer & Hoggart 2018).

It is important to emphasise that abortion has long been a significant cause of maternal mortality, and in many countries where some form of abortion is now lawful, legislators were motivated to lift the abortion ban by the prospect of protecting women's lives. Chile has one of the lowest rates of maternal mortality in Latin America: 26 per 100,000 live births, comparable to the U.S. rate of 24 per 100,000 (Molina & Cartes et al. 2013). There are probably many reasons for the decline of maternal mortality over the years: among the most significant factors we can count government subsidised birth control, post-abortion care, and also access to safer but illegal abortion procedures like the use of misoprostol (See, for instance, Laufarie et al. 2005; Zambarlie et al. 2012). In Chile, as elsewhere, the banning of abortion does not do away with its practice; it simply drives it underground. As one might expect, there is no certainty about the numbers of clandestine abortions (estimated between 65,000 and 160,000) (Casas & Vivaldi 2013). The safety of clandestine abortions varies depending on cost, social contacts, and personal networks.

Furthermore, the case of misoprostol involves the exposure of women to black markets. In Chile, the public commercialisation of misoprostol was restricted in 2001, and nowadays it is not possible to buy it in pharmacies. However, the pills are clandestinely sold on the Internet, and can be bought in other countries. While there are some international NGOs which send misoprostol to Chile by mail, the majority of women seeking the drug in Chile must navigate the black market, with no guidance as to where and how to buy it. Additionally, as most abortions remain hidden and the rate of death due to abortion complications is low (Molina & Cartes et al. 2013), some have argued that the prohibition of abortion does not have a real impact on mortality or morbidity. Consequently, they argue that there is no need to liberalise the current legislation, thus contributing to the perpetuation of present hardships for women (Koch et al. 2012).

The social situation generated by the use of misoprostol is ambivalent, and touches on key issues of agency or even resistance against medical and legal power. On the one hand, the use of misoprostol promotes women's control over their own reproduction: the fact that a doctor is not needed to perform an abortion is not new, but it is of great significance. Certainly, women have attained abortions for a long time and in a variety of ways (Jiles/Rojas 1992). However, misoprostol is safer and easier than many of them. The doctor or midwife (and hence the state) is no longer needed, and women can perform the abortion in their own homes and in the company that they choose. This independence, of course, is not free of difficulties.

The same situation can be seen from a different perspective. In the private realm, the woman is responsible for her own abortion, and in light of this, the problem is the way this situation places the entire burden on women's shoulders. Moreover, this situation liberates the Chilean State from the responsibility of providing any standard of abortion healthcare. Of course, what exactly this standard would amount to is a contentious issue, not just in Chile. Take, for instance, the work of Myra Ferree et al., who compares the feminist positions in the United States and Germany (2002). In the case of the United States, as abortion is founded on the right to privacy and choice, feminists such as MacKinnon (1989) have asked for more State intervention in the provision of women's welfare, including politics of fertility control, methods of contraception, and medical support. In contrast, in Germany the foetus is constitutionally protected and, although counselling is needed, the State must provide the infrastructure and care that is required for the woman's welfare. In the case of Germany, the need for counselling has been criticised for being too paternalistic and patronising to women. In the case of Chile, the politics and policies regarding sexual education, contraceptive methods, and medical confidentiality have been in permanent dispute (cf. Shepard 2000; Araujo 2005). Paradoxically, those who oppose the abortion liberalisation have also opposed policies geared towards controlling reproduction, such as sex education (Palma et al. 2013).

This pattern of vulnerabilisation by means of the retreat of the involvement of the State in public welfare matches a trend of late neoliberal rationality, which makes individuals "responsible for themselves," involving, as stated above, a paradoxical process of liberty accompanied by increasing vulnerability. In the words of Wendy Brown, neoliberalism "figures individuals as rational, calculating creatures whose moral autonomy is measured by their capacity for 'self-care'—the ability to provide for their own needs and service their own ambitions" (Brown 2009, 42). In extreme cases, this vulnerability can lead to criminal charges. For instance, the Office of the Public Prosecutor reported as many as 310 cases that were investigated and tried between January 2011 and September 2012 (Casas & Vivaldi 2013). Most cases are denounced in public hospitals, therefore those women who cannot afford private healthcare are most exposed to criminal prosecution if they have any complications. In Chile, it is not difficult to encounter in the media, healthcare practitioners denouncing women who show signs of misoprostol use or who confess to using it to induce an abortion.

In sum, the use of misoprostol as an abortive method has the paradoxical social result of promoting both autonomy and vulnerability in women. This fits well with a certain critical reading of late neoliberalism, in which matters of social, public, or national relevance (motherhood itself and the medical and legal procedures related to it) are left to the market, including clandestine practices and black markets. In general terms, the use of misoprostol for

clandestine abortions represents an instance of medical devices, in which the "meaning" or "truth" is being transposed to other fields of practical application: from the treatment of gastric ulcers to unregulated but safe abortions (at least much safer than the alternatives). These reinterpretations seem to follow individual or collective patterns of agency that collide in different ways (more or less foreseeably) with social structures. As in the other cases, women have to deal with the unintended consequences of prohibition, which involve not only activity transgressing or at the margins of the law common to other cases of drug prohibition, but also problems associated with gender-profiling and the commodification of bodies and reproduction (who decides the cost and reach of medical procedures, how it is decided and what procedures should be guaranteed by the state, etc.) Next, I will consider the case of the Free Abortion Hotline, highlighting the ramification of political resistance associated with this event.

INFORMATION, SOLIDARITY, AND RESISTANCE: FREE ABORTION HOTLINE

Since 2009, there has been a Chilean abortion hotline, Linea Aborto Libre, created by the Lesbians and Feminists for the Right of Information Collective (www.infoabortochile.org) which provides legal advice and information on misoprostol-based abortion. What we know about the hotline is mostly the product of private conversations with the people involved or the media. There have not been, to my knowledge, specific research projects about the Chilean case. An important reference is the case of Chicago's clandestine abortion services under the name of JANE (1968–1973), which also resembles the case of Open Door and Dublin Well Woman in Ireland (see below). In the case of the abortion hotline in Chile, as well as in other countries in Latin America, the NGO called Women on Waves trained the first volunteers to prepare them to receive calls.

In regard to the information provided by the hotline, a strict protocol designed to keep the hotline within the confines of the law was implemented: legally they cannot give any information about how to get or where to buy the pill. The information they provide is given only to persons of legal age and is based on World Health Organisation guidelines. In December 2012, the Collective published a handbook with this information, and lead workshops in different cities of Chile. According to their information, from May 2012 to May 2013 they held 32 such events for 820 women and men in the cities of Santiago, Valparaíso, Antofagasta, Iquique, Concepción and Temuco. Certainly, the volunteers are aware that the information given by the Collective is far from a definitive solution for women looking for help in the process of getting an abortion. The volunteers working at the hotline have declared many times that they are usually asked about how to get the pill, but all they can do is spread information guiding women about how much pain is normal to feel, how to avoid being discovered in case they need to go to the hospital or clinic, and so on. Moreover, many callers express concerns about the quality of the product and about the possibility of being victims of a scam. A further problem has to do with the access to the hotline itself because information about it is mainly disseminated online, as the volunteers themselves have reported. Individuals with limited access to online services are therefore less likely to access this information. For this reason the Collective have devised other ways to spread the information, such as workshops in universities and unions; stickers; painting the number in different walls of the cities; and flyers distributed in strategic locations. Additionally, since 2016 feminist activists have created new groups that provide more direct help to women who are seeking abortions, such as Con las amigas y en la casa (with friends and at home) or Miso pa todas (Misoprostol for everyone). However, as we can see, there are many legal obstacles to safe access to abortion for women in Chile. For instance, problems with the distribution of and access to information; problems with the distribution of and access to the drugs; a lack of assurance as to the quality of these drugs. Despite being fundamental for women's wellbeing, these aspects are surrounded by conflict, which is ultimately detrimental to the safety of women.

I would like to further analyse the strategies of the Collective under two clusters of concepts: on the one hand, the idea of a shared experience and awareness, of interdependency and solidarity; on the other hand, the idea of political agency in the margins of politics and the State, which, furthermore, can be interpreted in terms of resistance.

Regarding the first point, there are at least two feminist strategies presented explicitly by the Collective: the first is to raise awareness and political consciousness about abortion as a common place in which the body is the locus of oppression but also as a shared experience. The second is to support self-induced abortion by transmitting the misoprostol method as *practical knowledge*. Operating outside the law, academia or direct medical power, the Collective shares information and knowledge which promotes women's agency and autonomy (in the sense sketched above in relation to misoprostol in general). Moreover, as a solidarity network designed to counteract the effects of the ban and provide abortion support, the Collective provides a means of taking care of each other with a logic that recalls the difference between a logic of care and logic of instrumental rationality as we see in recent work in feminist economy (Pérez-Orozco 2014). The Collective's opposition to neoliberal individuality is crucial: it is a network of women organising themselves around novel styles of care and knowledge for which the end is to support each other on the issue of abortion. In particular, the Collective's idea is to "socially decriminalise abortion" (Interview by Catalan 2013, 236) by showing that most women perform abortions during their lifetime and it should not be something traumatic. This traumatic element may be tackled in two ways. On the one hand, as one of the members of the Collective declared in an interview, even though the number of people they can help might be quite small, they trust the value of their "symbolic gesture" (Catalan 2013, 236). While these words might be interpreted as modest, the "symbolic" point is significant if we also consider the fact, highlighted by the same volunteer, that they are lesbians providing the service and that in Chile abortion is seen as a symbol of oppression.

In this sense they are not challenging the content of medical or legal knowledge but the way in which the knowledge is used practically on the self, in an intimate relation between care of the body and care of the soul. In other words, the effects of power are resisted creating new strategic practices of the self.

In addition, the goal of *socially decriminalizing abortion* is pursued in public events, as exemplified by the poster calling for the past 8th of March demonstration: "*Sin doctor ni policía nuestro aborto es alegría*" (Without the police or doctors, our abortion is joy). This message incorporates important ideas of the Collective. First, if an abortion is practiced following the appropriate instructions, it is a safe procedure: doctors are not needed and also the pill leaves no trace, so the police cannot detect it. Secondly, they identify the abortion as *ours*, to highlight that abortion is a shared experience for many women. And finally, the notion that abortion may go hand in hand with joy challenging the imaginary that associates abortion with trauma and loss.

Regarding the second point, and in relation to the State, the Collective has no political connections and does not lobby for legislative reform, rejecting any dialogue with the government. They do not consider the State as a valid interlocutor. They have declared that the State is patriarchal and oppressive and they prefer to rely on the type of independent networks that can provide effective support. There is evidently a profound mistrust of the state apparatus per se, and also of the real possibility of accomplishing changes through the implementation of laws or state policies. They are aware that decriminalisation is important because women still face the risk of being criminally prosecuted, however, they have chosen "to put their energy into the cultural work that is to disarm the taboo of abortion and guilt" (Catalan 2013, 236, my translation).

It is important to note that Collective volunteers have faced three criminal inquiries instigated by pro-life religious groups (Catalan 2014). The first two inquiries were stayed and the third was shelved after police questioned two volunteers. However, as the Collective only provides publicly available information, its work is completely above legal reproach. As mentioned above, this case resembles that of Open Door and Dublin Well Woman, two Irish non-profit organisations that were restricted by the Irish High Court and

Supreme Court from providing pregnant women with information on abortion facilities outside Ireland. In 1992, the European Court of Human Rights found that such restrictions constituted unjustified interference with the right to impart or receive information, contrary to article 10 of the Convention on the Protection of Human Rights and Fundamental Freedoms. The key point, one that the Chilean hotline has also argued in its own case, is that the information can be legally spread even though abortion is prohibited.

Interestingly, those selling the product online have not been prosecuted and religious groups do not seem to be concerned with them, even though they are not difficult to trace (Catalan 2013). This fact in itself gives reasons to believe that, in the minds of the accusers, women spreading knowledge and *normalising* abortion are seen as more dangerous and/or easier to attack than those who profit from it in the black market. It could also be a reflection of the paradox of a society based on the concept of *free market*, in which monetary profit is more accepted than communitarian networks of self-determination.

Now, besides the paradoxical promotion of women's autonomy and vulnerability, this case has been significant for feminism in developing new ways of communication and social awareness that can be further analysed in terms of resistance in a Foucauldian sense. Indeed, we have seen that the autonomy which the use of misoprostol promotes has to be considered side by side with the vulnerability attached to self-medicating, black markets and criminal prosecution. How, then, might the hotline be considered a form of resistance?

We have to be careful in not too readily categorizing something as either "resistance" or "complicity," reducing the Foucauldian analysis of freedom to a mere dichotomy between active/passive, voluntary/involuntary. The idea is to "see how people adopt rationalities and logics, how they negotiate them in specific domains of life" (Bell, 2015:58). Indeed, these kinds of feminist movements are an example of resistance in terms of the local questioning of dominant discursive categories, and thus negotiating the freedom of women in new ways (Bell 1993, 56). Indeed, there is resistance in the Foucauldian sense when there is a series of exercises that shape the way of living of women commonly facing a relation to the "powers" of the Church, the law and State. The work of the Collective (and other similar projects) makes possible and enacts a reshaping of feminist agency. The hotline offers a much needed channel of communication for women living the vulnerability of having to clandestinely take care of their own reproductive rights. At the same time, the Collective "has to be resigned to the understanding that it contains all the contradictions and power/knowledge links that other ways of speaking contain" (Bell 1993, 176). They are not just a means to a predetermined end, but a relation both affective (humane) and rational (articulating) that moulds the present of those involved. A key aspect involves the fact that political strategies might operate in a productive and normalising way through struggles, through efforts to gain control, to regulate, to mask, or to sanction what is acceptable and useful. (cf. Foucault 1978, 105–6; Bell 1993, 19). Finally, Foucault's conceptualisation elucidates a real possibility of resistance, disobedience, and opposition under current circumstances. This real possibility does not reside in an unconditional or natural capacity or right, but in agency itself:

> Liberty is a practice. . . . The liberty of men is never assured by the institutions and laws that are intended to guarantee them. . . . Not because they are ambiguous, but simply because "liberty" is what must be exercised. (1991a, 245)

CONCLUSIONS

This historical review of abortion in Chile shows us how feminist movements have been involved in the struggle for abortion and how abortion has been differently understood in different periods: At the beginning of the last century abortion was directly related to the economic resources and the material conditions for having a baby and thus it was mainly seen as a class problem. Later on, the possibility of choosing whether to continue pregnancy was seen as a problem related with patriarchy and the choice whether to be a mother or not was reconceived as a choice that every woman has the right to make. The revision also enables us to recognise how the prohibition of abortion was directly related to the irruption of Pinochet's coup which, besides (but intimately related to) its political violence, imposed the prohibition of abortion and the implementation of an economic model of deep social reach and an ideological apparatus underpinning legislation supporting the interests of conservative and religious groups which still influence Chilean society today.

Regarding the more recent feminist organisations that help women to have abortions, there is a question of whether the Hotline constitutes resistance if there is no effective support for finding misoprostol, preventing scams, and supporting and guiding women during the abortive process itself. Undoubtedly, the "symbolic gesture" of the Collective represents a form of resistance in the sense of reshaping power strategies. This reshaping is reactive in the sense of being inseparable from power and subjugation. But it is active in the sense of producing a change in the conditions of possibility of action. It creates a space in which solidarity grows as the shared experience of abortion is revealed: women realise that there are other women in the same situation; they can empathise and collaborate around a common plight. These alternative strategies might nevertheless have as consequence the normalisation of women's agency in the terms of the market, in such a way that in the future it could force women to pursue this autonomy in an even more exposed and vulnerable position. However, if Foucault is correct, and if the conditions of power relations (in this case, information) change, the new conditions will offer a space of resistance for feminism.

NOTE

1. For information in more detail about gender related public policies and the transition period see Richard 2001; Blofield & Haas 2005; Haas 2006.

REFERENCES

Araujo, Kathya. 2005. "Sobre ruidos y nueces: debates chilenos en torno a la sexualidad." *Revista Iberoamericana* 5 (2): 109–125.
Baldez, Lisa. 2002. *Why Women Protest: Women's movements in Chile*. Cambridge: Cambridge University Press.
Bascuñán Rodríguez, Antonio. 2004. "La Licitud del Aborto Consentido en el Derecho Chileno." *Revista de Derecho y Humanidades* 10: 143–181.
Bell, Vikki. 1993. *Interrogating incest: Feminism, Foucault, and the law, Sociology of law and crime*. London, New York: Routledge.
Bell, Vikki. 2015. Studying provocations, the researcher's care for what exists. Interview with Vikki Bell. In: Hansson, S., Hellberg, S., and Stern, M. (Eds.) *Studying the agency of being governed: Methodological reflections.* New York: Routledge.
Berer, Marge and Hoggart Lesley. (Eds.) 2018. "Medical Abortion" [Special Issue]. *Contraception Journal*, 97 (2): 79–190.
Brito, Alejandra, Cid, Beatriz, and Donoso, Carla. 2012. "Ruling the Womb: The Sexual and Reproductive Struggle during the Bachelet Administration." *Latin American Perspectives*, 39 (4): 145–162.
Brown, Wendy. 2005. *Edgework: Critical essays on knowledge and politics*. Princeton: Princeton University Press.
Brown, Wendy. 2009. Wounded Attachments. *Feminist Legal Studies,* (1): 396–419.
Caffarena, Elena 1935. *MEMCH: A las mujeres* (letter) Sent to the women, 28 May 1935. Memoria Chilena archive. From http://www.memoriachilena.cl/archivos2/pdfs/MC0065896.pdf
Casas, Lidia, and Shepard, Bonnie. 2007. "Abortion Policies and Practices in Chile: Ambiguities and Dilemmas." *Reproductive Health Matters*, 15 (30): 202–210.
Casas, Lidia, and Vivaldi, Lieta. 2013. "La penalización del aborto como una violación a los derechos humanos de las mujeres." *Informe Anual sobre Derechos Humanos en Chile 2013.* Santiago: Universidad Diego Portales. From: www.derechoshumanos.udp.cl/wp/wp-content/uploads/2013/10/libro_DD_HH_capitulo2.pdf
Catalan, Iván. 2013. "Viviana Díaz: "Desde la más pobre a la más rica, el riesgo de morir o irte presa por abortar está puesto solamente en las últimas." *Revista Nomadías,* (18): 235–240.
Del Campo, Andrea. 2008. "El debate medico sobre el aborto en Chile en la década de 1930." Zarate, Soledad (Ed.) *Por la Salud del Cuerpo*. Santiago: Universidad Alberto Hurtado, 1311–188.
Eguiguren, Pamela and Ferrer, Marcela. 2014. "Aborto y Salud Publica en Chile: Argumentos para una legislación que espera desde hace casi 80 años." Articulación Feminista por la Libertad de Decidir AFLD (eds.) *Voces Sobre el Aborto: Ciudadanía de las mujeres, cuerpo y autonomía.* Santiago: AFLD; Escuela de Salud Publica "Dr. Salvador Allende G. Facultad de Medicina, Universidad de Chile.
Ferree, Myra Marx, Gamson, William, Gerhards, Jürgen and Rucht, Dieter. 2002. *Shaping Abortion Discourse: Democracy and the Public Sphere in Germany and the United States*. Cambridge: Cambridge University Press.

Foucault, Michel. 1977. *Discipline and punish: The birth of the prison*. New York: Pantheon Books.

Foucault, Michel. 1978 *History of Sexuality, Volume 1: An Introduction*. Translated by R. Hurley, New York: Random House.

Foucault, Michel. 1991. *The Foucault Reader*. London: Penguin.

Foucault, Michel. 2008. *The Birth of Biopolitics: Lectures At The Collège De France, 1978–79*. New York: Palgrave Macmillan.

Gane, David. 2012. "The governmentalities of neoliberalism: panopticism, post-panopticism and beyond." *The Sociological Review*, 60 (4): 611–634.

Gaviola, E., Largo, S., Palestro, S.1994. *Una historia necesaria: mujeres en Chile 1973–1990*. Santiago de Chile: S. N.

Haas, L. 2006. The Rules of the Game: Feminist Policymaking in Chile. *Revista política* 46: 199–225.

Harvey, D. 2005. *A Brief History of Neoliberalism*. Oxford: Oxford University Press.

Jiles, P., and Rojas, C. 1992. *De la Miel a los Implantes: Historia de las Políticas de Regulación de la Fecundidad en Chile*. Santiago, Chile: CORSAPS, Corporación de Salud y Políticas Sociales.

Jiménez, G., and Marshall, P. 2010. La píldora del día después y las potestades públicas. *Revista Hemiciclo* 2: 43–64.

Kirkwood, Julieta. 1982. "Feminismo y participación política en Chile." *Documento de Trabajo FLACSO:* N 152.

Kirkwood, Julieta. 1990. *Ser política en Chile: los nudos de la sabiduría feminista*. Santiago: Editorial Cuarto Propio.

Koch, Elard, et al. 2012. "Women's education level, maternal health facilities, abortion legislation and maternal deaths: a natural experiment in Chile from 1957 to 2007." *PloS One,* 7 (5): https://doi.org/10.1371/journal.pone.0036613

MacKinnon, Catherine. 1989. *Toward a Feminist Theory of the State*. Cambridge, MA: Harvard University Press.

Maira, Gloria, Molina, Siomara, Santana, Paulina. 2008. *Violencia sexual y aborto: conexiones necesarias*. Santiago, Chile: Red Chilena contra la Violencia Doméstica y Sexual.

Marshall, P., Zúñiga, Y., Accatino, D. and Bordalí, A. 2008. Sentencia sobre inconstitucionalidad del decreto supremo N° 48 del ministerio de salud en la parte que autoriza la distribución de la píldora del día después en el sistema público de salud. *Revista de Derecho (Universidad Austral)* 21 (1).

Matamala Vivaldi, María Isabel. 2014. "Aborto en Chile: Cuerpos, Derechos y Libertades." Articulación Feminista por la Libertad de Decidir, AFLD (Eds.) *Voces Sobre el Aborto: Ciudadania de las mujeres, cuerpo y autonomia*. Santiago, Chile: AFLD; Escuela de Salud Pública "Dr. Salvador Allende G." Facultad de Medicina, Universidad de Chile

Maturana, Kesten. (2014) "Aborto: derechos humanos de las mujeres frente al parlamento chileno." Articulación Feminista por la Libertad de Decidir, AFLD (Eds.) *Voces Sobre el Aborto: Ciudadania de las mujeres, cuerpo y autonomia.* Santiago: AFLD; Escuela de Salud Pública "Dr. Salvador Allende G." Facultad de Medicina, Universidad de Chile.

McGuire, James. 2010. *Wealth, health, and democracy in East Asia and Latin America*. Cambridge: Cambridge University Press

MEMCH, 1938. Estatutos del Movimiento Pro-Emancipación de la Mujer Chilena. Valparaíso: Impr. Valparaíso. From http://www.memoriachilena.cl/archivos2/pdfs/MC0023661.pdf.

Molina-Cartes Ramiro. Et Al. 2013. "Profile of abortion in Chile, with extremely restrictive law." *Open Journal of Obstetrics and Gynecology* (3): 732–38.

Mottier, Natalia and Gerodetti, Veronique 2007. "Eugenics and social democracy: or, how the European left tried to eliminate the 'weeds' from its national gardens." *New formations*, (60): 35–49.

Muñoz, Fernando 2014. "Morning-after decisions: Legal Mobilization Against Emergency Contraception in Chile." *Michigan Journal of Gender and Law*, (21): 123–175.

Observatorio Género y Equidad. 2009. *Primeras Organizaciones de Mujeres en Chile: Las Pioneras del Feminismo*. http://www.observatoriogeneroyliderazgo.cl/blog/?p=395

ODEPLAN. 1979. *Politica poblacional* aprobada por su excelencia el Presidente de la República y publicada en el plan nacional indicativo de desarrollo (1978–1983) en noviembre 1978: política de población.

Palma, Irma, Reyes, Daniel & Moreno, Claudia. 2013. "Pluralismo y libertad de elección que esconde una propuesta gubernamental conservadora." *Docencia* , 49 (Mayo): 14–24.

Pérez-Orozco, Amaia. 2014. *Subversion de la Economia Feminista: aportes para un debate sobre el conflicto Capital-Vida.* Madrid: Traficante de Suenos

Pieper, Jadwiga. 2009. *The Politics of Motherhood. Maternity and Women's Rights in Twentieth Century Chile*. Pittsburgh: University of Pittsburgh Press.

Rios, Marcela. 2003. "'Feminism is Socialism, Liberty and Much More': Second-Wave Chilean Feminism and its Contentious Relationship with Socialism." *Journal of Women's History.* 15 (3), (Autumn): 129–134.

Salazar, Gabriel. 1985. *Labradores, peones y proletarios: formación y crisis de la sociedad popular chilena del siglo XIX.* Santiago, Chile: Ediciones Sur.

Shepard, Bonnie. 2000. "The 'double discourse' on sexual and reproductive rights in Latin America: the chasm between public policy and private actions" *Health and Human Rights* 4 (2): 110–143. 2.

Valdés, Teresa, Weinstein, Marisa, Toledo, María Isabel, Letelier, Lilian. 1989. "Centros de Madres 1973–1989 Sólo discipliamiento?" *Documento de Trabajo Flacso-Chile*, Number 416.

Valdés, Juan Gabriel. 1995. *Pinochet's Economists: The Chicago School of Economics in Chile*. Cambridge: Cambridge University Press.

Yuval-Davis, Nira, Anthias, Floya, Campling, Jo. 1989. *Woman, nation, state*. Basingstoke: Palgrave Macmillan.

Chapter Three

Political Participation of Women

Potentialities, Limits, and Challenges

Yanira Zúñiga

INTRODUCTION

The struggle for the full inclusion of women in the social contract has been the guiding thread of feminist ideology and practice throughout its history. Women's movements have learned valuable lessons during this long and eventful journey. They have discovered that suffrage does not guarantee female citizenship and that even though they can vote, women do not manage to enter the political decision-making processes as men do.

Through the creation of new frames of reference, feminists have managed to make the low presence of women in positions of power a part of contemporary discussions on democracy. The notion of "the glass ceiling," coined during the eighties, highlights the chain of invisible maneuvers, practices, and material and symbolic mechanisms which result in women being systematically dismissed in electoral processes. Ever since, feminists have questioned the modern form of representative government and the bases of liberal democracy, arguing that the delegation of decision making to representatives atrophies good government and excludes half of humanity. They denounce the liberal democracy as another institution made to uphold the political domination of men over women. The convergence of various other social concerns about the crisis of representation on the legitimacy of the democratic system amplifies this criticism. Thanks to this favorable conjuncture, the unequal distribution of political power between the sexes engaged women and the male monopoly of power came to be seen as a democratic anomaly that needed to be corrected.

In the public sphere, the most visible legacy of this process of creating new frameworks of analysis has been the expansion and diversification of the tools for the promotion of female representation throughout the world. These have evolved rapidly. In place of voluntary mechanisms, mandatory quotas have been widely adopted in Latin America. In a small but increasing number of countries, these quotas have grown into requirements of parity or balanced representation, all in no more than four decades.

There is no doubt that measures to encourage female political participation constitute one of the most valuable assets of contemporary feminism. However, quotas and parity have had varying effectiveness in significantly increasing the presence of women in political positions, and their potential to question the cultural elements of sex-gender system has yet to be realized.

Evidence accumulated over almost four decades suggests that the effectiveness of these measures varies depending on the cultural and institutional contexts of each country. As of June 2017, the following percentages of presence in national parliaments were registered (single and combined houses of parliament): Nordic countries, 41.7%; Americas, 28.1%; Europe (including the Nordic countries), 26.5%; Europe (excluding the Nordic countries), 25.3%; Sub-Saharan Africa, 23.6%; Asia, 19.4%; Arab countries, 17.4%; and the Pacific region, 17.4% (IPU 2017). A scan of this information reveals that the mechanism employed does not by itself determine success. For example, in 1995, eight of the ten countries with the largest presence of women were European and of those, five were Nordic. Twenty years later, although there is greater balance between the regions with four of the countries with the greatest advances located in sub-Saharan Africa and three in the Americas, the Nordic countries continue to occupy the first ten positions, bordering 40% female representation despite having non-compulsory mechanisms (IPU, 2015). On the other hand, the parity model was first implemented in the National Assembly of France, which, 17 years after the introduction of the model, reached a record of 38.8% female representation after the June 2017 election. This figure, an improvement over the previous record of 26.9%, is still far from the goal of equal access for men and women in elected office set by the Article 1 of the French Constitution.

Anyway, it is possible and desirable to extract conclusions on the impact of quotas and parity based on the current configuration of the relationships between power and gender in order to elucidate the best paths to follow and the challenges to address in striving toward full female citizenship.

This chapter will examine the potential for these measures to destabilize the sex-gender system, focusing on their stated justifications to identify their conceptual boundaries, evaluate the objectives they claim to pursue and highlight their limitations. Chile's recent approval of a quota offers a concrete example of how discourses that favor female political participation, as well as other discourses which are critical of the current power structure, are not immune to appropriation and ideological distortion.

This chapter will be structured as follows: Section (I) will clarify the differences between quotas and parity. Section (II) will argue that parity as it has been formulated in recent feminist discourse can be conceived as a transformative policy, in contrast to quotas which are more of an affirmative policy. Section (III) will identify some limitations of the parity discourse derived from its excessive emphasis on access to power and its neglect of the problems linked to its exercise. To demonstrate the shortcomings of this approach, Section (IV) will focus on the emerging phenomenon of political violence against women. Finally, starting from the Chilean case, I will postulate that norms and discourses that promote a greater female presence in positions of power can mask forms of legitimization of the current order. Furthermore, the study of the leadership of Michelle Bachelet provides some elements that confirm the advantages associated with the politics of presence, but also raises questions about the true impact of new female leaders in the deconstruction of gender patterns.

FROM QUOTAS TO PARITY: SPEECHES AND NORMATIVE IMPLICATIONS

In the mid-nineties the notion of parity emerged in Europe. The first normative formulation of this idea appeared in international documents such as the Athens Declaration (1992) and the Beijing Declaration (1995). However, its conceptual development was intimately linked to the French parity movement. This movement of feminist origin sought to renovate French republican universalism to allow for sexual diversity. Accordingly, the notion of parity is presented as a universalist alternative to the concept of quotas coming from the United States. In the French discourse on parity, sexual difference is considered specific and irreducible, the only kind of difference with sufficient pedigree to rise as a criterion for the configuration of citizenship.

The French movement has not succeeded in increasing the presence of French women in positions of power to the level of parity, but it is undeniable that it has had a fundamental transnational influence in recent debates on female citizenship. As the American historian Joan W. Scott (2005) has pointed out, the great success of the movement for parity has been the transformation of the fundamental sexual duality of humanity into not only a social slogan, but a real theoretical, political revolution, making it possible to overcome the difficulties that the dilemma of equality versus difference had historically presented for feminism.

A brief review of the evolution of regulation regarding female underrepresentation in recent decades confirms that despite its ups and downs, the parity project is in good health. Since the year 2000, France has progressively expanded its parity policy to various types of elections including municipal, national, European and regional, while Belgium (2002) and Spain (2007) have swelled the list of European countries committed to the principle of balanced representation of power. In Latin America, a significant number of countries have replaced legal quotas with mechanisms associated with parity. For example, Bolivia (2008), Ecuador (2009), Costa Rica (2009) and Mexico (2014) have made such changes in their legislative or constitutional regulations. On the African continent, Senegal (2010) and Tunisia (2012) also subscribe to parity norms.

At this point, it seems appropriate to explain what makes parity different from quotas. Although it is not unusual for quotas and parity to be used synonymously, the literature differentiates between the two conceptually and practically. The most frequently described difference is the existence of a half-to-end relationship between quotas and parity (Bareiro 2007). Quotas are often described as a tool to arrive at the ideal model: parity democracy. A second differentiation is the ratio of women to men required in each model. In parity, the objective is to balance the presence of each group in positions of political representation with relatively equal proportions. That is to say, parity strives for close to equal representation by sex, while quotas oscillate around 30% female participation. A third difference between quotas and parity is the internal logic of each of these tools. In the words of the Belgian political scientist Bérengère Marques Pereira (2013, 282):

> The quotas represent a measure of recovery that seeks to compensate the imbalance produced as a result of the social division of labor, which produces effects that are detrimental to women. Parity, on the other hand, is a measure that is not transitory, but definitive, and whose objective is to guarantee the distribution of political power between men and women. For this reason, parity has a symbolic scope more noticeable than quotas, since, this measure denounces the male monopolization of political power, proposing its distribution instead of a simple participation of women in deliberative, consultative and decision-making institutions of public and political life.

From this perspective, parity has more ambitious objectives than quotas because it seeks to restructure public office by restructuring the traditional order of gender. A more detailed examination of the symbolic and material implications of this approach is important. For those who defend parity, this is the paradigmatic expression of humanity as sexual duality. The paritarists emphasize that women are not a category or a group, but one of the two ways in which the people can present themselves. According to this logic, equal female political participation cannot be structured in terms of temporary remedies such as quotas, but must be guaranteed fully. Parity, therefore, is seen as a new, fundamental, permanent organizational principle for political power.

On the other side, using a gendered concept of *the people* and a miroir or descriptive representation as the backbone of the argument for balanced distribution of power between men and women has been seen by some feminists as a dangerous use of the same sexual dimorphism that has historically oppressed women. There is no doubt, however, that this shift has earned the parity discourse a good part of its success. Regardless, the criticisms that have risen within feminist thinking warning of the dangers of the rationale behind parity should be noted. Several feminists think that there is a high price to pay for a rather questionable success. The first being the minimization of the anti-discriminatory dimension of these measures in favor of a discourse that presents parity as an instrument of good political representation. Second, the natural regression that the reinvention of people as a sexed entity entails (Bereni and Lépinard 2004). Finally, the way in which the emphasis on sexual difference diffuses other factors of political exclusion, such as race, ethnicity or social class. In the words of Barrère (2013, 65) parity has ended up being confused with mere presence, promotes a uniform representation of women, and has ceased to be conceived as an instrument against oppression to become an end in itself.

It can be accepted that the sexualization of *the people* on which rests the principle of balanced distribution of power, carries the risk of reinforcing the belief in a difference in aptitude between the sexes and a danger of naturalistic regression. However, attempts to reformulate the principle of equality have generated similar problems for the theory and practice of feminism. From this perspective, there are doubts that a discourse focused on equality could offer better prospects. As Joan Scott (1998) has warned, the historical construction of female citizenship has been paradoxical since it has required affirming and at the same time refuting sexual difference. The debate on equality has constantly tried to determine if feminists should prefer sameness, or if it is necessary to accept or integrate the cultural or biological differences that distinguish women.

The emphasis on the goal of presence produces a distortion of the problem of female underrepresentation and limits the transformative potential of parity, a dilemma that is discussed later in this chapter. Even so, the justification for parity can be shown to be more positive than this criticism indicates. The next section will explore this further.

POLITICAL INJUSTICE AND PARITY AS A TRANSFORMATIVE POLICY

If we consider, as Nancy Fraser (2008) does, that problems of representation are problems of justice, parity can be understood as a transformative solution, overcoming the affirmative solution embodied in quotas. In this approach, affirmative solutions are characterized as trying to correct the undesired effects of social agreements without affecting the frameworks that produce them, while transformative solutions seek to destabilize such frameworks, attacking the origin or cause of the injustice (Fraser 1997, 38–39).

Feminists have emphasized that the most influential contemporary theories of justice have focused on the distribution of material goods, and have started from individualistic presuppositions (Young 2000). They have not referred to the interrelationship between distribution, recognition and representation, nor have they adequately explored the links between the injustices that occur in the public sphere and those that happen in private and familial spaces (Fraser 2008; Okin 2008). For these theories, the lack of women in political positions is not an anomaly in itself. The problems of redistribution, recognition and representation, in most cases, are different and unrelated problems, and the gender distribution of domestic responsibilities does not have an impact on the systematic discrimination suffered by women.

The parity discourse is part of this feminist critical tradition. By placing the emphasis on the way in which democracies organize and distribute political power, parity has drawn links between political injustice and the mechanisms of domination/subalternity underlying the social order of gender. The parity discourse makes the transversal impact that the asymmetry of access to power has on the lives of men and women visible. It shows how the injustices that affect women give rise to a vicious cycle: political injustice corroborates and perpetuates economic and status injustices, and these contribute to the failure of female political representation (Fraser, 2008). In short, the parity discussion highlights the mechanisms that determine who participates in politics and poses the questions about who decides, what is decided and whom those decisions benefit.

Consequently, the parity policy is fairer not only because it reflects the sexed composition of society and contributes to the deconstruction of politics as a predominantly masculine activity, but because it significantly improves the chances that the interests of women are properly understood and protected by the political process. This reasoning has been developed in depth by Anne Phillips (2000), through her famous distinction between the politics of presence and the politics of ideas. The politics of presence is a more appropriate vehicle than the politics of ideas to address the problems of historically marginalized groups because it allows them to better identify and protect their interests. The inherent belonging of the representative to this class of groups reduces the epistemic gap between representatives and represented, and dissolves the conflict between representative democracy and participatory democracy.

If we understand parity under this reference framework, it can be said to have three advantages when it comes to the relationship between women and the political process: it includes them in the public sphere, it allows a better representation of their interests and it allows women to be restored positively as a group.

It is reasonable to conclude that parity has a greater potential than quotas to restructure gender relations from the outset. This advantage lies in the way in which the proposals approach the political system. The discourse in favor of quotas shows a certain optimism, sometimes naïve, about the capacity of the political system to incorporate traditionally excluded groups. Advocates of quotas seem to assume that the political system is inclusive by nature, and consequently, it would suffice to optimize its functioning in a yet undefined way to favor an increase in female participation. They profess a blind faith that leads them to conclude that, sooner rather than later, the entry barriers that affect women will naturally fall and that quotas will then cease to be necessary.

In contrast, many feminists who defend parity adopt a more pragmatic approach. They assume that politics refers to attributes of the masculine symbolic universe, such as leadership and the ability to govern, in such a way that gender operates as an identity marker that delimits access to political power. Consequently, politics is a primary structure that shapes the social processes that determine the individual's positions of privilege and disadvantage. Therefore, it is necessary to structurally transform its institutional functioning that ensures the almost monopolistic occupation of power by men. The discourse of parity postulates that the just solution does not consist in the participation of some women in the political power exerted paradigmatically by some men in a transitory and remedial manner but in an equitable and permanent distribution of political power between both sexes.

THE LIMITATIONS OF PARITY, OR THE DISPLACEMENT OF THE RESISTANCE

Some parts of the frameworks around which the concept of parity is built suggest it to be a transformative policy. However, the transformative potential of parity cannot be isolated from the way in which it has been taking shape, and this creates an intricate entanglement.

Both quotas and parity claim to increase the presence of women in positions of power, and in doing so, focus too much on the barriers that women face in gaining political power. This leaves out the conditions that affect the exercise of political power, which are derived from its masculinized paradigmatic form. As Celia Amorós observes, "it does not seem credible that . . . such subtle schemes have been devised to prevent or stop our transit to the public world and that such ideas, the product of long held beliefs, have been interrupted in their effects once this critical transit has been completed" (2006, 384).

The evidence corroborates Amorós' suspicions. Several works focused on the Latin American experience show the proliferation of diverse practices of avoidance to outwit the measures that favor female political participation (Ríos 2008; Archenti and Tula 2013). It matters little whether it is quotas or parity policies. Even in those countries that embrace measures such as guaranteed positions in the electoral lists, strong sanctions against non-compliance, financial incentives and a favorable electoral system that have large multi-member districts with closed and blocked lists, political parties apply these measures in a minimalist and bureaucratic way, considering the minimum legal percentage as a maximum, presenting the bulk of women in territories that they estimate less competitive, or using legal loopholes to replace an elected woman with a man, circumventing the purpose of these rules. In the period from 2000 to 2014, at the height of the measures to encourage female political participation in Latin America, the average number of seats held by women in the lower houses of deputies increased barely 11%, very far from thc 50% that parity pursues.

Other research shows that women who manage to develop a political career are confronted with multiple obstacles related to the exercise of political power. Several works on Hillary Clinton, a politician from the United States, have highlighted that female politicians continue to be the subject of intense public scrutiny that is dominated by gender stereotypes that operate at a normative level (McGinley 2009; Leslie 2015). This suggests that social representations of politics and the political are still traversed by gender perceptions that inhibit greater female presence in political decision-making spaces. While it is true that at present this remains latent or at least significantly reduced when it comes to accessing political power, in part thanks to the existence of parity and quota measures and greater female empowerment in the social space, the bitter resistance to a greater feminization of politics unfolds openly when women try to exercise this power.

According to Celia Amorós (2006), the great problem faced by women who manage to develop a political career is that they are considered unable to hold the social authority that makes the power exercised by someone seem plausible, credible or reliable. In the collective imagination, women are considered unable to hold power, whatever their version, and when some of them come to exercise it is seen as undeserved. This means that the decisions and opinions of female politicians are the subject of a scrutiny that checks whether they are susceptible to being ratified by a man. It does not matter if the man is above the woman in the hierarchical scale, is her peer, or is even in a lower rank (Valcárcel 1997, 116).

The above explanation evokes the delightful story that Rebecca Solnit offered us in *Men Explain Things to Me* (2016). In this book, the author coined the expression *mansplaining* to refer to the masculine practice that consists of undervaluing a women's opinion, regardless of social position. Recently, some female advisors to former President Obama told the *Washington Post* that, under the first Obama administration, they designed a particular strategy that sought to counteract the difficulties that women have accessing power circles and being heard. They agreed that, whenever one of them formulated an idea in a meeting of advisors, the others repeated it and gave the credit to its author. The objective of this practice was to amplify their respective voices and prevent men from monopolizing the discussion and appropriating their ideas (Juliet Eilperin 2016).

One of the most flagrant examples of the resistance to a greater female presence displaces our focus from the access to power to the field of its exercise. This is the phenomenon of violence against women in politics.

VIOLENCE AGAINST WOMEN IN POLITICS

The phenomenon of violence against women in politics (hereinafter VAWP) has been attracting growing interest in Latin America, particularly since 2012 when Bolivia approved a law against harassment and political violence against women (Ley 243). This law defines political harassment as a type of conduct, direct or indirect, individual or collective, which takes the form of pressure, persecution, harassment or threat directed at female candidates or women holding public office. Political violence, in contrast, consists of physical, sexual or psychological attacks directed against women. In both cases, the prohibited action seeks to shorten, suspend, prevent or restrict the proper exercise of the rights or functions by a woman (Article 7).

The Bolivian VAWP law has promoted regional discussion on this phenomenon. In 2015, the VI Conference of States Parties to the Convention of Belém do Pará, also known as the Inter-American Convention against Violence against Women, adopted the Declaration on Violence and Political Harassment against Women. It urges Latin American States to adopt norms, actions, programs and public policies that prevent and eradicate political violence and harassment against women, address and repair the effects, and protect their rights. Also in 2015, a reform of the Constitution of Mexico City included a clause declaring any election or process of citizen participation void if the existence of gender based political violence is proven (Article 27, D 2). However, the Legislative Assembly of the Federal District (ALDF) published a clarifying note in June of 2017 which seeks to eliminate the expression “on the basis of gender” established in the aforementioned constitutional text, and also other passages that described various actions constituting this kind of violence.

At the global level, the International Knowledge Network of Women in Politics (iKNOW Politics) published a 2016 report with the results of an online discussion on this phenomenon. This document includes testimonies from female politicians from France, Canada, Scotland and Israel, among other countries, who denounce the existence of a culture of violence that permeates political activity. According to this report, VAWP does not only occur during election campaigns. As women assume different political positions, they may be pressured to renounce their positions due to their gender or be verbally threatened or intimidated. VAWP can also take on other forms, including sexist images and stereotypes, which proliferate in the digital age. These focus on women’s bodies, sexuality and traditional roles, rather than on their competence, ability and contribution as leaders (iKNOW Politics 2016, 1).

Although scant, the literature on the subject usually shows a continuum of VAWP, ranging from electoral violence to the prevention of the exercise of representative functions, Krook and Restrepo (2016, 139) consider that there are certain particularities between two kinds of violence for which it is important to differentiate. While electoral violence includes actions against female candidates, activists or voters during the electoral process, strict political violence is committed against women, both during and after campaigns, when women assume positions of power.

Strict political violence, therefore, occurs in the phase in which a woman has already overcome barriers to access power and is attempting to exercise it. This violence is characterized by an attack aimed at refuting the belonging of women to the public space. The motivation for this kind of attack is to dissuade other women from pursuing a political career. Those who suffer this violence are usually painted as fish out of water. Either they are too feminine to withstand the rigor of political activity, or they are too harsh or too authoritarian to be seen as real women.

The exploitation of feminine stereotypes plays an essential role in the materialization of this kind of violence. The expulsion of women from politics generally rests on representing them as usurpers of a power that does not legitimately belong to them, and that denounce their transgression from the sexual division of labor and the gender hierarchy. The questioning of the sexual morality of political women or the fulfillment of their family duties is this kind of violence. The exaggerated attention paid to the way political women dress also operates as a strategy of hypersexualization that seeks to emphasize that women, wherever they are and whatever they do, are always sexual objects.

Although VAWP usually adopts symbolic forms, it can also include manifestations of physical harm. The recent Latin American experience offers several examples of murders, threats of death, kidnapping, rape, sexual harassment and financial coercion. In summary, VAWP may consist of symbolic, physical, sexual and economic violence. (Lena Krook and Restrepo Sanín, 2006, 143–144).

SOME REFLECTIONS FROM THE CHILEAN CASE

In Chile, the political underrepresentation of women has traditionally been associated with institutional consequences of the military dictatorship and with socio-cultural characteristics such as machismo, Marianismo, and Catholicism. The issue of the underrepresentation of women in political decision-making began to be considered as a problem with the return of democracy. Several of the political parties that formed the center-left bloc called Concertación de Partidos por la Democracia established some type of voluntary quota. Soon after, however, they adopted a practice of resistance to the quotas they had voluntarily established in their statutes.

As a result, from 1990 onward, the presence of women in the Chilean parliament has increased slowly, from 5.8% to 15.8%. This last figure is below the Latin American average of 25.25%, and very far from Argentina, Bolivia or Costa Rica, which stand at around 40%. The low female presence in town halls is especially worrisome. At present, only 12.5% of Chilean municipalities are headed by women, a percentage that is lower than the 12.9% achieved following the 2000 election (UNDP 2018)

The study of the Chilean politics reveals several factors that explain the low presence of women in political positions. These are similar to those identified for other Latin American countries, which include socio-economic, cultural and political-institutional variables (Ríos 2008, 14). Many of the obstacles that Chilean women have faced have been associated with the political-institutional factor and, in particular, with the characteristics of the Chilean electoral system.

From the return to democracy until 2015, Chile applied a binominal electoral system. This was introduced by the military dictatorship in order to form two large political blocs, and replaced the proportional system of Chilean parliamentary elections until 1973. Under this system it is only possible to nominate two candidates per seat. A majority of 66% of the votes is needed to obtain a seat or it is in dispute. This electoral system has had a notable negative effect on the presence of women in congress. According to data from the Chilean Electoral Service, the largest number of female candidates for parliamentary elections have historically been presented by small parties or coalitions that have had little chance of winning a seat.

The Law of Quotas

In the last two decades, several bills have been submitted to establish some kind of legal incentive for female presence in positions of power. Among these initiatives, it is worth mentioning a project presented in 2007 under the first administration of Michelle Bachelet (Bulletin 5553–06). This referred to the balanced participation of men and women in power, and established a 30% quota for the underrepresented sex, applicable to parliamentary, municipal and internal elections of political parties. This project was not successful.

In 2015, the binominal electoral system was replaced by a proportional system and a gender electoral quota was introduced (Ley 20840). The law states that neither male nor female candidates may exceed 60% of the candidates on the ballot from a political party. If this requirement is not met, the list is considered not submitted. This gender quota will only be applied for four successive parliamentary elections in 2017, 2021, 2025 and 2029. Similar temporary restriction affects the economic incentives provided for the political parties whose candidates win.

The Chilean gender quota is disconcerting if it is examined in the face of comparative evidence. After several decades of application of mechanisms to encourage female presence in political decision making, studies suggest that the mere presence of women, even when reaching the highest thresholds, is not able to neutralize the sex-gender system. The advancement of measures designed to increase female presence in positions of power does not imply a complete leveling of the opportunities for men and women to access and exercise power, nor the disappearance of resistance. Rather, they diversify and shift it from the electoral stage to the exercise of power, and from the official to the informal.

Consequently, the accumulated evidence does not support the Chilean legislator's hypothesis that the 12 years from 2017 to 2029 would be enough to produce a cascade of social transformation that would ensure equal access to the positions of power for men and women. Such optimism is suspect considering that the 2007 project, also presented by President Bachelet, was more ambitious than the one approved under her second administration. That project did not include an expiration date for the quota mechanism. It included the municipal and internal elections of the political parties in addition to the parliamentary elections, and it used the language of parity.

A cursory scan reveals that the gender quota approved by the Chilean parliament is not designed to produce the result that it declares to pursue. If the objective of the Chilean law is not to ensure a stable presence of women in power, then it has some other purpose in reality. The mismatch between public discourses in favor of a balanced distribution of power and the elusive practices of political parties has been a common phenomenon. This reveals that the reasons that lead political parties to consent to the installation quotas are generally strategic in nature. They tolerate and use the presence of outsiders such as women, youth or members of ethnic minorities to legitimize their parties as a tool for self-preservation. This drive increases in moments of scandal for the political class.

It is not by chance that almost thirty years after the return of democracy, the Chilean political class has approved two major reforms aimed at democratizing politics at the same time: the reformation of the binominal system and a gender quota. This coincides with the most serious crisis of representation that the Chilean system has seen since the end of the dictatorship. The combination of consequences from the student movement, the emergence of new social movements critical of the post-dictatorship neoliberal consensus, the scandals of political financing that exposed collusion with business, and the corruption that permeates the armed forces have generated a deterioration of the image of representative institutions, and the Chilean Congress in particular. Considering this, the sudden inclusiveness of Chilean politics can be interpreted as a strategic concession of the political class, particularly with the high volatility in voter turnout introduced by the reform that did away with compulsory voting.

If this hypothesis is correct, the Chilean gender quota reveals a greater obstacle that the construction of a full feminine citizenship must face: the masculinized power is only willing to incorporate women on condition that it is interim, precarious and unstable. This is problematic because, in this time of gender pattern transition, the achievements obtained with one hand can be easily be undone by the other. Discussing greater female political participation in terms of marginal and interim presence can easily end up serving the same gender order that this discourse is supposed to subvert. In other words, a gender quota set up as a provisional tool and subject to expiration can become a real poisoned gift.

The Legacy of Bachelet

But the case of Chile also shows some promise related to issues of female leadership. In fact, the most studied aspect in the recent Chilean political experience regarding the relations between gender and politics is Michelle Bachelet. She has been elected president twice, serving between 2006 and 2010, and between 2014 and 2018.

The leadership of Michelle Bachelet has attracted special attention in the field of gender studies because it constitutes a clear example of the use of gender as political capital. Bachelet is the first woman to ascend to the government of a Latin American country without having a familial relationship with a man who has previously held a relevant political position. That is, without enjoying a derivative legitimacy. Therefore, Bachelet's legacy challenges the accumulated historical experience that suggested that the few women who came to power, such as Bhutto, Ghandi and Chamorro, did so accidentally, thanks to their family ties and in the context of moments of great political turmoil. In contrast, Bachelet's political career rests on a leadership that vindicates being a woman.

Apart from factors such as her family history, her past as an exiled and tortured politician, her position in the previous government or an incipient disaffection with the political elite that could have facilitated her triumph in the 2005 elections, Bachelet's electoral success is explained by her ability to develop a discourse that connected her status as a woman with the possibility of making politics closer to citizens (Fernández Ramil 2007; Valdés 2010; Marques Pereira 2015; Valenzuela 2015). Bachelet used the same arguments that have been used to install gender quotas and parity in the heart of democratic discussions. She highlighted the obstacles women face in accessing politics, claimed their gender belonging as something positive, symbolized her triumph as a break from gender discrimination and connected it with a deepening of democracy.

Additionally, she redefined gender stereotypes and managed to use them in her favor. Particularly in the discursive record of her first presidential campaign, it is possible to observe the use of the feminine as a metaphor for closeness, trust and even moral supremacy. She mobilized some elements of the rhetoric of Latin American Marianism, and embodied them in the figure of a divorced, agnostic and plain-spoken mother (Vera Gajardo 2008; Marques Pereira 2015). All this identified her with a large segment of the female population, especially single mothers and heads of reconstituted families who, through her, felt included and legitimized in society (Valdés 2010, 258).

Paradoxically, the same factors that facilitated her election turned against her in the form of questions about her lack of leadership and political expertise during her first government. As Marques Pereira (2015, 163) warns, in the case of Bachelet, gender status has strongly revealed its oscillating nature. Her second government has also been negatively affected. Her agenda of foundational reforms in education, taxes, politics and the constitution lacked the public support that the great popularity that led her to win the 2013 election predicted. It does not seem possible to explain this result from a gender perspective alone. There are other elements, such as the ambivalent relationship of Chilean society with neoliberalism, or the crisis of representation, triggered by the recent episodes of political corruption, which have more potential to explain the frustration of these projects (Araujo 2017; Garretón 2016).

In terms of the impact of political leadership on the deconstruction of gender patterns, it is obvious that Michelle Bachelet has helped to reconfigure the relationship between women and politics. She has made it seem likely that women entering politics will become less of an exception and more of a common occurrence.

It is also clear that her two terms have been committed to the promotion of a gender agenda. Despite the difficulties associated with it, a large part of the most transcendent products of her gender agenda are concentrated in her last term. In the first part of her second term, the Chilean parliament approved the gender electoral quota, with the limitations mentioned above. In 2016, the Ministry of Women and Gender Equity was created, which absorbed the former National Service for Women, significantly strengthening this institutional framework. In September 2017, the law decriminalizing the voluntary interruption of pregnancy in the case of danger to the life of the mother, lethal fetal unfeasibility and rape was enacted. Although the system this law creates is conservative in nature, its approval was a great political triumph for Bachelet in that it managed to overcome the resistance coming from her own coalition of government, and the constitutional objections raised by a group of conservative parliamentarians and filed before the Chilean Constitutional Court. It is worth remembering that, in 2008, the court struck down an emergency contraception distribution policy driven by Bachelet.

During her first term, as part of her gender equity agenda, she appointed the first ministerial cabinet with gender parity. This was a significant increase in the number of women who held ministerial positions. She also strengthened the social network of nurseries and kindergartens and reformed the pension system in 2008 to include a pillar of gender equality through the recognition of female domestic work.

Although it is difficult to prematurely draw conclusions about the transformative impact of her two governments, what seems certain is that Michelle Bachelet has revealed mechanisms for deconstructing a highly masculinized political model, which can open up opportunities to redefine relation ships between gender and politics. She has achieved a reasonable balance between rhetoric and practice, and even with the ghost of essentialism always present, has helped to modify the limits of power, offering a promise of shared political territory (Fernández Ramil 2011, 144).

Bachelet's example has demonstrated that the mere presence of women in positions of power is not sufficient for the promotion and protection of women's interests, but is a necessary condition to progress substantively in this area. It remains to be seen if the strength of her leadership, remaining in office despite the numerous attacks suffered during her two governments, is capable of overcoming the personification of power. It may be possible that Bachelet transfers her political capital to women as a collective, and thus helps prevent the relative illegitimacy that affects women in the political sphere It is also possible that Bachelet's leadership is seen as unique and unrepeatable. A swallow that does not make a summer. Only time will tell.

FINAL REFLECTION

The feminist idea that increasing the presence of women in politics is the radicalization of democracy has had an inconclusive effect. Translated into a simple numerical representation, a provisional quota has very limited potential to transform the gender order. As a new arrangement of political justice, structured as a new principle for the articulation of power, the principle of balanced distribution has more potential to interrupt the relative illegitimacy that affects women, as long as attention is paid to the protecting the exercise of power, and is not only focused on barriers to access.

The emergence of new female leaders can contribute powerfully to reclaiming politics from masculine territory, provided that we take note of the risks of regression involved in the *naturalization* of a feminine form of politics. The study of Chile, and Michelle Bachelet in particular, shows us, on a cultural and historical scale, the potential for and limits of the recent conversion of discourses and strategies to combat female underrepresentation.

REFERENCES

Amorós, C. 2006. *La gran diferencia y sus pequeñas consecuencias para la lucha de las mujeres*. Madrid: Ediciones Cátedra.

Araujo, K. 2017. "Sujeto y neoliberalismo en Chile. Rechazos y apegos." *Nuevo Mundo Mundos Nuevos*, Questions du temps présent, October 1, 2017. http://nuevomundo.revues.org/70649

Archenti, N. and Tula, M.I. 2013. "¿Las Mujeres al Poder? Cuotas y Paridad de Género en América Latina." *Seminario de Investigación #9*. February 22, 2013. Salamanca: Instituto de Iberoamérica -Universidad de Salamanca.

Bareiro, L., Soto, C. and Soto, L. 2007. *La Inclusión de la Mujer en los Procesos de Reforma en América Latina.* Santiago: Banco Interamericano de Desarrollo, Departamento de Desarrollo Sostenible.

Barrère, M. 2013. "Versiones de la democracia, feminismos y polítca radical." In *Democracia y participación política de las mujeres: Visiones desde Europa y América Latina*, edited by Mestre i Mestre, R. and Zúñiga, Y., 45–80. Valencia: Tirant lo Blanch.

Bereni, L. and Lépinard, É. 2004. "Les femmes ne sont pas une catégorie. Les stratégies de légitimation de la parité en France." *Revue française de science politique* 54, no. 1: 71- 88.

Eilperin, J. 2016. "White House women want to be in the room where it happens." *The Washington Post,* September 13, 2016. https://www.washingtonpost.com/news/powerpost/wp/2016/09/13/white-house-women-are-now-in-the-room-where-it-happens/?mc_cid=23f41632c6&mc_eid=4cd64fb794&postshare=6251473762897800&utm_term=.1e38c7d0600f&wpisrc=nl_daily202&wpmm=1

Fernández Ramil, M.A. 2007. *Bienvenida, Paridad.* Santiago: Cuarto propio.

——— .2011. "El género post-Bachellet: La pérdida de un territorio compartido," *Revista Anales* Séptima serie no. 2: 131–147.

Fraser, N. 1997. *Justitia Interrupta. Reflexiones críticas desde la posición postsocialista.* Bogotá: Siglo del Hombre Editores-Universidad de los Andes.

———. 2008. *Escalas de Justicia*. Barcelona: Editorial Herder.

Garretón. M. A. 2016. "Le second gouvernement de Bachelet: projet de transformation et crise politique." *Le "modèle" chilean: des ruptures en trompe-l-oeil, Problèmes d'Amérique Latine,* no. 102: 13–33. Paris: Editions Eska iKNOW Politics. 2016. *Discusión en línea sobre violencia contra mujeres en política. Nota conceptual.* http://iknowpolitics.org/sites/default/files/edvawip_sp.pdf

Inter-Parliamentary Union (IPU). 2015. *Women in Parliament: 20 years in review.* http://archive.ipu.org/pdf/publications/WIP20Y-en.pdf

Inter-Parliamentary Union (IPU). 2017. *Women in national parliaments.* http://archive.ipu.org/wmn-e/classif.htm

Krook, L. and Restrepo, J. 2016. "Género y violencia política en América Latina. Conceptos, debates y soluciones." *Política y Gobierno* 23, no. 1: 127–162.

Leslie, S.J. 2015. "Hillary Clinton is the only man in the Obama Administration»: dual character concepts, generics, and gender." *Analytic Philosophy* 56, no. 2, (June): 111–141.

McGinley, A. C. 2009. "Hillary Clinton, Sarah Palin, and Michelle Obama: Performing Gender, Race, and Class on the Campaign Trail." *Denver University Law Review* (vol. 86) 709–725.

Marques-Pereira, B. 2013. "Caminos y argumentos a favor de las cuotas y la paridad en Belgica y en Francia." In *Democracia y participación política de las mujeres: Visiones desde Europa y América Latina*, coordinated by Mestre i Mestre, R. and Zúñiga, Y., 281–304. Valencia: Tirant lo Blanch.

Marques-Pereira, B., Paternotte, D. and Valenzuela, M. 2015. "El género como recurso político: el uso estratégico del género por Michelle Bachelet (Chile) y Laurette Onkelinx (Bélgica)." *Revista de la Academia* 20: 155–182.

Okin, S. 2008. *Justice, Genre et famille.* París: Champs Essais.

Phillips, A. 2000. *Democracy and the Representation of Differe nce and The Politics of Presence: Problems and Developments.* Aalborg: Aalborg Universitet.

Ríos Tobar, M. 2008. *Mujer y Política. El impacto de las cuotas de género en América Latina.* Santiago: FLACSO-IDEA-Ed. Catalonia.

Scott, J. 1998. *La citoyenne paradoxale. Les féministes françaises et les droits de l'homme.* Paris: Albin Michel.

Scott, J. 2005. *Parité! L'universel et la différence des sexes.* París: Albin Michel.

Solnit, R. 2016. *Los hombres me explican cosas.* Madrid: Capitan Swing.

UNDP. 2018. *Participación política de las mujeres. Auditoría a la Democracia.* http://www.cl.undp.org/content/chile/es/home/ourwork/democraticgovernance/infografias/participacion-politica-mujeres.html

Valcárcel, A. 1997. *La política de las mujeres.* Madrid: Ediciones Cátedra.

Valdés, T. 2010. *¿Género en el poder? El Chile de Michelle Bachelet.* Santiago: Observatorio Género y Equidad- UNDEF-UNIFEM-Corporación de Estudios para el Desarrollo de la Mujer.

Valenzuela, M. 2015. "La pertenencia de género como capital de legitimación discursiva; el caso de las presidentas Michelle Bachelet (Chile) y Cristina Fernándes (Argentina)." *Revista de la Academia* 19: 165–186.

Vera Gajardo, A. 2008. "Les discours de genre dans la campagne présidentielle de Michelle Bachelet: une critique féministe." *Raisons Politiques* 31: 81–103.

Young, I. 2000. *La justicia y la política de la diferencia.* Madrid: Ediciones Cátedra.

Chapter Four

Torture and Domestic Violence

A View from Cases of Terroristic Torture and Intimate Terrorism

Paula Hollstein

Some horrendous tales between partners made public on police news have mostly been labelled as domestic violence in Chile. Nonetheless, there is room to argue that these same facts should have been regarded as torture. Consider the following testimony from Nabila Rifo, a victim of an unfortunate and prominent case of domestic violence in Chile:

> He started to argue, I told him: I am going to leave you tomorrow! He was insolent, unbearable. When I turned around I felt that he hit me with a stone on my head. With the first hit I fell down, it shook my head, I sobered up in a second; the second blow was with a very large stone and after the third one, I lost consciousness. The first strike threw me to the grass and from there I no longer resisted, I played dead to make him stop beating me." (*El Mostrador* 2017)

Some feminists have already made the links between both of these notions. For instance, MacKinnon suggests that understanding some types of domestic violence within the recognized profile of torture would contribute to the recognition of such abuses as a serious human rights concern (2006, 17). Are feminists right to make this point? Chilean experience can shed some light on this issue. In spite of the presence of both phenomena in Chilean history, the previous association has not been analyzed yet. There are some reasons that prevent taking that approach. Domestic violence (hereinafter DV) and torture are distressing topics. The stigma that is attached to these acts also means that they are invariably met with strong human emotions: shame, fear, and despair.

With respect to torture, most societies infer it to be one of the most serious injustices a human can inflict upon another being. Most Latin American countries, including Chile, have suffered from one particular, atrocious and unique type: terroristic torture. It was designed to disable and intimidate the enemies from the left in the context of dictatorship (1973–1989). This kind of torture "cannot satisfy the constraint of possible compliance because its purpose—the intimidation of persons other than the victim—cannot be accomplished and may not even be capable of being influenced by the victim" (Shue 1978, 132).

On the other hand, we think of DV as violent behavior between two individuals who are not enemies. They are lovers. Feminists usually associate DV under the rubric of violence against women. This outlook does not treat this topic separately from other kinds of wrongdoings (e.g., rape, gender discrimination, women's objectification, etc.). However, it is also possible to isolate DV as a unit of analysis, and therefore it can be morally censured as such. In this sense, DV has been defined as "a pattern of coercive control in which the perpetrator asserts his power over the victim through the use of threats, as well as actual violence" (Dutton & Goodman 2005, 743).

As in the vast majority of the world, DV is a serious problem in Chile, not only in terms of frequency, but also in terms of the brutality of the actions that the victims' testimonies describe. Indeed, often DV results in death. According to the current data there have been 41 femicides and 1 femicide suicide so far in 2018. Moreover, Chilean society was shocked and stunned by the cruelty of Rifo's case, who was found unconscious with various fractures, broken teeth and, even more shocking, her eyes missing. After several days in a critical condition, Rifo managed to survive but she had completely lost her eyesight. Rifo's case has become an emblematic symbol of the country's uphill battle against DV.

The main aim of this paper is to make a conceptual comparison between torture, especially terroristic torture, and DV, two phenomena highly prevalent in recent Chilean history. In order to do this, I am going to define torture and DV separately, showing a representative sample of fragments of stories from Chilean experience in both concepts. Finally, I will draw a parallel between these two kinds of acts, and then, address the political consequences of that appraisal.

I will sustain that torture and DV share some elements that make them similar. At least, the wrongness and the outcomes (in agency) equate both behaviors. Consequently, I claim that the seriousness of these two kinds of actions should be reflected in the attention they receive from Chilean public policy. At this point I would like to emphasize the necessary introductory nature of that final section since the complexity of institutional responses justifies the writing of a separate article.

TORTURE

The word torture has its origin in the idea of "twisting." Torture originally consisted of tormenting the body until it twists uncontrollably (Davis 2005, 163). Nowadays the idea of torture seems conceptually more teleological.[1] At its very least, torture involves the deliberate infliction of severe pain on an unwilling person for purposes that the person does not share. If we take this definition at face value, there are two main ways in which it can be condemned as wrong: one utilitarian and the other Kantian. The former objects to torture as long as it gives rise to great suffering that fails to be compensated by any utility. The latter—based on Kant's categorical imperative in the form of the formula of humanity—posits that torture is wrong because it involves using someone as a mere means to another's purposes (Sussman 2005, 5; 13–14).[2]

What makes torture wrong is related to the following elements: 1) The kind of relationship it enacts (because it implies a violation of the victim's autonomy); and 2) the fact that torture involves the infliction of pain. Sussman's account of torture includes those two elements; moreover he offers a sophisticated description of the way in which the torturer and his victim relate to each other, which is useful for the purposes of this chapter. This account posits that torture turns out to be the pre-eminent instance of a kind of forced self-betrayal, which not only frustrates the victim's autonomy, but perverts it (Sussman 2005, 4–19), as I will now describe in more detail below.

Pain

With torture the victim's cooperation is achievable because of the nature of pain. To be in pain requires responding to a type of request to do something, an internal voice of our agency, a kind of imperative. We can have nonspecific discomforts that we have no idea how to deal with, yet even here we feel a need to do something in response: we writhe, grimace, or groan (Sussman 2005, 20). Thus, pain is something found somewhere between an exercise of agency and exogenous act. The torturer has control of his victim's pain, and through this his victim's body, and so can command it to express the torturer's will.

Atrocious forms of causing severe pain were used in Chile. Not only blows, but electroshocks were administered to sensitive body parts (Metiendo Ruido 2012), cuts and "special methods" were frequently mentioned in accounts, such as the following:

> Torture methods included shocks and electric shocks to all the most sensitive parts of the body, such as the breasts, eyes, anus, vagina, nose, ears, and fingers. They also used a torture method called "pau de arara" ("parrot's perch" in Portuguese), in which the feet and arms were tied, the body hung upside down, and an electric shock given to the anus. Another torture method was "the telephone," where both of my ears were beaten simultaneously. (Pascoe 2004)

As we can see, Chilean torturers used extreme ways to get the alliance of the victims. It seems that the torturer's idea was to directly manipulate sensitive body parts in order to effectively establish collaboration or intimidation. Although perverse, this appears to be a very conscious choice. Suffering was a tool used to achieve the torturer's aim.

Dilemma

Along with pain, torture implies a sort of instrumentalisation of the victim's feelings. These feelings are expressed in terms of questioning about submission or resistance. On the one hand, there is a hard choice to make between two undesirable alternatives (e.g., giving information that will harm loved ones or bearing electroshocks to the genitals). That element is more commonly seen in interrogational torture. But torture is more than a mere tough negotiation. To the victim he/she is not only accountable for the final answer (choice); but also for some possible strategies within the process (e.g., how or when to submit properly) (Sussman 2005, 10).

Furthermore, the dilemma is not binary: It also includes remorse (e.g., giving information about the loved one); anger (e.g., towards the sardonic attitude of the torturer); frustration (e.g., if the victim could not resist enough); little triumphs (e.g., if the victim gains temporary mercy from the torturer); and contradictory feelings (e.g., if the victim becomes friendly with the torturer). Thus, the act of torture not only establishes two scenarios to achieve some end; it also exposes the victim to the difficult choice of exploring his/her capacities and attitudes toward the torturer. Confusing tactics, such as fake executions and good cop/bad cop routines encourage the victims to think that to some extent they could *handle the situation*, but at the same time this can break their emotional resistance, as the dilemma becomes more complex.

As previously mentioned, terroristic torture "cannot satisfy the constraint of possible compliance, because its purpose—intimidation of persons other than the victim—cannot be accomplished" (Shue 1978, 132). In this case, even though there is not a clear purpose from the torturer the dilemma is equally present and probably stronger. Furthermore, when there is no specific information or action required the victim will be totally at the mercy of the torturer depending on whether they fulfill his needs or not. The victim will have to figure out what is required from the torturer.

These types of tactics were used systematically in Chile as reported in the *National Commission Report on Political Prisoners and Torture* (hereinafter NCPT): "A large number of attendees to this Commission said they had been subjected to firing drills" (2005, 237). In addition, the torturer's purpose was hardly ever clear. Obscure and mysterious requests were usual in the Chilean dictatorship, as can be appreciated from this testimony: "Many times they tortured me without any interrogation. I did not know why they kept torturing me" (Pascoe 2004).

As can be seen, along with pain, Chilean victims suffered strong and complex dilemmas. They not only dealt with the classic double choice of submission or resistance, but they also dealt with constant questioning on many details within a very tough process. Furthermore, it can be stated that as terroristic torture was an official and systematic method of repression in the Chilean dictatorship, most of the victims' psychological processes had most probably collapsed by incisive explorations on what to do in that context.

Victim Participation: Self-Betrayal

Due to the extreme circumstances the victim will try to please the torturer in order to avoid any extra harm. As previously mentioned, when there is no action required the victim will be totally at the mercy of the torturer's satisfaction; yet, even in the cases where the torturer has a clear goal, the victim will not merely develop specific actions to fulfil demands; instead he will read the torturer's mood, interests and demands. In that scenario the victim will make positive efforts to understand and gratify his torturer, and will pay attention to every detail. That pressure level shifts—to some extent—who feels in charge of the situation. The victim represents his own feelings as a problem; as something he is responsible for (Sussman 2005, 10).

Again, the case of terroristic torture is a good example to illustrate the victim's involvement. The victim's participation becomes explicit and a requirement. In the Chilean dictatorship, the victim was usually forced to actively participate in the act of torture to feel the dilemma strongly. For example: one woman testified that she was forced to have sex with her father and brother, who were also detained (NCPT 2005, 249–250). Another person affirmed that she had to erect three soldiers by means of oral sex at the age of 14 (Metiendo Ruido 2012).

As it can be seen, Chilean victims not only suffered their own explorations of the torturers' attitudes as part of the classic torture process; torturers also wanted to make sure of the victim's contribution by suitable (and perverse) methods. As discussed, in that way, the person who feels in charge of the situation changes. This psychological trap was explicitly reported in the NCPT: “Many people referred . . . to the blame of having spoken during the torture, for endangering their families and loved ones; to the shame and guilt of being raped and abused; the impotence and the guilt of being forced to witness how they tortured others, without having been able to prevent it” (NCPT 2005, 599).

Analogies

To Sussman “our sexual desires and responses are particularly apt avenues of torture.” This potential arises not only from the influence of sexual seduction, but also from its aptness to cause shame. The sexual act offers one of the deepest forms of closeness, self-revelation, and trust: “As such, it is readily perverted into a mode of self-estrangement and self-betrayal” (Sussman 2005, 27–28).

Rape (by torturers, other prisoners and animals), nakedness, and forced masturbation were frequent methods of torture in the Chilean dictatorship, especially amongst women (Metiendo Ruido 2012; Lobos 2014). The NCPT reported those kinds of acts in an exclusive chapter: Nakedness (2005, 276) and aggression and sexual violence (2005, 278). Even pantomimes of relationships were present in prisoner camps: Commander Pacheco, who was in charge of Tres Álamos, “constantly abused me, subjecting me to sexual harassment for almost two years. He liked walking around the concentration camp with me at his side” (López, 2016).

Sussman goes further when he points out that the wrongness of torture “may also be found in rape and many kinds of spousal and child abuse. I suspect that in a comprehensive analysis, these latter would be best understood as special types of torture” (Sussman 2005, 3 footnote 9). Victims of those kinds of acts are frequently gripped with the idea they did not resist sufficiently, as we can see in this testimony: “I felt guilty and I did not know why. All I wanted was to get away from him. I did not write a single letter to him, because he was also in jail. He told me that he loved me and I could not tell him anything . . . (about having been raped). I could not” (NCPT 2005, 605).

As we can see, it is not difficult to make a link between sexual violence and Chilean torture. There are not only sexual connotations in some of the ways that degrading treatments were used by Chilean torturers, but also some sexual attacks were used directly as a form of torture, especially among women. The National Commission on Political Prisoners and Torture reported on those situations: “This Commission received the testimony of 3,399 women, corresponding to 12.5% of all the testimonies. . . . Almost all women reported having been subjected to sexual violence regardless of age and 316 reported being raped. However, it is estimated that the number of women raped is much higher than the reported cases, because of the above considerations and because there are many testimonies which reported having witnessed rapes committed in a large number of detention facilities" (2005, 291).

Domestic Violence

Focusing exclusively on the notion of DV (in contrast with any broader approach), Michael Johnson (2008) has outlined four different concepts. We must highlight that the presence of coercion is crucial to identify the behavior which is associated with DV.

> In intimate terrorism, the perpetrator uses violence in the service of general control over his or her partner; the partner does not. In violent resistance, the partner is violent and controlling—an intimate terrorist—and the resister's violence arises in reaction to that attempt to exert general control. In mutual violent control, both members of the couple use violence in attempts to gain general control over their partner. Thus, three of the four types of intimate partner violence are organised around attempts to exert or thwart general control. In the fourth type of intimate partner violence, situational couple violence, the perpetrator is violent (and his or her partner may be as well); however, neither of them uses violence to attempt to exert general control. (Johnson 2008, 5)

In the same vein, the "general theory of social power" by Dutton & Goodman's conceptualization has defined DV as "a *pattern of coercive control* in which the perpetrator asserts his power over the victim through the use of threats, as well as actual violence" (Dutton & Goodman 2005, 743). Consequently, coercive control is the core idea in the definition of DV which can be conceptualized as "a dynamic process linking a demand with a credible threatened, negative consequence for noncompliance" (Dutton & Goodman 2005, 743–746). It is important to emphasize that any particular violent incident may not involve control.

In the case of DV, we do not need to settle for information about one particular act. We are not looking at an isolated encounter between two people, but a pattern of encounters that extends over a period of time and involves a variety of circumstances. To define whether the violence is in fact part of a pattern of DV, we have to ask if other elements are present. Dutton and Goodman (2005, 745) point out that coercive control requires a credible threat, setting the stage, surveillance, compliance and resistance .

Demand and Threat

Coercion involves a demand and a threat. A potential negative outcome involved in coercion depends on the victim's failure to comply with the partner's demand. However, inherent to the definition of DV is the vagueness of its boundaries because practically all affairs include persuasion and influence (French & Raven 1959). Demands may be communicated explicitly (e.g., "you'd better be home when I get here!") or implicitly (e.g., just a glimpse showing disconformity with an opinion). Assessing coercive requests in DV requires not only identifying obvious demands, but also those that are integrated into the day-to-day interactions (Dutton & Goodman 2005, 749–750).

Chilean experiences reveal numerous examples of demands and threats: "If she reports him to the cops, or the boys report him to the cops, he will burn the house down while she and the children are sleeping"; "he told me that if I meet a man, he will do something to me. Yes, I always lived in threat" (Astudillo and Santana 2014, 73–87). Sometimes threats are made in a bizarre symbolic manner, such as the case of Carla: 'I was terrified of his reactions, especially because he frightened me with a knife at least once a day. He used to sit on the bed with a stone, sharpening the blade: "With this one I will kill you, if you cheat on me, he said" (Rojas 2016).

Setting the Stage

Raven (quoted by Dutton & Goodman 2005) argues that coercion may require *setting the stage*, where the perpetrator exhibits that he has the means to exert coercion. This usually occurs in a history of growing DV. Once an act of DV happens the probability remains that it will occur many times in the future. Four ways in which a partner can set the stage include: (1) creating the expectancy for negative consequences; (2) creating or exploiting the partner's vulnerabilities; (3) wearing down the partner's resistance; and (4) facilitating dependency (Dutton & Goodman 2005, 748).

Creating the Expectancy for Negative Consequences

An example of setting the stage is found in the following testimony: "[the husband] started to take his anger out on things, he broke the computer, the cooker, and he shattered a video player. He said "I pay for them, I buy them and I break them." The plants and my dog were also victims. My dog was also hit, I had to defend it. He hurt me that way" (*Mercurio de Calama* 2007). In that case the perpetrator creates the expectancy of penalties, not only by the suggestion that any of her appreciated objects will be harmed if she fails to comply, but also by the implicit message that he is willing to inflict the same act of cruelty on her.

Creating or Exploiting the Partner's Vulnerabilities

Perpetrators also use more subtle techniques, many of which involve forms of psychological abuse. As Johnson (2008, 88) reports, there are many sophisticated ways to undermine the self-esteem of individuals. The Chilean media is full of detailed accounts of relentless psychological abuse: "Once he took all the things from the bedroom and threw them into the dining room. He did not want to sleep with me because he considered me to be a prostitute. I used to get up at 5.30 to go to work and at that time he used to attack me psychologically and in other ways. For example, I was taking a shower and to annoy me he turned off the water heater" (*Mercurio de Calama* 2007).

Wearing Down the Partner's Resistance

Public acts of humiliation are also effective ways of wearing down the partner's resistance: "I have a friend who behaves this way: The phone rings and he shouts to his girlfriend in front of everyone saying: 'can you stay quiet for a while or not, ah?' They have been together for five years, and she is unfortunately resigned to this" (SERNAM 2009, 73). The will to resist is also weakened by the defense of acts of violence that shifts the blame to the victim or legitimates the use of violence: "When they say bad things to you, you think the problem is you. They make you think that you are the problem, it hurts more than when they hit you" (Latin American Foundation for Social Innovation 2010, 26).

Facilitating Dependency

It could be tricky to see facilitating emotional dependency as an element of DV since relationships involve interdependence in many aspects of everyday life (e.g., advice with decisions or support with problems). However, when dependence in the relationship is uneven, the individual who is less dependent has greater power (Dutton & Goodman 2005, 749). In a Chilean case (which culminated in suicide) dependency was set by different means. Her sister gave the testimony: "This guy kept Elena drugged by pills. . . . He made her sign documents under the influence of pills and in that way took away all her properties. He never worked!"; "Elena transferred the restaurant and its licenses into his name, [. . .] and the van's papers were also put into his name. The truck was also hers [. . .] he spent all the money from her credit cards, made her totally dependent; he controlled all the couple's money" (Astudillo and Santana 2014, 94–96).

Surveillance

Monitoring is an element that reveals the controlling aim of the perpetrator. The perpetrator needs evidence of the partner's behavior to know whether or not he should punish the victim (Dutton and Goodman 2005, 745–750). Chilean testimonies also frequently mention control and surveillance as elements of DV: “He was calling the house all day, all the time, like every one to two hours, and then, he used to ask: How are you? Did you go out? And where did you go?” (SERNAM 2009, 73). In Elena’s case the perpetrator used to control not only his victim, but also her family in order to keep her isolated: “He was the owner of the house and the condominium; so, some people kept him informed of everything: ‘They are going out, they are coming back!’ He knew everything. And when we went out, he used to go into the house. What is more, he took down the curtains” (Astudillo and Santana 2014, 95).

Dilemmas around Compliance or Resistance

Victims subject themselves to immense questioning when they face an intimidating request in the context of DV. Research around behavioral response to coercion reveals that reactions can involve compliance or resistance, but usually both. Dutton and Goodman found that battered women use increasing levels of both resistance and conciliating tactics as the violence escalates in its intensity (2005, 745–746).

That hesitant attitude from the victim exposes the complexity of the process. Firstly, the DV victim has to decide day by day if she will follow the rules imposed by the partner who wants to exercise control over her. Those rules are usually imposed over a long period of time and involve a variety of circumstances. If controlling behavior is frequent and intense, the victim’s life can become very stressful. One can clearly appreciate the intricacy and toughness of a day by day dilemma in this example: “[I had sexual relations without wanting it]. That was the worst thing that I did. I cried. I hated him. I told him off. But then I moved forward for my daughter. I just have to bear it, since I have three girls and my mother is poor” (Astudillo and Santana 2014, 85).

In addition, the decisions are not always binary (submission or resistance). Firstly, obedience to requests can sometimes turn into day-to-day rules without a clear negative appraisal from the victim. That kind of judgmental deficit is reinforced since there are previous acts that aim to set the stage (e.g., “I accepted that he manages my money because of my poor financial skills”). In that way, submission to requests can become routine—with those actions taking on the appearance of being “voluntary” (Dutton & Goodman 2005, 752). That cognitive deficit can be appreciated in the following testimony from a victim’s sister. The victim saw DV acts as being part of a normal couple’s conflicts: “She always told us not to get involved; ‘that is the way relationships are’ [. . .]. She always protected him. ‘Do not worry Dad. I’m okay, we’re super good’” (Astudillo and Santana 2014, 96).

Thirdly, the victim will more or less try to control the situation: In some cases, non-compliance is oblique. The victim does not confront the abuser with a direct rejection (Dutton and Goodman 2005, 752): For instance, when victims lie to their partners when compliance comes at the expense of another important risk. This situation can occur when the victim has been isolated from her family and friends, but the victim nevertheless visits them to hide the restrictions imposed by the abuser. In Teresa's case (murdered together with her three children), she used to talk with her sister in spite of the prohibition: "[Teresa] never asked anyone for help. She just talked with my daughter Flor, but they did it discreetly. However, she did not want me to know about what was happening to her." (Astudillo and Santana 2014, 77).

Yet, as previously stated, the victim is not merely a passive element of the scheme. Indeed, at the other end of the scale the victim can commit violent resistance as well, moreover, the victim can get involved in "mutual violent control" (Johnson 2008, 5).

Furthermore, the possibility of total surrender seems impracticable: it is a labyrinth with no way out. Unlike torture, the objective of DV seems broader. It seems difficult for control to be completely satisfied; at most it can be temporally fulfilled by obedience to certain acts. In that way, the victim cannot *choose* to yield her freedom completely. The failure to comply is about *giving up*; feeling desperate and with no energy to respond to a partner's demands, such as in Elena's final decision: "On the last day, when she talked to him on a Friday night, he asked her to come back home, because 'we have children.' He said that he would forgive her because she was sick and crazy, but she told him that she would never go back to him. And then, the next day she committed suicide" (Astudillo and Santana 2014, 99). So, there is no chance of solving the dilemma in the context of the relationship. It seems that the only possibility of escaping the questioning is to leave.

Fear Arousal

Cognitive appraisals of threat are normally associated with distress reactions including PTSD. Increased provocation can influence the victim's judgments and behavior. For example, dread may focus the victim's care on the perception of immediate risk, rather than on the long-term consequences of her response to it (Dutton & Goodman 2005, 752).

One example of this sort of distress reaction can be found in this testimony:

> Once, I was so tired because of the scandal and psychological abuse that he was putting my daughters under, that I went to the kitchen, I took a knife, I chased him and he came out into the street. In a few minutes he came back, and then I grabbed him and began to stab the knife into his neck. My girls began to cry and told me to stop, I looked at them but I did not see them, and

> then I realised that I was willing to kill him. I saw no other solution for the harmony of the house." (*Mercurio de Calama* 2007)

In terms of autonomy, DV can leave the victim feeling absolutely inept or uncertain as to who she is, what she believes, or what is real and what is not:

> We went on a weekend, and we proposed to her "shall we go for lunch?," and she said: "I do not know, if you want, I'll have lunch." Then, the father said "but daughter what do you really want? We have come here for you, we want you to be well. . . . " Thereafter Elena replied "but if you say that you want to eat empanadas, I'll eat empanadas." We replied "but we will do whatever you want." Finally Elena answered "It's just that I do not know what I want." Elena could not make up her mind. He took away her personality. (Astudillo and Santana 2014, 94)

Perversion of Agency

In the case of DV, the element of pain is not necessarily present. Nonetheless, there are other elements that can make the victim a participant of the progression of DV. First of all, the development of the process is something that can take some time. Through setting the stage, the perpetrator is taking control of the victim by terrorizing her, thus making her more vulnerable and dependent. While this step takes place, the victim has made decisions, and among them, she has permitted acts of control (e.g., "I didn't stop Joseph in his acts of jealousy when I'd spent time spent with others"). *The capture* of the victim was made possible by her day to day acquiescence.

Secondly, as previously stated, the dilemma around submission and resistance is not really dual. The victim is going to try to control the situation; she can possibly try to overcome the difficulties with comings and goings (*honeymoon* period). The fight for control can escalate to violent resistance or mutual violent control, where the victim will have been completely involved in the process. She will have become the other perpetrator of a reciprocal wrongdoing.

Moreover, in DV there is already an existent amorous bond. The perpetrator and victim were previously involved in a close relationship where both body and emotions are completely unprotected. The perpetrator can use those elements as long as there is dependency from the victim. In addition, the sexual act offers one of the deepest forms of closeness, self-revelation, and trust (Sussman 2005, 28).

The above, together with an effective stage of wearing down resistance, can be used to manipulate the victim's own perceptions of reality, as is relayed in this testimony: "He always said that my sister was crazy, so, he had to control her and give her medicine. He even carried out a sleep treatment. She slept for three days, day and night"; "he [the perpetrator] said that he would forgive her because she was sick and crazy" (Astudillo and Santana 2014, 94–99); "verbal violence is harder to recognize because they usually say to you: no, I did not mean that" (Latin American Foundation for Social Innovation 2010, 43).

SIMILARITIES FOUND BETWEEN TORTURE AND DV IN THE TESTIMONIES OF VICTIMS

Intention

While the conscious and direct intention to distort the victim's willpower appears palpable in torture, the case of DV is different, since its direct end is to exercise an open and relentless control. However, it is worth mentioning that general and inexorable control can bring about the same consequences of torture in terms of psychological effects. It could cripple the victim's will. If that is the situation then control can be seen as a means to distort the victim's will, which in a way equates both conducts.

Furthermore, it is possible to argue that the intention to pervert the victim's will can be found in the setting the stage process, which is designed to weaken the victim's resistance, and facilitate dependency. Consequently, it can be claimed that the immediate goal in DV is equally to break or pervert the victim's will, in order to gain control later on. Something not dissimilar occurs in torture, when the will is perverted in order to get what is needed (information, intimidation, etc.). Yet, it is also possible that the degree of violence could tip the balance in terms of the equivalence of those conducts. DV is a broad concept and implies (mostly) a slower process that encompasses many situations. For that reason, it is important to stay cautious in this matter.

The Relationship between the Perpetrator and Victim

At least in the beginning, the relationship between the torturer and the victim is a distant one: it is a relationship between strangers. Officially speaking, acts of torture have been perpetrated by official agents, soldiers from the enemy side and terrorists. Conversely, in DV there is an already existent relationship. Both perpetrator and victim are involved in one of the closest relationships that people can be involved in. Both body and emotions are usually completely exposed. In the context of such a relationship intimates usually expect care and respect.

Dilemma

As can be seen, both torture and DV involve dilemmas that inevitably implicate the victim's exercise of agency. The dilemma in torture is over two bad outcomes that disrupt the fundamental values of the tortured; but the dilemma is also over the way that the victim will exercise his agency in the context of pain and fear: pre-eminently decisions related with *giving in* (when, how). The victim in DV has to deal with a dilemma too as that situation can be presented more explicitly after the victim's realization of her partner's wrongdoing. The questioning includes the set of reactions against acts of control in the context of attachment and dependency. A normal progression of the dilemma should involve the decision of whether to leave (or not) the relationship.

Perversion of Agency

As one can see, both torture and DV have elements that can trigger the victim's participation. Torture makes use of pain, fear and uncertainty. DV uses elements that arise from the nature of any close relationship: exposure of feelings, trust and dependence, but also fear that comes from the setting stage. Therefore, both torture and DV make the victim an agent of the progression of the acts, and then, imposes the feeling of self-betrayal in him/her.

Effects

It has been observed that if DV exceeds a threshold of continuity and severity it can produce the same effects as torture: "Continuing, frequent and extreme acts of domestic violence produce equally damaging and long-term effects in victims of abuse" (Youngs 2003, 1221). Psychological and physical sufferings of women experiencing violence in their everyday lives are no less devastating than the torture inflicted by state agents (Youngs 2003, 1222; Quereshi 2009, 39).

With respect to psychological effects, the concept of "complex post-traumatic stress syndrome" (C-PTSD) has been forged by Judith Herman (1992). Herman shows the equivalence between private violence such as rape and public disturbances such as terrorism. The concept describes the psychological signs of torture both upon the victims of DV and upon political convicts (Herman 1992, 77–119). Furthermore, Herman said that DV psychological effects can be worse than those produced by a strange state oppressor (Herman 1992, 76–79). In a similar vein, Copelon argued that "women victims suffer anguish, humiliation, fear, isolation, and disintegration of self, similar to the psychological conditions of a prisoner in a concentration camp or those of a political captive" (Copelon 1993–94, 313).

Current Situation in Chile

As we have seen, torture and DV share important elements. The wrongness of the conducts and their outcomes are very similar. Some of them are especially relevant in order to evaluate the current understanding about both concepts in general, but particularly in Chile. In this regard, Chile can offer a good representative sample, since both phenomena are present in our recent history. That way, the comparison can be done in people who share some cultural background, which can make our preliminary approach sounder, for future developments in the area.

In addition, the conceptual parallel is relevant since both torture and DV are taboo topics in Chile. First, the Valech Report (officially the already referred to National Commission on Political Imprisonment and Torture Report)—a record of abuses committed in Chile between 1973 and 1990 by agents of Augusto Pinochet's military regime—has been classified, and will be kept secret for the next fifty years (starting November 29, 2004), in contrast to the "Archives of Terror" in Paraguay and Operation Condor. For the above, the records not only cannot be used in trials concerning human rights violations, but also, they cannot be used for research that allows for a better understanding of these phenomena.

As far as DV is concerned, although there has been a law in place that regulates what is called family violence (L 20,066) since 2005, the problem is still prevalent and currently affects a wide range of the Chilean population. There were 127,682 DV crimes in Chile in 2016.[3] However, Camila Maturana Kesten, a lawyer at Corporación Humanas, says those numbers are only a part of a much bigger problem: "In Chile there is a high number of criminal complaints, more than 100,000 women per year report domestic violence. But that percentage is lower than the actual cases' percentage, because many do not complain. They take years to recognize they are in an actual situation of violence" (Sepúlveda 2017).

As Maturana says, going beyond the arousal of the victim's fear, what prevents victims from complaining or leaving the violent relationship is an initial deficit in the cognitive appraisal of the DV phenomenon. Many do not know what is going on or how serious the consequences that DV can bring are. People usually recognize wrongdoing in a relationship when physical violence comes into it, but as we have seen, some DV mechanisms have taken the victim and weakened her resistance at the same time the violence developed. For that reason, it is crucial to delve deeply into the DV concept, because that exploration could be the most effective way to prevent those acts.

Policy Implications

Based on the conclusion of the great importance of this preliminary conceptualization, it is possible to start a discussion around the status of both actions. All of this, in order to be consistent in what is grounded in the Chilean legal system. Significant progress has been already made by feminist activists.

Coherence of the Criminal Justice System

As some feminists noticed, men's suffering was labelled as torture while women's pain was set at the private sphere. Later on, when acts of violence perpetrated by (mostly) husbands were seen as atrocious, feminists advocated for the intervention of criminal justice. Therefore, due to similarities between torture and DV, it is possible to argue that DV deserves the same concerns and status as torture in criminal law.

Nowadays, while torture is considered a crime punishable under the Chilean Criminal Code (paragraph 4, title III of the second book) and as a "crime against humanity"—the highest status in terms of seriousness—in contrast DV is regulated by a double and complex regimen. Acts of DV may be tried by family courts or by criminal justice. Family courts jurisdiction is given in cases where the DV action does not constitute a punishable act. Thus, these courts deal with psychological abuses, or physical maltreats that do not cause injuries, or if it is a one-off act. Criminal justice is in charge of abuse that also constitutes a crime, such as repeated abuses, different kinds of injuries, or death.

It is important to note, that in the case of the family court process, the legislation also provides for the *conditional suspension of the sentence*. This mechanism grants the opportunity to continue the relationship between perpetrator and victim. The rule applies when there is recognition of the DV facts by the offender and when there are antecedents that allow the judge to reasonably presume that the perpetrator will not commit DV acts in the future. Such a situation is impossible to imagine by those who have been torture victims.

For that reason, feminist scholars have continued to draw attention to this disparity: "DV as torture situates intimate violence in the category of state-sponsored violence" (Copelon 2003, 871) and "torture is torture regardless of the setting, identity and the gender of the persons involved" (Qureshi 2013, 44).

Promotion of Autonomy

Although the feminist approach has the merit of consistency, it can be seen as controversial that the exact same exercise of punitive power can be the proper intervention for both conducts. It is possible to think that no punitive interventions should be set in the field of DV. First of all, there are some intrinsic problems with DV's criminal procedures: "Survivors of domestic violence frequently refused to testify against their batterers and substantial evidence against the batterer was often hard to produce and defend. Although increased criminal justice intervention still represented significant gains, advocates were finding that the strategy often failed" (Ben Ishai 2009, 313).

As a result of the awareness of the above difficulty, a new approach that focused on the care of the victims was suggested. The purpose is to overcome the criticisms of the criminal system but also to promote the victim's autonomy. For example, Sally Sholz says that advocates for DV victims will need to care for those victims and this involves working to help them in a way that allows the victim to recover her sense of autonomy and so to make her own decisions (Sholz 1998, 46, 53, 58).

According to Bramer that perspective seems closer to the purposes of the Kantian State. In the DV ambit these resources have been mentioned: "policies, laws, and agencies that will help restore and promote the autonomy for victims of IT [Intimate Terrorism]" (2011, 13). Likewise, Sarah focuses her approach on the capacity of independence of DV victims:

> As citizens of the state who are potentially unable to maintain themselves when they first leave their abusers, victims of IT have a right to be supported by the state. They have a right to services and policies that will help restore their autonomy and promote their agency. These services and policies will include financial assistance, housing assistance, possibly educational assistance, and physical and legal protection from their former partners. (Bramer 2011, 12–13)

In this respect, although there are social programs for treatment of DV victims in Chile, among them "Prevention and Care of Violence against Women" (see Cámara de Diputados de Chile 2015, 81 and the following); those programs are at best focused on prevention, instead of reparation. In addition, resources are too scarce to respond to the high demand of victims. The special service (SERNAM) does not have the capacity to receive high-risk victims in each of the country's regions.

In this context, the current programmatic offer was criticized due to its fragmentation between protected groups (women, the elderly, people with disabilities, children and adolescents) and the different dimensions of their needs (education, health, psychosocial support, labor, among others). This could cause over-intervention in the families and the reduction of women to their role as *caretakers*: mothers of their children, without providing the necessary tools for them to achieve economic independence and autonomy (Cámara de Diputados de Chile 2015, 115).

CONCLUSION

As we have seen through this chapter, there is a great similarity between torture and DV. These conducts share crucial elements. A huge and relentless dilemma, an instrumentalization of the victim's agency, and pervasive psychological effects are present in both kinds of acts. Nonetheless, the relationship between perpetrators and victims are different in these wrongdoings. Torture is a process between unknown people, mostly declared enemies. In contrast, in DV there is a pre-existent bond between known participants: they are intimates. This implies that the victim's psychological immersion can be stronger that of torture victims, since perpetrators have important access to the victim's feelings, body, and thoughts. That can be a risk for greater dependence, and thus control. Moreover, the wrongness of the everyday DV acts does not appear so obvious at first, but over a long time, when it becomes apparent that the victim's personality has been strongly weakened.

For those reasons, DV can be, in a certain way, a more sophisticated way of victim annihilation. At least, torture victims already know the wrongness of the experienced act. To go into greater depth in this preliminary comparison, Chile can offer a good representative sample, since both kinds of violence are present in our history. While the Valech Commission found that 38,254 people were imprisoned for political reasons and most of them were tortured, in 2016 there were 127,682 DV crimes in Chile. Although links between those crimes have not been analyzed in Chile, in my view that task must be addressed in order to unearth phenomena which are behind the barriers of certain taboos and ignorance. That way we can get a better understanding of these acts, and then, open up the doors to sound public policy to prevent them (if that is possible) or repair the victims properly. To that end, the first thing to do is start a discussion around the status of both crimes: while torture is considered a crime against humanity, DV is regulated by a double regimen: Family and Criminal Law. In the case of the family courts process, the regulation also permits the conditional suspension of the sentence. This mechanism grants the possibility of another opportunity for the couple in order to continue their relationship.

Although feminist scholars have drawn attention to this inequality, it can be seen as controversial that the same exercise of punitive power can be the best response for both these actions. It is possible to think that care interventions have to be set in the field of DV, since there are some problems with DV's criminal procedures (refusing to testify against perpetrators) due to the special complexity of DV, as we have seen. The purpose of the care approach is to overcome the criticisms of the criminal system but also to recover the victim's autonomy. Victims have a right to be supported by the state, through services and policies (financial and housing assistance, possibly educational assistance, and physical and legal protection from their former partners).

Suggestions in Cámara de Diputados de Chile report (2015) are partially in the same vein.

NOTES

1. For example, see article 1 of the United Nations Convention Against Torture and other Cruel, Inhuman or Degrading Treatment or Punishment.

2. An alternative account is explained by Henry Shue (1978) who says that torture infringes a principle of just-combat killing which consists in the prohibition of the cruel assault upon "the defenceless" (Shue 1978, 125).

3. The percentages per kind of crime are the following: injuries (47.18%), threats (37.13%), reiterated abuse (9.73%); offence of contempt of court (3.40%); sexual abuses (0.30%); parricide (0.07%); femicides (0.07% with 96 cases); homicide (0.03%); and other crimes (1.43%) (Ministerio Público de Chile 2017, chart 23).

REFERENCES

Astudillo, Lorena, and Paula Santana. 2014. Extreme violence against women in Chile (2010–2012) . Santiago. Red Chilena contra la Violencia hacia las Mujeres and Heinrich-Böll-Stiftung Cono Sur. http://www.nomasviolenciacontramujeres.cl/wp-content/uploads/2015/11/ViolenciaextremacontralasmujeresRED.compressed.pdf

Ben-Ishai, Elizabeth. 2009. "The Autonomy-Fostering State: 'Coordinated Fragmentation' and Domestic Violence Services." *Journal of Political Philosophy* 17, N° 3: 307–331. https://doi.org/10.1111/j.1467–9760.2008.00315.x

Bramer, Marilea. 2011. "Domestic Violence as a Violation of Autonomy and Agency: The Required Response of the Kantian State." *Social Philosophy Today: Poverty, Justice, and Markets* 27: 97–110. DOI: socphiltoday2011278

Cámara de Diputados de Chile, Assessment of the 20,066 Act, by Comité Evaluación de la Ley/OCDE. Valparaíso—Chile. March 2015. http://www.evaluaciondelaley.cl/foro_ciudadano/site/artic/20140909/asocfile/20140909160016/informe_evaluaci__n_ley_n__20_066.pdf

Copelon, Rhonda. 1994. "Recognizing the Egregious in the Everyday: Domestic Violence as Torture." *Columbia Human Rights Law Review* 25, N° 2 (Spring 1994): 291–368. https://heinonline.org/HOL/Page?handle=hein.journals/colhr25&div=16&start_page=291&collection=journals&set_as_cursor=0&men_tab=srchresults

Davis, Michael. 2005. "The Moral Justifiability of Torture and other Cruel, Inhuman, or Degrading Treatment." *International Journal of Applied Philosophy* 19, N° 2: 161–178. DOI: 10.5840/ijap200519215

Dutton, Mary Ann, and Lisa A. Goodman. 2005. "Coercion in Intimate Partner Violence: Toward a New Conceptualization." *Sex Roles* 52. N° 11–12: 743–756. http://dx.doi.org/10.1007/s11199–005–4196–6

Herman, Judith. 1992. *Trauma and Recovery: The Aftermath of Violence—from Domestic Abuse to Political Terror*. New York: Basic Books.

Latin American Foundation for Social Innovation, commissioned by SERNAM. Exploratory research on violence in adolescent relationships . Santiago, Chile. November 2010. https://estudios.sernam.cl/documentos/?eMjMxNDA5Mg==-Investigaci%C3%B3n_exploratoria_respecto_a_la_violencia_ocurrida_durante_las_relaciones_adolescentes

Lobos, Elkjaer. 2014. "El escalofriante relato de Nieves Ayress, torturada en Tejas Verdes y Londres 38." *24 horas*, December 16, 2014. http://www.24horas.cl/nacional/el-escalofriante-relato-de-nieves-ayress-torturada-en-tejas-verdes-y-londres-38--1524811.

López, Mario. 2016. "El increíble caso de niña adolescente: La Ana Frank chilena: a los 15 años, presa política." piensaChile.com, January 11, 2016. http://piensachile.com/2016/01/el-increible-caso-de-nina-adolescente-la-ana-frank-chilena-a-los-15-anos-presa-politica/.

Mackinnon, C. A. 2006. *Are women human? And other international dialogues*. Cambridge, Mass. London: Belknap Press of Harvard University Press.

Mercurio de Calama. 2007. "Los crudos testimonios de dos mujeres agredidas," *Mercurio Calama*, March 25, 2007. http://www.mercuriocalama.cl/prontus4_nots/site/artic/20070325/pags/20070325041411.html.

Metiendo Ruido. 2012. "8 Relatos para no olvidar jamás: voces de lxs sobrevivientes a la dictadura." Metiendoruido.com, June 11, 2012. http://metiendoruido.com/2012/06/8-relatos-para-no-olvidar-jamas-voces-de-lxs-sobrevivientes-a-la-dictadura/.

Ministerio Público de Chile. Annual statistical report January–December 2016. January 2017.

Miranda, Oriana. 2013. "Violencia sexual contra mujeres en dictadura: un crimen invisibilizado." diarioUchile, September 3, 2013. http://radio.uchile.cl/2013/09/03/violencia-sexual-contra-mujeres-en-dictadura-un-crimen-invisibilizado/.

El Mostrador. 2017. "El desgarrador testimonio de Nabila Rifo que inculpa a Ortega: 'Con el primer golpe me botó al pasto, era una piedra muy grande y con la tercera yo quedé inconsciente,'" *El Mostrador*, March 23, 2017. http://www.elmostrador.cl/noticias/pais/2017/03/23/el-desgarrador-testimonio-de-nabila-rifo-que-inculpa-a-ortega-con-el-primer-golpe-me-boto-al-pasto-era-una-piedra-muy-grande-y-con-la-tercera-yo-quede-inconsciente/

National Commission on Political Prisoners and Torture (NCPT), Report. 2005.

Pascoe, Andrés. 2004. "La defensa del idiota." Crónica.com.mx, November 28, 2004. http://www.cronica.com.mx/notas/2004/155306.html.

Qureshi, Shazia. 2013. "Reconceptualising Domestic Violence as Domestic Torture." *Journal of Political Studies* 20, N° 1: 35–49. https://www.questia.com/library/journal/1P3-3109787261/reconceptualising-domestic-violence-as-domestic-torture

Rojas, Jorge. 2016. "La historia que inspiró la ley de violencia intrafamiliar." The Clinic online, May 29, 2016. http://www.theclinic.cl/2016/05/29/la-historia-que-inspiro-la-ley-de-violencia-intrafamiliar/.

Sepúlveda, Paulina. 2017. "127 mil delitos de violencia intrafamiliar ocurrieron en 2016." *La Tercera*, July 6, 2017. http://www.latercera.com/noticia/127-mil-delitos-violencia-intrafamiliar-ocurrieron-2016/.

SERNAM, Department of Studies and Training. Working Paper N° 105: Analysis of Violence in Young Couple Relationships. Santiago, Chile. January 2009. https://estudios.sernam.cl/documentos/?eOTQ3Nzkz-An%C3%A1lisis_de_la_Violencia_en_las_Relaciones_de_Pareja_entre_J%C3%B3venes

Shue, Henry. 1978. "Torture." *Philosophy and Public Affairs* 7, N° 2 (Winter, 1978): 124–143. http://people.brandeis.edu/~teuber/Shue-on-Torture.pdf

Sussman, David. 2005. "What's Wrong with Torture." *Philosophy & Public Affairs* 33, N° 1 (Winter, 2005): 1–33. http://www.jstor.org/stable/3557941

Chapter Five

The Response to Sex Work

A Regulation with a Voice of Their Own

Paula Nuño and Ximena Valencia

INTRODUCTION

Sex work is a complex phenomenon (Satz 1995, 136) that has existed, at least in Western societies, since the beginning of patriarchy and of private property (Gimeno 2012, 16), and of which connotations and degrees of social acceptance have varied over time. As to feminism, sex work has been the focus of a deeply polarized debate between anti-prostitution feminists and sex work pro-regulation feminists, two apparently irreconcilable positions (Gimeno 2012, 26; Scoular 2004, 349). However, these discussions have almost always omitted the voices of sex workers themselves, who claim the recognition of their activity as work, and the freedom to decide over their own bodies and their sexual self-determination, all of which are essential conditions to be considered and treated as citizens.

The object of this chapter is to examine the situation of sex workers in Chile, addressing their issues and vindications from the point of view of citizenship. In the case of Chile, the invisibility of sex work begins with the absence of explicit legal recognition—or prohibition—and lack of systematic regulation of this activity, which impairs sex workers' full enjoyment of rights as citizens. In spite of this, sex workers in Chile are a highly organized group and are active in the promotion of their rights. In the opinion of the authors, although prostitution is a practice that reaffirms structural inequality between men and women, the right of women to decide over their own bodies and their sexuality cannot be ignored. Moreover, in a patriarchal and neoliberal system, sex work appears as a legitimate work alternative that merits recognition and protection. Therefore, the State should adopt the necessary measures to collect the vindications of sex workers, and to promote, protect and guarantee their rights, so that they can fully enjoy their citizen status.

This chapter will start with a brief explanation of the main approaches towards sex work: namely, abolitionism and regulationism, to further take into consideration the claims of sex workers themselves in the matter. Then, we will examine the relationship between sex work and citizenship in Chile, observing the experience of sex workers in our country. In this section we will see how due to the lack of full citizenship, sex workers in Chile have been forced to form associations. Further, we will describe the main problems sex workers experience that affect the enjoyment of their citizenship. Equally, we will explain how the exercise of citizenship by sex workers in Chile is paradoxical. Then we will generally explore the solution proposed by sex workers themselves to achieve full citizenship, namely the development of regulation that reflects their own voices. Finally, the last sections will be dedicated to revealing the conclusions of this chapter.

ABOLITIONISM VERSUS REGULATIONISM

As noted already, sex work is a contested issue within feminism. A sector of feminism opposes prostitution[1] as well as the recognition of such activity as "sex work." They argue that prostitution is gender violence (MacKinnon 1993, 14) and that those who practice it are victims of a form of servitude or sexual slavery, as the decision to engage in sex trade is never truly a free choice for women (MacKinnon 1993, 28). They further argue that prostitution reaffirms and perpetuates patterns of structural inequality between men and women (Scoular 2004). Such would be the case that equality would be impossible as long as prostitution continues to exist (Gimeno 2012, 26). Other arguments are the objectification of women, and the relationship between sex trafficking and prostitution (Lamas 2016), among others that will not be examined in this chapter.

A part of the anti-prostitution sector, known as abolitionism, has opposed the recognition of sex work as work, arguing in favor of its elimination and for the criminalization of "johns" (clients) and pimps. Sweden would be the paradigmatic example of this. Meanwhile, a more radical sector known as prohibitionism, of which the United States and China are examples (Canales 2005, 7), insists upon the criminalization of sex workers, pimps and johns altogether. This sector of feminism tends to be defended by radical feminism (MacKinnon 1993), and has even found support in more conservative political sectors (Lamas 2016, 26).

On the other hand, there are sex work pro-regulation feminists, for whom the exercise of sex trade is proper "work." Thus, they argue it should be legally recognized and regulated. In defense of this approach it has been argued that sex workers are not victims, as the opposite would mean denying their agency and their freedom to decide over their own bodies. It has also been expressed that sex work is an ambivalent practice that, although it contributes to perpetuating gender inequality, may also be viewed as "an activity that challenges the boundaries of heterosexist and matrimonial monogamy" (Scoular 2004, 384).

Within this sector, some have argued that sex work is a complex and intersectional phenomenon rooted in patriarchy, yet in a neoliberal capitalist context, it gives a possibility of emancipation and greater freedom to women who would otherwise be exploited in the formal labor market (Kempadoo 2003, 2). Therefore, the permanence of sex work is strongly determined by the prevailing economic model. In the words of Marta Lamas, "if the socioeconomic circumstances that lead to sex trade are not resolved, prohibiting it or attempting to eradicate it would sink or marginalize those who sell sex services" (Lamas 2016, 26). This is the approach we support.

In our opinion, and as Satz explains, the problem with contemporary sex work is that "[c]urrently prostitutes are overwhelmingly women and their clients are almost exclusively men. In conceiving of a class of women as needed to satisfy male sexual desire, prostitution represents women as sexual servants to men" (1995, 144). Ultimately, we argue that sex work harms the collective of women in general, as it molds the way in which "men perceive women and on how women perceive themselves" (Satz 1995,146). In addition, it reaffirms the widespread belief according to which "men have strong sex drives that must be satisfied, largely by gaining access to some woman's body" (Satz 1995, 146). According to Satz, "[t]his belief underlies the mistaken idea that prostitution is the oldest profession, a necessary consequence of human (i.e., male) nature" (1995, 146). In this regard, we believe that male sexuality, conceived as an insatiable drive for which satisfaction channels must be guaranteed, which would justify the existence of a collective of women engaging in sex work, is a social construct, not a natural instinct.

Furthermore, this role that the sex workers' collective would be destined to fulfill is problematic from a gender equality point of view. Firstly, "because in our culture there is no reciprocal social practice that represents men as serving women's sexual needs" (Satz 1995, 146). Secondly, because it objectifies women and it embodies the idea that they are inferior. In this sense, sex work cannot effectively be considered as any other kind of work since it is not neutral. Although it is a complex practice founded in patriarchy, in the context of neoliberal capitalism sex work opens possibilities of emancipation and greater freedom to women who would otherwise be exploited in the formal labor market (Lamas 2016).

On this subject and on the role of feminism therein, we share the view expressed by Marta Lamas, in terms that

> the ethical-political aim of feminist research must be the criticism of certain practices, discourses and social representations that discriminate, oppress or violate persons based on the symbolization of sexual difference. The collective of prostitutes is one of the most convincing examples of this. That is why it is not only a matter of making comprehensible the various forms of the social existence of prostitutes, marked by the double standard existing in Judeo-Christian culture [. . .] but it is also essential to support them in the fight for their human, civil and labor rights. (Lamas 1993, 132)

It should be noted that both abolitionism and the pro–sex work approach are approaches that pursue the protection the rights of persons who engage in sex work, yet they differ as to which ought to be the correct strategy for such purpose. Notwithstanding the above, we consider this a debate that cannot evolve without hearing the voices of sex workers themselves. Feminism—as theory and political action program—cannot be isolated from the practical consequences supporting and implementing one approach or the other. Finally, the agency of a group of women such as sex workers, who have freely and voluntarily decided to engage in this activity and who have also, as will be further explained, demonstrated the ability to organize themselves and to act collectively, cannot be denied.

In sum, we suggest that sex work, as with most labor, is not gender neutral, yet it differs as to the negative consequences it has for the women collective. However, and precisely considering the consequences of the absence of regulation of sex work—which will be further addressed—and the work opportunities offered to women, we argue sex work is a legitimate and reasonable work option. Finally, we suggest that a piece of regulation on the matter must be developed with the participation of sex workers themselves.

SEX WORK AND CITIZENSHIP IN CHILE

The concept of citizenship has been the subject of feminist critiques given its universalist and allegedly neutral character, which in practice privileges the male political subject (Einhorn 2013, 33), and because it conceives, for the purposes of full citizen status, a number of elements which are not gender neutral. Thus, diverse strategies to construct a notion of citizenship have been adopted by various feminist authors (Orloff 1993; Munday 2009). However, we consider that the notion of citizenship is still useful to analyze the place and experience of sex workers in Chile.

Indeed, since sex work is a complex and intersectional phenomenon, in which discourses and practices such as human rights are unable to transcend race, class and gender factors, the concept of citizenship is capable of overcoming these differences that impede the realization of gender equality (Einhorn 2013, 33). For instance, the human rights discourse is one of rights, and as such, it has also been criticized by feminism. Firstly, because rights are too individualistic (Murno 2007, 75–76) and ultimately allocate to women the responsibility of claiming gender equality before national and international courts and tribunals, rather than enshrining it as an essential political goal of which we are all collectively responsible for (Einhorn 2013, 34). Secondly, rights are too abstract and their conduct prescriptions may, *inter alia*, oversimplify social problems and/or present theoretically laudable solutions that in practice fail to address effectively the issues they attempt to solve (Murno 2007, 77–78). In this regard, it should be noted that, although sex workers require the State to regulate their trade so as to conform to the international human rights norms to which Chile is bound, we believe that addressing sex work from the perspective of citizenship would be more suitable to tackle the complexity of the phenomenon, mainly because the notion of citizenship implies both the recognition of agency—in this case that of sex workers—and of an active role in the potential solution to the issue of the regulation of sex work.

In addition, the notion of citizenship allows a complex understanding of the subject to whom citizenship is recognized, which not only involves including the notion of a collective primarily composed of women, but it also makes women who often remain in the shadows visible (Munday 2009, 255).

With regard to the concept of citizenship, the authors share the opinion of Jennifer Gordon and R. A. Lenhardt, for whom citizenship is a multidimensional concept that encompasses many aspects, such as, *inter alia*, formal citizen status, possession of certain rights or benefits, political participation, and social inclusion, all of which may operate independently from one another. The State may recognize only some of these aspects in a particular group, and at the same time exclude other essential ones (Gordon and Lendhardt 2017).

We also share the idea that citizenship is not simply a status, but a process that requires active involvement with the purpose of achieving political changes (Einhorn 2013, 31). As Barbara Einhorn points out, the State has a crucial role in the implementation of the conditions for gender equal citizenship (Einhorn 2013, 35). Thus, citizenship implies active participation of persons and the adoption by the State of the necessary measures to promote and guarantee full participation and inclusion in society (Einhorn 2013, 35).

THE EXPERIENCE OF SEX WORK IN CHILE

In Chile, as in the rest of Latin America and the Caribbean, "there are structural problems that all poor women share: the lack of work and educational opportunities, gender inequality, sexism, the impossibility to earn a decent livelihood, economic necessity migration, amongst many other circumstances" (RedTraSex, 2015b, 6). Specifically in the work sphere, the participation of women currently reaches 48.3%, and it is characterized by development in conditions of inferiority compared to their male counterparts, which is reflected in various aspects: differences in salaries, limitations in the possibilities of promotion, segregation and feminization of certain areas of the economy associated with lower wages, among others. As a result of the gendered division of work, more women are seen in precarious jobs and in flexible forms of work, where the intensification of work becomes the general rule (Acevedo, Biaggi and Borges 2009). In this context, sex work appears as a work option that accommodates the needs and situation of many women.

"We Are Not Victims to Be Rescued"

According to the Chilean Ministry of Health, in Chile there are currently six thousand women, both Chilean and foreign, engaging in sex work. However, it is estimated that this figure only represents one third of all sex workers (Viñals 2015).

Sex workers have repeatedly pointed out that sex work means—for them—a work option that offers independence, self time management and greater income than the formal labor market. Sex work is more comfortable than a traditional job, and it allows them to attend to their family obligations, especially for those who are heads of household. That the exercise of sex work is a free and voluntary choice is something they constantly have to explain to authorities. They are adamant in arguing that they are women who have chosen this activity "by [their] own consent, from a rational decision, as free and as conditioned as many others we human beings make in our lives" (RedTraSex 2015b, 6). This is not only a response to institutional discrimination, but also to a sector of feminism that refuses to consider sex work as work (Scoular 2004, 347).

With regard to the abolitionist sector of feminism, the current president of Fundación Margen, Herminda González, has pointed out that the majority of sex workers consider themselves feminists, yet they believe that abolitionist feminism, apart from separating "good women from bad women," is very paternalistic. Neither do they understand why they are considered victims of sex work, when in fact sex workers are the masters of their own destiny. Furthermore, they assert that sex work is only one aspect of their lives, and that many of them also fulfill other social roles and responsibilities as mothers, heads of households, grandmothers, parents and neighbors (Robles 2016).

Sex Workers, Organized Citizens

In Chile, sex workers are currently organized in two associations: Fundación Margen and the Sindicato Nacional Independiente de Trabajadoras Sexuales Travestis, Transgéneras y Otras "Amanda Jofré" (Independent National Union of Transvestite, Transgender and Other Sex Workers "Amanda Jofré").

Fundación Margen is the continuation of the "Asociación por los Derechos de las Mujeres Ángela Lina" (Association for the Rights of Women Angela Lina), association created in 1993 after Angela Lina, a sex worker, was murdered while performing sex services. Later—and due to the emerging needs—they decided to establish an interdisciplinary body, which led to the creation of Fundación Margen in 1998 (Bolena n.d.). As pointed out by the current president of the organization, Herminda González, notwithstanding they receive professional support, the Foundation is entirely directed by sex workers. Fundación Margen is also the Chilean focal point of the Red de Mujeres Trabajadoras Sexuales de Latinoamérica y el Caribe (RedTraSex) (Network of Women Sex Workers of Latin America and the Caribbean), an organization whose work focuses on "the promotion and defense of the Human Rights of Women Sex workers, education in sex and reproductive health matters, prevention of HIV/AIDS and STD, and peer support for sexual health control and the counseling space" (RedTraSex n.d.).

For its part, the "Amanda Jofré" Union was founded in 2004, and it also carries the name of a transsexual sex worker who was brutally murdered in 2002. Through this union trans sex workers mainly address the human rights violations and transphobic violence of which they are victims.

The existence of these sex workers' associations has been fundamental for the exercise of their citizenship, not only towards the State, but also towards civil society. Sex workers are categorical in pointing out that the recognition of sex workers' organizations is necessary "for their voices to be legitimized in labor policies discussions and to guarantee their participation in the elaboration of the regulations regarding the application of the law and to create mechanisms to denounce arbitrariness and to guarantee our protection" (Fundación Margen 2015).

Precarious Work

Sex work can be exercised both in open and in closed spaces. In the first case, sex workers look for their clientele on the streets, whether or not under a labor subordination link to a third party (pimp). The second case refers to workers who perform their functions whether in premises (night clubs, saunas, bars, etc.) under the orders of a third party, or in other closed spaces (private apartments, hotels) on their own. None of these modalities are prohibited under our legislation, except for the existence of brothels, yet in all of them of sex work takes place in highly precarious conditions (RedTraSex 2015b, 7).

In the case of women who work in "*cafés con pierna*,"[2] the main problems relate to employers' failure to comply with working day limits and breaks, as well as hygiene and safety infractions (Dirección el Trabajo 2012).

With regard to the lack of security in the exercise of sex work in closed spaces, for example, the established limits regarding the noise levels in workplaces are not respected, the poles workers use to dance are not safe so labor accidents are very frequent, etc. These situations often result in professional illnesses, which in case of informal work, it makes it impossible for them to resort to the social security system.

Without prejudice to the aforementioned, it is fair to note that some improvements with regard to self-care measures developed by sex workers have been observed, particularly in lower rates of alcohol consumption in the workplace (Gallo 2017).

Institutional Violence

Sex workers are victims of institutional violence exercised both by agents of the public security forces, as well as by agents of justice (RedTraSex 2017).

Frequently members of police forces enter the premises where topless shows are performed or "*cafés con piernas*" without a court order. There, they illegally check the belongings of sex workers. On some occasions the inspection involves depriving sex workers of their condoms, which as will be explained below, has serious consequences for the prevention of sexually transmitted diseases.

In this regard, the role of sex worker associations has been decisive. Sex workers, who work on their own, tend to be victims of police abuse, whereas women who have knowledge of their rights normally resort to their corresponding organization, so that the latter may intervene in their aid with the assistance of legal counsel. Sex workers point out that when this happens, the authorities carrying out abusive operations cease the conduct.

For their part, trans sex workers are even more vulnerable and also experience other kinds of violations. Given that in Chile there is still no gender identity act, identity checks many times derive in situations of humiliation for them, as showing their identity cards reveals a different sex to the one they consider to be theirs. This, together with the removal of condoms and clothing, becomes "the prelude of naked body humiliation" (Bolena n.d.). Furthermore, they are denied support in situations of aggression, since the police often fail to turn up where a trans sex worker has been harmed (El Desconcierto 2017).

Furthermore, migrant sex workers are also victims of mistreatment, being subject to discrimination on the grounds of nationality, gender or race. They claim that it is not the clients who commit the abuses, but the police, who often intimidate them and tell them to go back to their countries, and often force them to engage in sexual intercourse under the threat of detention and deportation (Miranda 2017).

Additionally, although sex work is not regulated in Chile, municipalities in Santiago such as Las Condes and Providencia, to name a few, have adopted measures to prohibit and eradicate sex trade from their territories. They have done so by deploying more municipal security staff on the streets, by closing down premises and by expulsing sex workers from private buildings where they perform their trade. In the absence of legal grounds to adopt such measures, these have been justified on the maintenance of public and/or moral order (Bertin 2017).

Another relevant issue is the lack of access to justice for sex workers, particularly in cases of aggression and violations. They claim that, on the one hand, they are afraid of denouncing these and thus prefer to remain silent on the matter, and on the other hand, if they file a claim, the prosecution office does not persist in its investigations, and if it does proceedings hardly ever end in convictions. They also add that family law judges often deprive them of the care of their children, in cases when the fathers request so based on the fact that the mother is a sex worker (MACHI 2017).

Without prejudice to the above, sex workers agree that the street is less adverse than it used to be decades ago. In the opinion of the leaders of Fundación Margen, the reality of sex workers has greatly changed since the creation of the first union. They largely attribute these improvements to the successful action of their associations. As an example, until recently night detentions and the police abuse already mentioned were part of everyday dynamics (Gallo 2017). From the beginning, sex workers have carried out campaigns aimed both at sensibilizing public and private institutions as well as society in general, and also creating awareness amongst sex workers themselves as to self-care measures and knowledge of their rights. They claim these sensibilization efforts have been extremely important.

In addition, these associations have drafted documents with the purpose of providing information to the District Attorney Office, judges and police forces. As the vice-president of Fundación Margen notes, "us sex workers are always thought to be 'criminals, thieves, drunks, drug dealers and drug addicts.'" However, they claim that meeting with the authorities helps raise the visibility of sex workers "as persons" with rights who voluntarily exercise this type of work.

In a similar vein, they have worked with municipalities, with the government and with judges. They were recently invited to participate in the IV Conference of Chilean Women Judges organized by Asociación de Magistradas Chilenas (MACHI) (Association of Chilean Women Judges). In conjunction with this Association, sex workers have collaboratively worked to develop the first education workshop for agents of justice in the country, with the purpose of tearing down the myths and stigmas in male and female judges that prevent sex workers form having access to justice "like any other citizen" (Fundación Margen 2017).

Nevertheless, the way in which this citizenship is exercised has been a great challenge for sex workers, for it has meant breaking through institutional prejudices. In the speech given in the Conference referred to above, Herminda González highlighted the importance of organization for sex workers, as it has allowed them to place their demands on the table. However, she admits it is still difficult, because although sex work is not a crime, sex workers "have been convicted many times and many peers have had their children taken away from them because they are sex workers" (MACHI 2017).

HIV Epidemics and other Sexually Transmitted Diseases

One of the most deeply rooted prejudices is that sex workers are bearers of sexually transmitted diseases (STD), specifically the Human Immunodeficiency Virus (HIV). However, the reality is very different. In Chile, organized sex workers are highly aware of STD and HIV risks, and they carry out important HIV prevention campaigns. They train fellow sex workers in negotiation strategies to encourage clients to use condoms. Additionally, they organize STD awareness and prevention workshops addressed to civil society. They also participate in working groups within the government for the elaboration and improvement of public policies in the matter.

UNAids has recognized the relevant role of sex workers in this regard, and has pointed out that in order to eliminate the HIV epidemic as a public health threat it is necessary that governments address the structural and legal barriers that affect sex workers, by intensifying their efforts to protect the human rights of sex workers, and to ensure them access to HIV prevention and treatment services (2017).

In this regard, it should be noted that since 2007 sex workers in Chile are no longer required to obligatorily carry the Control de Salud Sexual (CSS) (Sexual Health Control card), which has been a significant advance for sex workers. Firstly, given that CSS was an obligation to which only sex workers were subject, its elimination has been essential to end the idea that sex workers are bearers of STDs. Secondly, it was precisely on the occasion of enforcing this obligation that police abuse and arbitrariness took place. According to UNAids, institutional violence towards sex workers in the form of removal of condoms has catastrophic effects on HIV prevention programs for the population (2017). Lastly, sex workers themselves assert that due to self-care awareness and to the valorization of a protected sexuality, they voluntarily go to health care centers to go through the necessary health controls.

Stigma

As Satz observes, "the idea of prostitution as a specialized occupation of an outcast and stigmatized group is of relatively recent origin" (1995, 137). From a citizenship point of view, the stigma of sex workers results in their marginalization in society.

An example of the manifestation of the stigma barrier is that sex workers may have money, yet since they cannot justify its origin, they are in a disadvantaged position to access certain goods, particularly to rent places where they may work or to purchase real estate property. Also, in this case, stigma weighs more than the law. The lack of recognition of rights that would be afforded to any other worker means sex workers are unable to retire or to access bank loans, to name a few examples (RedTraSex 2015b, 8).

Stigma manifestations can also be identified in the relationship of sex workers with the health care system. According to the testimonies of sex workers, health workers often discriminate, stigmatize and morally chastise them (RedTraSex 2015b, 8). This is a serious obstacle for the self-care and responsible sexuality culture that organized sex workers work towards, as the technical support of health professionals for this purpose is essential.

The case of trans sex workers is even more dramatic. According to the president of the "Amanda Jofré" Union, although there is no official figure, many trans sex workers live in poverty and have low life expectancy. Indeed, it notes that "as your options as a sex worker come to an end, you don't have a house of your own or the possibility of working as something else, many end up on the streets, as alcoholics, victims of transphobic attacks, killed, or dying of cold, hunger or HIV" (El Dinamo 2015).

In sum, despite improvements on the matter, the stigma surrounding sex work is still too strong in our country and it obstructs sex workers' access to the same rights enjoyed by any other worker.

The Paradox in the Recognition of Citizenship

From the evidence referred to in the sections above, it is possible to argue that sex workers' experience of citizenship in Chile is somewhat ambiguous. On the one hand, and as noted already, the Chilean legal system does not include any provision that expressly prohibits or recognizes sex work. It only regulates certain sanitary aspects of "persons who engage in sex trade" and it prohibits the existence of brothels (art. 41 Sanitary Code). From a criminal law point of view, Chilean law criminalizes procuring, human trafficking (Art. 411 ter Penal Code) and child prostitution (Art. 367 Penal Code). These scarce provisions are not enough evidence to claim that sex work in Chile is either regulated or that it is considered work as such. Indeed, although from a legal-formal point of view female sex workers are equal to any other worker, in practice they do not enjoy full citizenship. As sex workers themselves point out, the absence of their recognition as workers prevents them from fully enjoying and exercising their citizen status, the lack of which results in situations of abuse, institutional violence, precarious work conditions and discrimination (RedTraSex 2015a).

Furthermore, regardless of the absence of legal recognition of sex work and social stigma, sex workers in Chile have searched for ways to resist marginalization, to be heard and to actively participate in Chilean society as citizens through political action. Indeed, sex workers in Chile are currently highly organized either as foundations or unions. As such, they carry out activities to promote change. For example, they organize awareness workshops with public institutions such as Carabineros de Chile (Chilean Police) and Policía de Investigaciones, as well as with university students. They have also adopted an active role in sex education and in the prevention of the HIV and AIDS epidemic, which has involved reaching out to housewives.

In addition to these education and awareness raising activities which are addressed to society in general, the associations have assumed an essential role in the protection of sex workers, which ranges from, *inter alia*, assisting those workers who have been victims of institutional violence to inspecting closed spaces where sex trade is performed to ensure minimum safety conditions are met.

Also, the institutional acknowledgment of sex workers' organizations deserves to be highlighted. Indeed, with the purpose of revealing their realities and reclaiming their rights, they have appeared before the Economic Commission for Latin America and the Caribbean (ECLAC) and the Organization of American States (OAS); they have met with the Chilean President of the Republic, with the Minister for Women and Gender Equality, with congressmen and -women, mayors and judges. In 2016, the current president of Fundación Margen was granted the Elena Caffarena award in the "Trade Union Leadership" category, recognition given by the Government of Chile, through the Ministry of Women and Gender Equality and the Intendencia de Santiago, to women who have excelled in the promotion of women's rights (Intendencia Metropolitana 2016). Thus, in practice the sex workers' collective not only has relevant political and rights promotion presence, but it has also been acknowledged at both international and national levels.

The paradox is that although sex workers have a broad and propositional exercise of citizenship—in some cases even greater than other vulnerable groups—the absence of recognition of their rights as sex workers and the impact of stigma in the exercise of and participation in daily life, marginalizes and violates them. They continue to face barriers to access social rights that ensure the satisfaction of basic needs (Marshall 2012), such as housing, social security and other labor rights, to which the rest of working citizens in Chile have access. It may well be argued that sex workers are perceived as citizens, yet their participation in one of the public activities that citizenship status entails, such as remunerated work (Munday 2009, 253), is made invisible, and the rights derived therefrom are denied to them. Indeed, it would be fair to argue that sex workers enjoy only partial recognition of their citizenship, that is, only with regard to those aspects which are not related to their economic activity. In addition, as we have seen, the institutional acknowledgment from the State is not reflected in the recognition of social and labor rights for sex workers as workers. In this sense, we suggest that what is recognized is the association of sex workers, not the sex work as work, which would encompass the enjoyment of political rights, but not of civil and social rights in full (Marshall 2012). Thus, although sex workers are from a legal-formal point of view equal to other workers, in practice they do not have access to the same rights as the rest of citizens who also perform legal work (Robles 2016), which means they do not enjoy full citizenship.

A Regulation for the Benefit of Sex Workers

In Chile, the debate about the regulation of prostitution has had little prominence. There is no public policy addressed to sex workers, and since 1995 several bills have been presented, yet none of them has been an organic proposal to regulate sex work. Rather these have fundamentally consisted of amendments to certain provisions in the Chilean Penal Code, Sanitary Code and other acts. In Latin America, the only country that has an act on sex work is Uruguay, yet it only regulates certain sanitary aspects.

A Law with Their Own Voice

Sex workers have pointed out that any bill or regulation project must be developed taking into account "the point of view, the experience and recommendations" of sex workers themselves (Fundación Margen 2015). Furthermore, they have proposed contents that would be in accordance with the rights recognized and guaranteed in the various constitutions and with the international treaties ratified by the corresponding countries in Latin America and the Caribbean (Fundación Margen 2015).

In Chile, sex workers demand the recognition of their right to work in the sex trade. For this purpose, they consider essential the existence of a piece of regulation that defines what sex work is, who may legally exercise it and that the minimum conditions for its decent exercise be guaranteed, in accordance with Chile's international commitments on human rights (Fundación Margen 2015).

They propose to define sex work as "the conscious, free, voluntary, autonomous activity, performed on a regular or occasional basis by persons of legal age, who choose to exercise this work and offer and/or provide sexual services in exchange for money or other type of retribution for their own benefit" (Fundación Margen 2015). In addition, sex worker would be defined as "the person of legal age who voluntarily performs sex work" (Fundación Margen 2015). As can be observed, they suggest a definition of sex work and of sex worker that is clearly distinguished from human trafficking and which recognizes the agency of sex workers to decide freely and voluntarily to engage in sex work, and to exercise their sexual freedom.

For sex workers, one of the indispensable elements that a law that regulates sex work in Chile must contain is the recognition of sex work as autonomous work, thereby removing the figure of the pimp, one of the typical authors of the violence and abuse sex workers experience.

In their opinion, the regulation of sex work would be the appropriate means to end institutional violence and arbitrariness, the precarious labor conditions of sex workers, stigma, exclusion, abuses and the constant violation of their rights, as well as to improve the quality of life of sex workers (Fundación Margen 2015). This recognition would also entail the correlative obligations of any work activity, such as tax payment and social security and health contributions.

FINAL CONCLUSIONS

The aim of this chapter has been to propose a solution to the issue of the absence of regulation of sex work, that overcomes the current approaches surrounding abolitionism and regulationism of sex work, and above all, taking into account the voices of sex workers themselves.

In the first section, we observed that there are two main approaches towards sex work: on the one hand, abolitionism which ultimately argues for the disappearance of this practice; and on the other hand, regulationism which argues in favor of the recognition of sex work as proper work and as such that it should be regulated. We suggest it is necessary to recognize sex work as a complex and multi-causal phenomenon that is greatly determined by the predominant socioeconomic order. Thus, although sex work is not gender neutral and it contributes to inequality between men and women, we argue that feminism cannot propose solutions that ignore the voices of sex workers and the practical consequences that such proposals effectively have in their lives.

In the second section on sex work and citizenship in Chile, we mention the characteristics of the Chilean labor market, whereby sex work is a work option that accommodates the needs of many women, but wherein they constantly have to stress the freedom and consent with which they exercise this trade.

In addition, the concept of citizenship is useful to address sex work, since it transcends race, class and gender factors that effectively render sex work such a complex phenomenon. Citizenship is a multidimensional concept; therefore it is perfectly possible that some people, in this case sex workers, may only partially exercise their citizenship. With the purpose of reaching full citizenship, sex workers have organized themselves so that their voices can be heard by the State and by civil society. In spite of the important advances they have achieved, the persistence of precarious work, institutional violence and stigma, among other factors, prevent them from fully enjoying their citizen status.

The important work carried out by organized sex workers regarding HIV and other STDs has also been highlighted. This aspect of their work is also an example of how their level of organization has allowed them to have influence in the elaboration of public policies in this regard, which is ultimately a form of exercising citizenship.

Notwithstanding the progresses mentioned in the points above, it is suggested that the stigma associated to being a sex worker operates as an obstacle for sex workers to access and exercise the rights to which any other worker in Chile is entitled to.

It is suggested that although from a formal-legal point of view sex workers are equal to other workers, the contrast between the achievements attributable to sex workers' highly organized work and political action, versus the absence of effective recognition of their rights, is paradoxical since it does not translate into the full enjoyment of rights the status of citizen should provide. In order to solve this paradox, sex workers argue that the regulation of sex work would be the suitable answer to respond to their interests as citizens.

Finally, we suggest the need to elaborate a piece of regulation that considers the experiences and vindications of sex workers in their own voice. This should include the minimum contents as set out by them to ensure that the legal initiative effectively protects their rights as citizens, in accordance with Chile's international commitments on human rights.

NOTES

1. Terminologically, there are differences between those who use the term prostitution and those who refer to it as sex work. The term prostitute or whore operates with denigrating force in our culture, reinforcing stigma and social exclusion (Sánchez Miranda 2015; Morcillo and Varela 2016, 9).

2. "*Cafés con pierna*" are a typically Chilean case. They are cafés located in the center of the capital city that open during the day, and where the public are mostly men of different ages, who are waited on by women wearing clothing that "shows their legs." Although in some cases these cafés may lead to sex trade related services, it is not the general rule. However, women who work there consider themselves sex workers.

REFERENCES

Acevedo, Doris, Yajaira Biaggi, and Glanés Borges. 2009. "Violencia De Género En El Trabajo: Acoso Sexual Y Hostigamiento Laboral." *Revista Venezolana De Estudios De La Mujer* 14 (32): 163–180.

Bertin, Ximena. 2017. "Providencia Identifica 150 Edificios Donde Se Ejerce La Prostitución." *La Tercera*. April 4, 2017. http://www.latercera.com/noticia/providencia-identifica-150-edificios-donde-se-ejerce-la-prostitucion/.

Bolena, Ana. *n.d.* "La Lucha De Los Sindicatos De Trabajadoras Sexuales." *Fundación Savia*. Accessed May 28, 2018. http://www.fundacionsavia.cl/columnas-de-opinion/281#.Wwxehe6FOM-

Canales Nettle, Patricia. 2005. "La Regulación De La Prostitución En La Legislación Comparada." *Serie De Estudios De La Biblioteca Del Congreso Nacional De Chile* 325: 1–31.

Cho, Seo-Young, Axel Dreher, and Eric Neumeyer. 2013. "Does Legalized Prostitution Increase Human Trafficking?." *World Development* 41: 67–82.

El Desconcierto. 2017. "Trabajadora Sexual Trans Agredida Con Palos Y Martillos: 'Somos Personas También, Vivimos, Amamos, Queremos,'" May 4, 2017. http://www.eldesconcierto.cl/2017/05/04/trabajadora-sexual-trans-agredida-con-palos-y-martillos-somos-personas-tambien-vivimos-amamos-queremos/.

El Dínamo. 2015. "Las Críticas De Red Trans Chile Al Trámite De La Ley De Identidad De Género: 'Aún No Existimos En Este País.'" December 16, 2015. https://www.eldinamo.cl/nacional/2015/12/16/ley-identidad-de-genero-transgenero-alejandra-soto/.

Dirección Del Trabajo. 2012. "Dirección Del Trabajo Fiscaliza Los 'Cafés Con Piernas.'" January 19, 2012 http://www.dt.gob.cl/portal/1627/w3-article-100182.html.

Einhorn, Barbara. 2013. "Citizenship." In *Gender: The Key Concepts*, 1st ed., 29–35. Abingdon: Routledge.

Escribano Veloso, Irene. 2008. *Nunca Me Confieso*. 1st ed. Santiago de Chile: LOM Ediciones.

Gimeno, Beatriz. 2012. *La Prostitución*. Barcelona: Bellaterra.

González, Herminda. 2017. "Herminda González, Dirigenta De Trabajadoras Sexuales: 'Me gusta Guillier, es un caballero respetuoso.'" Interview by Macarena Gallo. *The Clinic*. July 24, 2017. http://www.theclinic.cl/2017/07/24/herminda-gonzalez-dirigenta-trabajadoras-sexuales-me-gusta-guillier-caballero-respetuoso/.

Gordon, Jennifer, and R.A. Lenhardt. 2008. "Rethinking Work And Citizenship." *UCLA Law Review* 55 (1161): 1161–1238. https://www.redtrasex.org/spip.php?page=imprimir_articulo&id_article=2641.

Intendencia Metropolitana. 2016. "17 Mujeres Fueron Destacadas Con El Premio 'Elena Caffarena 2016.'" March 16, 2016 http://www.intendenciametropolitana.gob.cl/n9752_10–03–2016.html.

Kempadoo, Kamala. 2003. "Globalizing Sex Workers' Rights." *Canadian Woman Studies/ Les Cahiers De La Femme* 22 (3–4): 143–149.

Lamas, Marta. 1993. "El Fulgor de la Noche: Algunos Aspectos de la Prostitución Callejera en la Ciudad de México." *Debate Feminista* 8: 103–134.

Lamas, Marta. 2016. "Feminismo y Prostitución: La Persistencia de una Amarga Disputa." *Debate Feminista* 51: 18–35.

MACHI. "IV Conferencia Anual De Magistradas De Chile, MACHI." 2017. Instituto de Estudios Judiciales, Santiago, Chile, 2017.

MacKinnon, Catharine. 1993. "Prostitution and Civil Rights." *Michigan Journal of Gender & Law* 1: 13–31.

Marshall Barberán, Pablo. 2012. "Notas Sobre Los Modelos Para La Extensión De La Ciudadanía." *Revista De Derecho Universidad Católica Del Norte* 2 (19): 119–143.

Miranda, Benjamín. 2017. "Violencia y Vulneración: La Radiografía del Trabajo Sexual en Chile." *The Clinic*. January 12, 2017 http://www.theclinic.cl/2017/01/12/violencia-y-vulneracion-la-radiografia-del-trabajo-sexual-en-chile/.

Morcillo, Santiago, and Cecilia Varela. 2016. "Trabajo Sexual Y Feminismo, Una Filiación Borrada: Traducción De 'Inventing Sex Work' De Carol Leigh (Alias Scarlot Harlot)." *La Ventana. Revista De Estudios De Género* 5 (44): 7–23.

Munday, Jennie. 2009. "Gendered Citizenship." *Sociology Compass* 3 (2): 249–266.

Munro, Vanessa. 2007. Law And Politics At The Perimeter. Oxford: Hart.

Neira, Montse. 2013. "Testimonio De Herminda González, Trabajadora Sexual En Bolivia." Blog. *Prostitución, Una Visión (Sub)Objetiva Compleja Y Global*. February 15, 2013 http://prostitucionrealidadessociales.blogspot.cl/2013/02/testimonio-de-herminda-gonzalez.html.

Orloff, Ann Shola. 1993. "Gender And The Social Rights Of Citizenship: The Comparative Analysis Of Gender Relations And Welfare States." *American Sociological Review* 58(3): 303–328.

Outshoorn, Joyce. 2014. "The Contested Citizenship Of Sex Workers: The Case Of The Netherlands." In *Negotiating Sex Work*, 1st ed., 171–194. Minnesota: University of Minnesota Press.

RedTraSex. 2013. "Ponte En Nuestros Zapatos: Guía De Buenas Práctica En El Personal Del Sistema De Salud." December 10, 2013 http://www.redtrasex.org/Guia-de-buenas-practicas-en-el.html

RedTraSex. 2015. "Una Ley Con Nuestra Voz. Contenidos Básicos Para Regular El Trabajo Sexual." October 24, 2015. http://www.redtrasex.org/Una-ley-con-nuestra-voz.html.

RedTraSex. 2015a. "5 Razones Por Las Cuales El Trabajo Sexual Debe Ser Regulado." July 28, 2015 http://redtrasex.org/Five-Reasons-Why-Sex-Work-Must-Be

RedTraSex. 2017. "Margen Se Reúne Con Presidenta De Asociación De Magistradas Chilenas—MACHI." May 18, 2017

RedTraSex. 2017a. "Derechos Humanos Y Trabajo Sexual: Del Protocolo A La Acción." June 7, 2017 http://www.redtrasex.org/Derechos-Humanos-y-Trabajo-Sexual

RedTraSex. n.d. "Nuestra Historia." Accessed August 16, 2017 http://www.redtrasex.org/spip.php?rubrique11.

Robles, Víctor Hugo. 2016. "Herminda González, a 20 años de la Fundación Margen: 'Las Autoridades Dicen Que Se Debe Regular El Trabajo Sexual, Pero No Sabemos Cuándo Y Cómo.'" *El Desconcierto*. November 18, 2016 http://www.eldesconcierto.cl/2016/11/18/herminda-gonzalez-fundacion-margen-las-autoridades-dicen-que-se-debe-regular-el-trabajo-sexual-pero-no-sabemos-cuando-y-como/.

Sánchez Miranda, Berta Massiel. 2015. *El Trabajo Sexual en Nicaragua: Apuestas Políticas y Caminos Compartidos con los Feminismos Locales*. Nicaragua: Fondo Centroamericano de Mujeres.

Satz, Debra. 1995. "Markets In Women's Sexual Labor." *Ethics* 106 (1): 63–85.

Scoular, Jane. 2004. "The 'Subject' of Prostitution: Interpreting the Discursive, Symbolic and Material Position of Sex/Work in Feminist Theory." *Feminist Theory* 5 (3): 343–355.

UNAIDS. 2017. "Protecting the Rights of Sex Workers." June 2, 2017 http://www.unaids.org/en/resources/presscentre/featurestories/2017/june/20170602_sexwork.

Viñals, Victoria. 2015. "Prostitución en Chile: Falta de Derechos, Violencia Policial e Inmigración." August 2, 2015 http://radio.uchile.cl/2015/08/02/prostitucion-en-chile-falta-de-derechos-violencia-policial-e-inmigracion/.

Walters, Joanna. 2017. "Campaigners Protest Against United Nations Stance On Prostitution." *The Guardian*. September 21, 2013 https://www.theguardian.com/society/2013/sep/21/united-nations-prostitution-sex-trafficking.

Chapter Six

Towards a Multicultural Jurisdiction

The Case of Mapuche Women

Luis Villavicencio

AN INAUSPICIOUS SOCIAL AND HISTORICAL CONTEXT

For a very long time, neither international nor domestic law were genuinely concerned about indigenous rights. So-called *indigenous populations* began to attract a measure of attention only after the creation of the International Labor Organization (ILO) and the 1957 adoption of ILO Convention 107, its evident assimilationist bias notwithstanding. A significant step toward fuller recognition of indigenous rights came with ILO Convention 169, in force since 1991 and ratified to date by 20 states, including 13 in Latin America (Aylwin, Meza-Lopehandía and Yañez 2013, 337–342).[1] The march forward of indigenous rights reached a milestone in 2007, as the United Nations General Assembly adopted the Declaration on the Rights of Indigenous Peoples, which included a right to self-determination.

Galvanized by Convention 169, indigenous peoples across most of Latin America began to question the *nation-state* paradigm on which these countries were founded and to assert the need for constitutional and law reform. "While implementation of reforms often lags behind the times, the region has seen progress in various contexts in terms of processes and policies recognizing indigenous lands and territories. This includes mechanisms to enable enfranchisement and/or autonomy in certain areas, such as justice" (Aylwin, Meza Lopehandía and Yañez 2013, 30).

As the only country in Latin America not to have extended constitutional recognition to a significant indigenous population, Chile's track record is a different story. To understand what is unique about Chile and the Mapuche nation, let us step back in time to the time of independence. As Clavero

(2000, 107–128) writes, relations with the *Wallmapu* (the Mapuche nation) were driven by the new Republic's pressing need to fix its borders as, at the time, south of the Bío-Bío River it was mostly *Wallmapu* territory. To address the issue, the leaders of independence revived the treaty negotiation practices the Spanish *conquistadors* had employed since the 16th century in their dealings with the Mapuche nation. The most important of those treaties emerged from the Parley of Tapihue and enshrined what amounted to a confederation. The landmark treaty, however, was later ignored in Chilean constitutions, notably the seminal Constitution of 1833. "In the Treaty of Tapihue, the *Mapu* and Chile recognized each other. The latter, though never the former, later spurned and squandered their mutual recognition. The indigenous side upheld the confederation against great odds until it was conquered and robbed of its territory, its resources, its rights and its self-rule" (Clavero 2000, 117; Toledo Llancaqueo 2006, 15–27; Bengoa 2014, 33–61).

This blatant breach of trust, plus the assistance of imaginative historians, helped build the narrative that Chile was from the start a homogeneous, unified nation-state, a myth that remains largely unchanged to this day.[2] Neither the inaptly named 1993 *Indigenous Law,* which recognized ethnicity rather than indigenous peoples,[3] nor the 2008 ratification of ILO Convention 169, which has yet to be implemented in full, have significantly altered this scenario (Contesse 2012; Habersang and Ydígoras 2015, 263–273). To date, Chile remains far from recognizing territorial and political autonomy to indigenous peoples in general, and to the Mapuche people in particular.

THEORETICAL CONTEXT

Modernity, the most ambitious emancipation effort undertaken by humankind so far, was exclusionary from inception on at least three counts: reasons of class that led to the structural oppression of the working class; reasons of culture that fostered the fiction of a unified, homogeneous polity;[4] and reasons of gender that produced Benhabib's (2002, 2006) substitutionalist universalism, when the "whole," i.e., the totality of human beings, is supplanted by the "part," i.e., white, heterosexual, property owners. While many of these factors have since yielded ground, an especially recalcitrant area of exclusion remains, crossing class, ethnic background and gender lines: the status of indigenous women.

At the present stage in the development of political philosophy, especially as regards individual agency, no one—not even in the liberal tradition—denies the role culture plays in the construction of identity, a concept built on both individual and community elements. It therefore comes as no surprise that individuals should expect their culture to be respected and for cultures themselves, as attested by their keepers and particularly if minority, to feel threatened by the assimilationist potential of dominant cultures. The challenge, then, is to articulate a connection between culture and individuality that addresses the dichotomy between the unreserved, abstract application of culturally insensitive rules and an essentialist cultural relativism that helps justify the violation of basic minority rights.

The overarching intent here is to explore the status of indigenous women as an issue that is highly reflective of the above tensions. Indigenous women are a disadvantaged group that is both vulnerable relative to the dominant culture and exposed to oppression and violence within their own communities, also for cultural reasons. This article will specifically review recognition of legal pluralism and indigenous jurisdiction, a key aspect of the implementation of ILO Convention 169 as it applies to Mapuche women.

The challenge, from the standpoint of the law, is to build mechanisms that ensure respect for the construction of identity and protect vulnerable groups. The aim is to enable members of minority cultures, especially national ones, to successfully argue from within that internal dissent is possible. As such, multicultural jurisdictions where two or more culturally differentiated systems of laws can coexist do the most justice to the first aspect at issue: recognition of cultural differences and the right of national minorities to their own laws and worldview. Yet, this is half of the challenge. Can gender violence be explained away for cultural reasons? Do multicultural jurisdictions have limits? Can they respect self-determination and protect their weakest members from the wielders of local power?

THE NEED TO OVERCOME THE NARROW LIBERAL CITIZENSHIP IDEAL

Both feminist theory (Sánchez 2002, 359) and the various flavors of multiculturalism (Kymlicka 2007, 61–86; Parekh 2002, 133–150; de Lucas 2001, 61–102; Banting & Kymlicka 2006, 9) hold that liberal citizenship stigmatizes groups that do not fit in. Liberal citizenship is noted for holding individuals as the ultimate source of political legitimacy and for regarding them as holders of certain rights in their capacity as abstractly equal moral agents (Song 2007, 68; Delanty 2010; Jackson 2005; Modood 2007; Zúñiga 2009, 2010). But the rights accorded to an "average citizen" do not align well with the needs of differentiated groups. These require more than the traditional redistributive policies of modern democratic states (Kymlicka 2002, 327–376), where economic and status hierarchies coexist. With standing in the economic hierarchy determined by relationships with markets and the means of production, the struggle against the inherent inequity generates *redistribution policies*. And as the hierarchy of status leads to stereotypical rules that discriminate against lower-ranking groups, the struggle against these hierarchies generates *policies of recognition or of the difference* (Fraser 2000, 107–120; Delanty 2010, 59; Modood 2007, 68–70).

While conceptually distinct, in the real world redistribution and recognition policies appear to overlap, even as the evidence suggests that hierarchy of status is not reducible to economic hierarchy. Groups that are financially comfortable but culturally stigmatized, such as gays, immigrants and members of some religions, are a case in point (Kymlicka 2002, 327–376). Especially relevant in this regard is Young's assertion about a new concept of oppression that "designates the disadvantage and injustice some people suffer not because a tyrannical power coerces them, but because of the everyday practices of a well-intentioned liberal society." Women's oppression consists partly in a systematic and unreciprocated transfer of powers from women to men. Women's oppression consists not merely in an inequality of status, power, and wealth resulting from men's cultural practice of excluding them from privileged activities, as the inequality is possible precisely *because women work for them.* Gender exploitation begins with the transfer of the fruits of material labor and of nurturing and sexual energies to men. This will not change unless the social and cultural structure changes (Young 2000, 89–93).

As Deveaux rightly notes (2000, 16–26; 2006, 54–88), liberal democratic citizenship is ill-equipped to harmonize social and cultural differences. Liberalism, she writes, has borne the brunt of the criticism coming from the new debate for its inability to treat women and members of ethnic and cultural minorities as equal citizens. The bulk of the criticisms emphasize liberalism's inattention to social and cultural particularity and its conceptual failure to secure justice for certain groups (Villavicencio 2007; 2009; 2010a; 2010b). As a result, Deveaux puts liberal theorists in a quandary: continue affirming individual rights and a culture-blind model of justice, or acknowledge the political relevance of certain demands for recognition and find ways to address claims for inclusion and autonomy.

The present challenge is larger, as the focus of the dispute has shifted to differences within minority groups and their impact on demands. This is the result of a more complex understanding of cultural identity by political philosophers (Deveaux 2006, 1–22), as cultural practices are increasingly construed as spaces where they can be challenged (Benhabib 2006, 336–338). The broad recognition of in-group disagreement requires recognizing the treatment afforded its most vulnerable members, the minorities within minorities that, as tends to happen in all groups, face the wielders of hegemonic power and control (cf. Eisenberg & Spinner-Halev 2005). This, in turn, requires examining the demands of cultural groups, especially communities whose practices reinforce illiberal traditions that, in light of constitutional standards and internal group norms, are discriminatory (Villavicencio 2014).

CATEGORIES OF DISADVANTAGED GROUPS AND THE IDEA OF CULTURE

Two issues face those espousing the need to transition to differentiated citizenship: determining which groups and differences count, and what should be understood as culture (Selamé and Villavicencio 2011).[5]

A disadvantaged group is a slippery notion. A possible definition would be a collective whose common identity places them in a position of severe subordination. Rather than its numbers, what characterizes these groups is its precarious position. But since such an abstract definition can apply to all manner of groups, the need arises to identify categories.

Broadly speaking, there are four types of disadvantaged groups. First, national minorities; historical nations strongly defined by a shared identity and language, often circumscribed to a given territory under a dominant state (Keating 2001, 1–28).[6] Second, migrant minorities; groups that, driven by need, travel more or less massively to another state, thus becoming exposed to assimilationist policies. Third, cultural groups other than national or migrant minorities that endure oppression because of certain distinctive shared traits, such as women and sexual minorities. Fourth, social minorities; groups that are severely hampered in the enjoyment of their rights, including the poor, persons with disabilities, prisoners, etc. (cf. Añón 2001, 217–233; Soriano 2002, 33–35).[7]

For the purposes of this chapter, cultures will be defined as being characterized by four specific traits:

(a) *The idea of process*. Culture, as Phillips (2007b, 15–29) notes, is "ordinary," part of the continuous and changing process through which any social organization develops and reproduces itself, building shared meanings transmitted from one generation to the next, and open to debate and amendment;

(b) *Culture shock as the unequal distribution of power*. From the standpoint of political theory, culture matters not so much as the study of difference in cultural practices but as inequality, i.e., determining what counts as just treatment of minority groups. Two questions arise: b.1. Recognition of unequal power relations between minority and majority groups, and the perception that states that impose a unitary political and legal framework often discriminate against minority cultural groups; and b.2. The often conflict-ridden nature of relations between minority and dominant groups;

(c) *The process of signification resides in agents, not in culture*. As Dhamoon (2007, 30–49) writes, the cultural is defined as the construction of meaning. This emphasis is decisive, as it shifts the analysis from the object of the distinct culture to the process expressing a diverse identity. The shift presupposes understanding that since signs are not permanent, what is at risk is not culture but the self-determination and ability of agents to fashion their own signification construction systems and shape their own meanings in a context of non-subordination; and

(d) *Cultures possess normative authority*. Groups are noted for imposing rules meant to regulate the conduct of its members (Shachar 2001, 2).

VIOLENCE AGAINST MAPUCHE WOMEN AND REPARATION AGREEMENTS, THE MULTICULTURAL JURISDICTION MODEL, DELIBERATIVE OPTIONS, INTERSECTIONALITY

A report from the Department on the Status of Women (SERNAM) notes that 17 cases of violence against women heard in 2011–2012 in the city of Temuco—in the Mapuche heartland—were settled with an apology under a controversial reading of Mapuche customs. These generally involve cases where both victim and offender are indigenous Mapuche and the Public Defender's Office invokes ostensibly traditional forms of conflict resolution to suggest a *reparation agreement.*[8] The threshold appears to be severe or habitual violence (Bravo 2017).[9] Is this reasonable? Does it meet the requirements of ILO Convention 169 and other international instruments? (Nash et al. 2014, 41–64) The challenge is to break through the binary solutions available and enable conciliation mechanisms that uphold the rights of women, as a minority within a minority. It is therefore imperative to advance toward a feminist discourse which, without denying the importance of culture, acknowledges women's subordinate status, stands for basic women's rights, and identifies the contextual circumstances that impact exclusion. The key is not to let the biases of one culture to prevail over another ex-ante and rush to argue the subordination of all women (Sandoval and Undurraga 2012, 32).

In my view, addressing this issue requires combining three mutually modulated theoretical propositions: multicultural jurisdiction, a culture-sensitive concept of deliberative democracy, and an *intersectional* perspective. The *multicultural jurisdiction* model advanced by philosopher Ayelet Shachar (cf Villavicencio 2014) is based on what she calls the paradox of *multicultural vulnerability*, the understandable reticence of liberal feminists about the potential oppression which, in the name of group rights, women may experience when well-meaning efforts to improve autonomy and respect cultural diversity actually make it harder to revert gender inequality—or even exacerbate subordination (Shachar 2001, 4–10). The goal is to overcome the paradox and protect vulnerable groups based on the entwinement of state and community jurisdictions under a dynamic interpretation of culture. This would help justify the accommodation of state jurisdictions to improve the status of subordinate groups and protect cultural differences by creating conditions for internal cultural change while discouraging intractable opposition in the larger dominant community. This would also help cement a rule of no jurisdictional monopoly ensuring that individuals can choose, on a case-by-case basis, the applicable law and jurisdictionally guaranteeing the individual rights of indigenous women who prefer the jurisdiction of the state over customs that, in their view, discriminate against them. The intent is to balance cultural normative autonomy and the effectiveness of basic rights protections (Shachar 2001, 117; Pérez de la Fuente 2004 423–425).

But in addition to the increased uncertainty and cost involved in implementing pluralistic jurisdictions, Shachar's model bears other relevant criticisms. First, a pluralistic model does not clearly distinguish between what is right and what is feasible, and could lead to confusing the strategic understanding of moral issues and what is considered just as a matter of principle (cf Chandran Kukathas 2012, 53–55). Second, sometimes the procedures necessary to entrench a multicultural jurisdiction seriously risk refeudalizing the law and undermining equal protections (Benhabib 2002, 128). There is a relevant difference between exceptions favoring specific groups based on purportedly shared grounds, and the presumption that the reasons that justify differential treatment no longer require to be generalized. In other words, if the capacity for constitutional principle to prevail at some point is not stated, rather than solving the paradox of intercultural vulnerability we might wind up recirculating it through the system of laws (Barry 2002, 38–50). Third, sacralization of the process remains a distinct possibility and can judicialize political and cultural dialogue.

Deliberative proposals, for their part, seek to revitalize an intercultural dialogue capable of enabling, from a non-reductionist view of culture,[10] the involvement in the public sphere of all groups, on an equal dialogic footing. Benhabib, for example, advances a notion of culture built upon social constructivism and characterized by a narrative view of actions and culture that requires drawing a distinction between the standpoints of social observers and social agents. Social observers, hand in hand with local élites, impose the unity of cultures as observed entities. Social agents, for their part, represent participants who experience their traditions through narratives that are shared, even if open to contestation. From within, cultures never seem a homogeneous whole (Benhabib 2002, 4–5). As such, multiculturalist stances must let go of static concepts of culture. A static culture would be inconsistent with the only plausible version of multiculturalism, ossify at the expense of the autonomy of some of its members, and prevent them from questioning their place within a culture. As Parekh (2006, 295–338) contends, cultures would cease to be externally pervious, rendering moot all arguments about how minorities within minorities should be treated.

To *deliberative proposals,* the right of exit does not suffice, as it shifts the burden of conflict onto the individual. When cultural identity truly counts, people are more likely to remain in their groups and stand up to the élites

(Phillips 2007a, 151–157; Shachar 2001, 40–42). As such, a more adequate response to the challenge is deliberative democracy characterized by two elements: (a) Marked emphasis on the public sphere as the locus of cultural disputes and political transformation; (b) Opening the public agenda so as to blur the distinction between the public and the private, between what belongs to all and what is the sole preserve of one's culture (Benhabib 2002, 106–114; Deveaux 2000, 138–179).

Deliberative proposals pack more punch but pose difficulties, especially those stemming from the more general objections about the deliberative model: Who takes part? Who is included, who stifled, who speaks for whom? Which norms does the approach assume, and are they exclusionary or genuinely shared? How should deliberations be conducted? What results to expect? (Deveaux 2005, 344–345) Beyond these general tensions, the ambiguity of proposals such as Parekh's remains: oppressed groups are unlikely to merely wait for the debate to become more amicable. Also, as Deveaux (2005, 360–361) notes, the deliberative approach has been unable to shed three perils: the contingency that process results will not be just; that the model relies on a concept of political legitimacy paradoxically at variance with the canonical views of the traditional groups whose practices are impugned; and a negative response by segments of the traditional communities to the effects of implementing an openly inclusive deliberation process.

Multicultural jurisdictions and deliberative proposals should therefore be modulated by an *intersectional* perspective (Villavicencio 2017, 155–167). Intersectionality (García and Villavicencio 2016) is a critical approach that helps understand the identity of individuals in diverse contexts, based on connections between gender, ethnic, and class structures whose intersection can result in complex contexts of inequalities which can, in turn, be analyzed in terms of power on various levels (Anthias and Yuval-Davis 1992; Anthias 1998; Andersen 2006; McCall 2005; Winker and Degele 2009). To Anzaldúa, ethnicity, class, and gender contribute to the way we perceive and are perceived, and are building blocks in the construction of identity. She offers a critique of the oppressive—to women—conditions inherent to the various cultural systems dominated by men. These experiences of oppression are not easy to disaggregate, as they often are concurrent: one cannot criticize racism without referring to sexism and class discrimination, and vice versa (Anzaldúa 1987).

As such, intersectionality is an alternative to identity politics that enables consideration of in-group differences by subverting the divide between gender, ethnicity, and class as disjunctive elements. The reference to cultural diversity seeks to underscore the need to understand it as based on its constitutively intersectional nature. As such, cultural diversity is shaped by many conditions in ways that cannot be defined *a priori*, which underlines its complex origin and interconnection with various conditions of social identification and discrimination, such as gender, ethnicity, and class. The principle is that no culture should be championed without also acknowledging its sexist, racist, or classist components.

Having examined the model, I will now turn to cases that illustrate the dilemma at issue. First, a distinction must be drawn between indigenous law as recognized by state justice (i.e., first-tier) and by separate indigenous jurisdictions (second-tier) (Melin et al. 2016, 71–86). Reparations are first-tier agreements. They exemplify the type of case in which the national courts, in applying laws and regulations to indigenous peoples, have "due regard [. . .] to their customs or customary laws" (ILO Convention 169, art. 8) and to "their economic, social and cultural characteristics" (ILO Convention 169, art. 10). Yet, use of the *Az Mapu* (the Mapuche system of law) to settle family violence cases faces two major hurdles: one, article 19 of Chile's Family Violence Act expressly disallows reparation agreements, and two, article 8.2 of ILO Convention 169 requires application of indigenous law to be compatible with human rights recognized in the national and international legal systems.

The reparation agreement issue brings into sharper focus the tensions coursing through ILO Convention 169, which requires states to ensure access to justice for indigenous peoples, with due regard for their customs or customary laws. While Convention article 8.1 requires that "In applying national laws and regulations to the peoples concerned, due regard shall be had to their customs," it notes that these may not be "incompatible with fundamental rights defined by the national legal system and with internationally recognized human rights."[11] In criminal matters, the underlying tensions take concrete form in the need to balance the duty of authorities and the courts to have due regard for the customs of indigenous peoples (art. 9.2) and the protected fundamental rights category. The reason to bar such agreements is as evident as it is plausible: in family violence cases, the power balance is skewed as a result of the violence itself (Aylwin, Meza-Lopehandía and Yañez 2013, 416–431; Villavicencio 2015).

These cases encompass several core issues that call for a more dynamic perspective. These are challenging cases whose implications extend far beyond the one-dimensional logic of the human rights discourse and the unresolved tension in Convention 169 between indigenous law and the expansive promise of fundamental rights. First, the human right of all women to be free from violence has indisputable transcultural force, however much it may be modulated in concrete situations for cultural, religious, or other reasons. Second, the obligation to respect indigenous legal systems converges with the goal of neutralizing the distinctive *assimilationism* of state law and recognize instead the existence of pluralistic legal systems (Aylwin, Meza-Lopehnadía and Yañez 2013, 416–417). Third, Convention 169 sets fundamental rights as a threshold for application of indigenous law. Fourth, class is a key issue in the way cases are evaluated. Fifth, gender is also relevant, especially because of the naturalization of violence against women by partners or relatives, with an impact on each of these areas. Can these tensions be properly balanced?[12]

In summary, the dilemma involved is the collision between the ban on culturally or transculturally situated violence and the normative consequences of this definition. Factors at play include ethnicity, gender, class, the hegemonic claims of human rights discourse, and the factual (even if not institutionalized) pluralism of normative systems. As noted, the proposition is predicated on intersectionality and on a deliberatively situated multicultural jurisdiction model.

Factors of ethnicity unquestionably play a key role. As such, as much light as possible needs to be shed on the Mapuche worldview on violence against women. A study published by the *Aukinko Zomo* Mapuche Women's Corporation (Mercado Catriñir et al. 2015) states that violence against women is a practice that no culture, including the Mapuche, should naturalize. Villegas and Mella (2017, 154) similarly conclude that "[A]mong the Mapuche people, family violence, its causes, frequency and victims do not substantially differ from non-Mapuche society."

Having ascertained that violence against women is transculturally condemned and has no relevant cultural peculiarities, an assessment of the *Az Mapu*'s response to it is in order (Villegas and Mella 2017, 153,163; Melin et al. 2016, 25–57). The Mapuche system of laws lacks a single dispute settlement mechanism. But while these vary across communities, they share certain basic traits: (a) Involvement of authoritative third parties, such as headmen *(lonkos)*, elders *(lof)*, or the extended family; (b) The role of discussion and participation in resolving a conflict and re-establishing the balance that allows an offender to *"chekonan"* or regain the condition of *che* (person); and (c) The *ngulam*[13] (advice) imparted by elders as the result of the talks (*nvxamkawvn*) or as reprimand.

The *Az Mapu* response to violence against women is clearly complex, comprehensive, and valid on a range of levels, and reparation agreements constrained solely to first-tier recognition of indigenous law do not do it proper justice. In state courts, the actors of the criminal justice system (defenders, prosecutors, judges), steeped as they are in an adversarial logic and in case strategizing, tend to resort to indigenous customs as an instrument of convenience. As prosecutors do their best to ensure offenders face the full weight of the state law, defenders strive to secure less onerous alternatives for their clients. Caught in the middle, judges often lack conviction that an actual plea agreement exists, wonder if the custom being invoked is a genuine part of indigenous law, and lack the knowledge or willingness to act as guarantors of a reparation agreement. Additionally, sometimes recourse to indigenous law is not even functional to the defense strategy, as it presupposes admitting the facts. Judges are often not conversant with the particularistic, community-based nature of *Az Mapu* and would like indigenous law to be codified and integrated into state law.

The outlook isn't much more auspicious among Mapuche women, who also feel victimized by state and institutional policies and programs that do not recognize their identity. They point to similarities between "police violence in the land claim territories and the violence used by state institutions. SERNAM, for example, is not regarded as trustworthy or able to address violence in its various forms in a way that guarantees the rights of Mapuche women. Access to information has helped encourage women to report offenders, but much more needs to be done to address male violence and sexism, starting with early childhood education. In short, only constitutional recognition of the Mapuche as a people will enable real policy transformations and a culturally-relevant approach to violence against Mapuche women" (Mercado Catriñir et al. 2015, 17).

Their views are especially instructive. Mapuche women seem dissatisfied with both state justice and their own system of justice, see themselves as vulnerable for ethnic, gender, and social reasons, and call for a dialogue that upholds their dual indigenous and female identity. In my view, this points to a clear need to work toward a pluralistic, second-tier, opt-in indigenous jurisdiction as part of an intersectional interpretation of indigenous law based on the transcultural distribution of the conditions that ensure participation in collective decision-making. As to reparations, related agreements need to include the actual, direct intervention of indigenous authorities and community members. Moreover, as currently available options for addressing violence protect neither women's nor indigenous rights, Chile must move "toward a justice system that respects indigenous punitive systems. This would not be incompatible with the right of all women to be free from violence. Since no culture is static, such rights can well form part of and be interpreted in the light of the indigenous worldview, and eventually become a real addition to indigenous conflict resolution methods" (Villegas and Mella 2017, 163).

CONCLUSION. BACK TO THEORY: FORMULATING A PLURALISTIC CONCEPT, INSTITUTIONAL ACCEPTANCE

Most likely to yield proper results is a pluralistic view capable of addressing the shortcomings (if taken in isolation) of the above propositions. Such a view should attempt to address the cultural vulnerability paradox and elucidate if an appeal to internal culture suffices to deny women a catalogue of the basic rights that provide the basis for genuine deliberation. As such, a triple balance is needed: recognition of the normative authority of indigenous communities (i.e., territorial and political self-determination); a multicultural jurisdiction that allows the applicable legislation to be chosen on a case-by-case basis, and access to all rights guaranteed in a deliberative democracy. This balance would provide an institutional guarantee that those who uphold more forceful intercultural stands but claim not to support essentialist views of cultures will be "taken seriously" and "up on their word." How to articulate this characterization of culture in the law? Surely, only through the fundamental rights that safeguard deliberation. Legal and institutional acceptance of such a triple balance specifically requires (cf Villavicencio 2014).

1. Building into the Constitution the gender perspective required to address its false neutrality and the structural discrimination that excludes women from *the groups that count* insofar as the legitimacy of the political system is concerned. This should at least translate into the enshrinement of gender in the Constitution's equality clause, a law-based electoral system that ends the underrepresentation of women, recognition of sexual and reproductive rights, and policies of mediation in matters of child rearing and care.
2. Ensuring equal participation by indigenous nations within a multinational state that grants territorial and functional autonomy. This is the only way to stably address the fact that indigenous identity is built at the intersection of general and community identities;
3. Entrenching the *nomoi* nature of indigenous communities through general recognition of second-tier normative authority, thereby creating a genuinely pluralistic jurisdiction that overcomes the constraints of articles 9 and 10 of ILO Convention 169;
4. Guaranteeing the ability of indigenous women to choose whether to submit to local or state jurisdictions on a case-by-case basis, within a context of full compliance with the conditions of deliberative democracy, including: (a) Reciprocity and political inclusion; (b) Broad, voluntary self-identification as indigenous; (c) Freedom of exit and association; (d) Non-domination, i.e., keeping the wielders of economic and social power—men—from coercing women and thus undermining political deliberation; and (e) Guarantees that agreements can be revised as often as necessary (Benhabib 2002, 131–132).
5. Once these conditions are met, both dominant and minority communities should be able to consider themselves as moral agents whose identities have a plural affiliation. In everyday life, this would enable the state and the dominant and minority groups to see themselves as mutable social entities that reciprocally influence one another (cf Shachar 2001, 118). Intercultural demands, which can challenge the basic assumptions of modern constitutional democracy, should release their potential for conflict through dialogue and negotiation in the public

> realm (Benhabib 2002, 115). In a dynamic deliberative and multicultural democracy, the maneuvering of lawyers, legal operators and judges using the tools of pluralistic legal models should not completely stifle cultural and political conflict or the learning opportunities it provides to all, including members of the dominant culture, the minority cultures, and their own internal minorities. As Deveaux (2005, 362) notes, while none of this guarantees that the result will be hailed as the most just by all concerned, the process of evaluating and reforming (if needed) contested practices should help generate more democratically legitimate and politically viable solutions.

Treating women with equal respect and consideration admits no simple or monist solutions. What is needed is a transition from essentializing culture to propositions that begin by ceasing to purport to speak for all women. Rather than within cultures, the violation of women's rights originates in the agents—men—leading these cultures and claiming to represent women in order to maintain control. It also originates in the well-intentioned states and international bodies that all too often neglect to ask and channel women's views. Rather than merely grant women rights administered by the dominant élites, the challenge is, as Gargarella (2014) aptly puts it, to let them—and other disadvantaged groups—into the constitutional "engine room."

NOTES

This article draws from "Indigenous Women as Minorities Within Minorities: A Hard Case for Theory and the Law," a research project funded by Chile's National Science and Technology Development Fund (FONDECYT) (Project No. 1150094).

1. This does not expunge the fact that for centuries the law was a powerful instrument in the service of reducing *Indians* to a "less than human" condition to justify policies of extermination or domination, as convenience dictated, or designed to forcibly assimilate and integrate the "savages." For an excellent analysis of ILO Convention 169, with emphasis on the Chilean case (Aylwin, Meza-Lopehandía and Yañez 2013, 337–443; 523–599).

2. The 2003 Final Report of the Commission on Historical Truth and New Deal for Indigenous Peoples is eloquent in this respect: "Formation of the Chilean nation-state required a systematic, deliberate effort to assimilate indigenous peoples. It was an attempt by 19th-century élites to build a society of loyal citizens. The Chilean nation was not the product of natural evolution inspiring the spontaneous emergence of a community" (531). Available at: http://bibliotecadigital.indh.cl/handle/123456789/268.

3. "Until recently, Chilean law did not recognize the existence of indigenous peoples or, save for the water rights of some Andean communities, their rights over ancestral lands, territories and resources. Neither did it recognize a right to an autonomous justice system or institutions" (Aylwin, Meza-Lopehandía and Yañez 2013, 32).

4. For an overview of critiques of the notion of *homogenous state* from a multicultural standpoint, see Villavicencio (2010, 2010, 2012, 2014).

5. Not to mention persuading skeptics that revising the common citizenship ideal will not distract from the ends of the democratic state.

6. National minorities can in turn be classified into civic nations (the product of a shared will, i.e., Québec) or ethnic nations (arising from firmer, more rigid traditions such as the Mapuche or Rapa Nui peoples).

7. This typology should result in different categories of minority rights. Rights more typical of national minorities include political autonomy, including special representation, the right to a wholly or partially specific system of laws, and self-rule. Cultural and migrant minority rights often translate into cultural differentiation (i.e., festivities, education, dress, religious practices, language) and freedom from discrimination by the dominant group. Social minorities claim certain entitlements providing access to more equitable resource distribution. What is both interesting and complicated is that a minority group often belongs to more than one category. Such is the case of Mapuche women, who are a national and ethnic minority (depending on place of residence), a sexual minority, and in all cases, a social minority.

8. Reparation agreements are decided by the Public Defender's Office. They hark back to an office for Mapuche defendants which became a specialized Mapuche Defender's Office in 2003. The practice has been validated by the case law of the Temuco Court of Appeals.

9. Excellent reviews from the perspective of multiculturally sensitive scholarship include Carmona 2015; Villegas 2012, 2014; Palma & Sandrini 2014; Couso 2013. For a comprehensive review of the persistence of indigenous punitive systems in Chile, see Villegas & Mella 2017). For a broader view and description of normative categories from the Mapuche worldview, see Melin et al. 2016). For a review of legal pluralism from the perspective of indigenous law, see Garzón López 2016, 213–261. Notably, article 19 of the Family Violence Act disallows reparation agreements, of which more later.

10. A *reductionist sociology of culture* based on faulty epistemology claims (a) that cultures are clearly delineable wholes; (b) that a noncontroversial description of culture is possible; and (c) that even if cultures and groups do not stand in one-to-one correspondence, this poses no important problems for politics or policy (Benhabib 2002, 4).

11. On its face, the liberal multiculturalist affiliation of ILO Convention 169 seems clear; as such, to a large extent the critique of Kymlicka's concept of a right of *accommodation* also applies (Villavicencio 2012). General Comment 28 (2000) on Equality of Rights between Men and Women (Human Rights Committee, International Covenant on Civil and Political Rights) issued in connection with article 3 of the Covenant, embraces the same principle: culture is not a valid pretext to violate women's right to equal protection of the law.

12. From a criminal law viewpoint, the conflict could be addressed by acquitting indigenous defendants, as their cultural practices and customs do not consider certain conducts as prohibited. My interest in this matter is to offer an approximation intended to help enrich the criminal scholarship analysis (Villegas 2012; Villegas 2014; Villegas and Mella 2017; Guzmán 2014; Couso 2013).

13. "A mechanism through which elders pass on guidelines and norms to young people or to anyone who wants to learn. They advise on specific matters, on how to act in a certain context or situation, or simply counsel people who have breached a rule" (Melin et al. 2016, 30).

REFERENCES

Andersen, Margaret. 2006. "Race, Gender, and Class Stereotypes: New Perspectives on Ideology and Inequality." *Revista Norteamérica* 1, 1 (January–June): 69–91.

Añón, María José. 2001. "La interculturalidad posible: ciudadanía diferenciada y derechos." *Cuadernos de derecho judicial* (6): 217–270.

Anthias, Floya. 1998. "Rethinking Social Divisions: Some Notes towards a Theoretical Framework." *Sociological Review* 46, 3 (August): 505–535.

Anthias, Floya, and Nira Yuval-Davis. 1992. *Racialized Boundaries: Race, Nation, Gender, Colour and Class and the Anti-Racist Struggle.* New York: Routledge.

Anzaldúa, Gloria. 1987. *Borderlands/La Frontera: The New Mestiza.* San Francisco: Aunt Lute Books.

Aylwin, José, Matías Meza-Lopehandía, and Nancy Yáñez. 2013. *Los pueblos indígenas y el derecho*. Santiago: LOM.

Banting, Keith, and Will Kymlicka, Eds. 2006. *Multiculturalism and the Welfare State: Recognition and Redistribution in Contemporary Democracies*. Oxford: Oxford University Press.
Barry, Bryan. 2002. *Culture and Equality*. Cambridge: Harvard University Press.
Bengoa, José. 2014. *Mapuches, colonos y el Estado Nacional*. Santiago: Catalonia.
Benhabib, Seyla. 2002. *The Claims of Culture. Equality and Diversity in the Global Era*. Princeton: Princeton University Press.
———. 2006. *El ser y el otro en la ética contemporánea. Feminismo, comunitarismo y posmodermismo*. Translated by Gabriel Zadunaisky. Barcelona: Gedisa.
Bravo, Millecer. 2017. "Tribunales validan disculpas verbales ante violencia intrafamiliar entre Mapuches." *Lexweb*. Last visited 23 September 2017 http://www.lexweb.cl/tribunales-validan-disculpas-verbales-ante-violencia-intrafamiliar-entremapuches.
Carmona, Cristóbal. 2015. "Hacia una comprensión 'trágica' de los conflictos multiculturales: acuerdos reparatorios, violencia intrafamiliar y derecho propio indígena." *Revista Chilena de Derecho* 42 (3): 975–1001.
Clavero, Bartolomé. 2007. "Reconocimiento de Estados (no indígenas) por pueblos (indígenas): Chile y Mapu, caso y categoría." In *Ciudadanía y derechos indígenas en América Latina: poblaciones, estados y orden internacional*, Laura Giraudo, Ed., pp. 107–128. Madrid: Centro de Estudios Políticos y Constitucionales.
Contesse, Jorge, Ed. 2013. *El Convenio 169 de la OIT y el derecho chileno. Mecanismos y obstáculos para su implementación*. Santiago: Ediciones Universidad Diego Portales.
Couso, Jaime. 2013. "Mapuches y derecho penal." In *Derecho y Pueblo Mapuche: Aportes para la discusión*, Helena Olea, Ed., pp. 155–21. Santiago: Universidad Diego Portales.
De Lucas, Javier. 2001. "La(s) sociedad(es) multicultural(es) y los conflictos políticos y jurídicos." *Cuadernos de derecho judicial,* (6): 59–102.
Delanty, Gerard. 2010. *Community* (2nd Ed.). Abingdon: Routledge.
Deveaux, Monique. 2000. *Cultural Pluralism and Dilemmas of Justice*. Ithaca: Cornell University Press.
Deveaux, Monique. 2005. "A Deliberative Approach to Conflicts of Culture." In *Minorities within Minorities. Equality, Rights and Diversity*, Avigail Eisenberg and Jeff Spinner-Halev, Eds., pp. 340–362. Cambridge: Cambridge University Press.
———. *Gender and Justice in Multicultural Liberal States*. Oxford University Press. 2006.
Dhamoon, Rita. 2007. "The Politics of Cultural Contestation." In *Sexual Justice/Cultural Justice. Critical Perspectives in Political Theory and Practice*, Barbara Arneil, Monique Deveaux, Rita Dhamoon and Avigail Eisenberg, Eds., pp. 54–95. London and New York: Routledge.
Eisenberg, Avigail, and Jeff Spinner-Halev, Eds. 2005. *Minorities within Minorities. Equality, Rights and Diversity*. Cambridge: Cambridge University Press.
Fraser, Nancy. 2000. "Rethinking Recognition." In *New Left Review*, No. 3 (May June): 107–120.
García, Sabina, and Luis Villavicencio. 2016. "Alcances y límites del multiculturalismo liberal desde un enfoque de género interseccional." *Convergencia Revista de Ciencias Sociales*, 72 (August): 13–38.
Gargarella, Roberto. 2014. "El 'nuevo constitucionalismo latinoamericano.'" *El País*, July 31, 2014. In http://elpais.com/elpais/2014/07/31/opinion/1406816088_091940.html
Garzón López, Pedro. 2016. *Ciudadanía indígena: del multiculturalismo a la colonialidad del poder*. Madrid: Centro de Estudios Políticos y Constitucionales.
Guzmán, José Luis. 2014. "Derecho penal y minorías étnicas: planteamiento y liquidación criminalista de un problema político." *Revista de Derecho Penal y Criminología* (11): 93–118.
Habersang, Anja, and Pamela Ydígoras. 2015. *El activismo internacional mapuche*. Santiago: Ceibo.
Jackson, Jennifer. 2005. *Minority Rights*. Cambridge, UK; Malden, USA: Polity Press.
Keating, Michael. 2001. *Plurinational Democracy. Stateless Nations in a Post-Sovereignty Era*. Oxford: Oxford University Press.

Kukathas, Chandran. 2012. "Exit, Freedom and Gender." In *On Exit: Interdisciplinary Perspectives on the Right of Exit in Liberal Multicultural Societies*, Dagmar Borchers and Annamari Vitikainen, Eds., pp. 56–34. Berlin/Boston: Walter de Gruyter.

Kymlicka, Will. 2002. *Contemporary Political Philosophy. An Introduction* (2nd Ed.). Oxford: Oxford University Press.

———. 2007. *Multicultural Odysseys. Navigating the New International Politics of Diversity*. Oxford: Oxford University Press.

McCall, Leslie. 2005. "The Complexity of Intersectionality." *Signs: Journal of Women in Culture and Society* 30, 3 (Spring): 1771–1800.

Melin, Miguel et al. 2016. *Azmapu: una aproximación al sistema normativo mapuche desde el Rakizuam y el derecho propio*. Temuco: Instituto Nacional de Derechos Humanos.

Mercado Catriñir, Ximena et al. 2015. *Sistematización de nvxamkawvn (encuentros de conversación) y definición de propuestas entre mujeres y organizaciones mapuche en torno a violencia contra mujeres mapuche y aplicación de sistemas de justicia propia*. Temuco: Corporación de Mujeres Mapuche Aukinko Zomo.

Modood, Tariq. 2007. *Multiculturalism. A Civic Idea.* Cambridge, UK; Malden, USA: Polity Press.

Nash, Claudio, Catalina Lagos, and Constanza Núñez. 2013. *Violencia contra mujeres indígenas en el marco de las relaciones familiares: pautas para decidir la procedencia de acuerdos reparatorios.* Santiago: Human Rights Center, University of Chile.

Palma, Rosario, and Renata Sandrini. 2014. "Mujer mapuche y retos de la justicia intercultural: aplicación del derecho propio indígena en delitos de violencia intrafamiliar." *Anuario de Derechos Humanos* (10): 151–161.

Parekh, Bhikhu 2006. *Rethinking Multiculturalism. Cultural Diversity and Political Theory* (2nd Ed.). Basingstoke: Palgrave Macmillan.

———. 2002. "Barry and the dangers of liberalism." In *Multiculturalism Reconsidered. Culture and Equality and its Critics*, Paul Kelly, Ed., pp. 133–150. Cambridge, UK; Malden, USA: Polity Press.

Pérez de la Fuente, Oscar. 2013. "Indígenas y derechos colectivos: ¿es el multiculturalismo malo para las mujeres?" *Derechos y libertades, Revista del Instituto Bartolomé de las Casas*, (13): 399–430.

Phillips, Anne. 2007a. Multiculturalism without Culture. Princeton: Princeton University Press.

———. 2007b. "What is 'culture'?" In *Sexual Justice/Cultural Justice. Critical Perspectives in Political Theory and Practice*, Barbara Arneil, Monique Deveaux, Rita Dhamoon and Avigail Eisenberg, Eds., pp. 15–29. Florence: Routledge.

Sánchez, Cristina. 2002. "Feminismo y ciudadanía." In *Estado, justicia, derechos*, Elías Díaz and José Luis Colomer, Eds., pp. 347–370. Madrid: Alianza.

Sandoval, Marcela, and Verónica Undurraga. 2012. "Mujeres y ciudadanía: revisiones conceptuales y estrategias políticas. ¿Qué significa ser ciudadana hoy en América Latina?." *Iniciativa Latinoamericana para el avance de los derechos humanos de las mujeres II. Mujeres, Ciudadanía y Multiculturalismo*. Santiago: Human Rights Center, University of Chile.

Selamé, Nicole, and Luis Villavicencio. 2011. "Liberalismo, multiculturalismo y Estado de bienestar." *Ideas y Valores. Revista Colombiana de Filosofía*, National University of Colombia 60 (147): 111–140.

Shachar, Ayalet. 2001. *Multicultural Jurisdictions. Cultural Differences and Women's Rights.* Cambridge: Cambridge University Press.

Song, Sarah. 2007. *Justice, Gender, and the Politics of Multiculturalism.* Cambridge: Cambridge University Press.

Soriano, Ramón. 2002. "Culturas, ideologías y derechos de las minorías," *Revista Facultad de Derecho de la Universidad de Granada* (5): 33–64.

Toledo Llancaqueo, Víctor. 2006. *Pueblo mapuche. Derechos colectivos y territorio: desafíos para la sustentabilidad democrática.* Santiago: Programa Chile Sustentable.

Villavicencio, Luis. 2007. "La concepción política de la persona y las visiones constitutivas del bien." *Ideas y Valores. Revista Colombiana de Filosofía*, National University of Colombia (135): 29–49.

———. 2009. "Algunas críticas a la idea de razón pública rawlsiana." *Revista de Derecho de la Pontificia Universidad Católica de Valparaíso* 32 (1): 533–557.
———. 2010a. "La relevancia moral de la identidad cultural." *Polis* 9 (26): 339–420.
———. 2010b. "Privatizando la diferencia: El liberalismo igualitario y el pluralismo cultural." *Revista de Derecho (Valdivia)* XXIII (1): 37–57.
———. 2012. "Un diálogo intercultural más allá del multiculturalismo." *Revista Opinión Jurídica*, School of Law, University of Medellín (Colombia) 11 (22): 31–44.
———. 2014. "Minorías étnico-culturales y derechos de las mujeres." *Revista de Ciencia Política* (Santiago) 34 (3): 605–621.
———. 2015. "Una concepción de la ciudadanía para una nueva Constitución. El caso de las mujeres indígenas." In *Propuestas para una nueva constitución (originada en democracia)*, Eduardo Chia and Flavio Quezada, Eds., pp. 301–325. Santiago: Instituto Igualdad - School of Law, University of Chile - Friedrich Ebert Stiftung.
———. 2017. "Interculturalidad, derechos de la infancia y Constitución." In *Constitución política e infancia: Una mirada desde los derechos de los niños, niñas y adolescentes en Chile*, Anuar Quesille, Ed., pp. 155–167. Santiago: UNICEF.
Villegas, Mirna. 2012. "Entre la justificación y la exculpación. Apuntes de legislación comparada latinoamericana sobre pluralismo jurídico y derecho penal." *Revista de Derecho (Valdivia)* XXV (2): 177–205.
———. 2014. "Sistemas sancionatorios indígenas y Derecho penal. ¿Subsiste el Az Mapu?" *Política Criminal* 9, (17): 213–247.
Villegas, Myrna, and Eduardo Mella. 2017. *Cuando la costumbre se vuelve ley: la cuestión penal y la pervivencia de los sistemas sancionatorios indígenas en Chile*. Santiago: LOM.
Winker, Gabriele, and Nina Degele. 2009. *Intersektionalität: Zur Analyse sozialer Ungleichheiten*. Bielefeld: Transcript Verlag.
Young, Iris Marion. 2000. *La justicia y la política de la diferencia* . Translated by Silvina Álvarez. Madrid: Cátedra.
Zúñiga, Yanira. 2009. "La 'generización' de la ciudadanía. Apuntes sobre el rol de la diferencia sexual en el pensamiento feminista." *Revista de Derecho (Valdivia)* XXII, (2): 39–64.
———. 2010. "Ciudadanía y género. Representaciones y conceptualizaciones en el pensamiento moderno y contemporáneo." *Revista de Derecho Universidad Católica del Norte* 17 (2): 133–163.

Chapter Seven

Frustrated Multiculturalism

(Neo)Liberalism and the Mapuche People

Matías Meza-Lopehandía

Indigenous peoples' rights have been an issue in Chilean politics since the beginning of the Republic. Mirroring the policies applied in the region, the State has employed different strategies to address the indigenous issue. These range from bare annihilation or assimilation to present-day attempts to improve this problematic relationship through actions promoting multiculturalism. This chapter explores these contemporary attempts, the adoption of which has facilitated the deployment of neoliberal policies in the Mapuche territory. Drawing from Charles Hale and Rosamel Millaman's critical approach, this chapter asserts the existence of an intimate link between multiculturalism and the criminalization of the Mapuche movement, which was wielded for the benefit of the long-term interests of the economic model, and the way in which this imposes limits on the full deployment of the multicultural program.

FRUSTRATED INTEGRATION

Since the independence of the Latin American states in the nineteenth century, their political authorities have tended to treat indigenous populations as a hindrance: a relic of the past that had to be overcome. Different strategies have been deployed, starting with extermination and moving to attempts to integrate the subaltern into hegemonic society.

In Chile, the assimilation project was pervasive, though the mestizo rhetoric, if it existed at all, was subordinate to the dominant class ideology that permeated the reformist and revolutionary movements (Richards 2010).

However, the short-lived socialist government of President Allende (1970–1973) was the first to recognize the existence of cultural diversity and the need for indigenous participation,[1] yet the whole assimilationist period has been labelled as frustrated integration (CVHNT 2008, 52).

Pinochet's regime (1973–1990), which overthrew Allende's government, adopted neoliberal policies in the late seventies. It focused its attention on the privatization of public services, balancing the fiscal budget and building comparative advantages for international trade. Regarding the issue of ethnicity, the dictatorship embraced a strict program of assimilation which was instituted in the infamous Decree-Law 2568 of 1979.

This legislation boosted the division of collective lands and the individual adjudication of land ownership. It also established that once the allocation of land had been completed, neither the former individual holder of collective ownership, the comunero Mapuche, nor his land would qualify as indigenous for any legal purpose. In this way, the dictatorship pursued the long held desire of the Chilean elite: the complete assimilation of the Mapuche people into the Chilean population, carrying out the white man's civilizing mission.[2]

In addition, dividing Mapuche communal lands and suppressing indigenous identity assisted in the expansion of the forestry industry on Mapuche's ancestral lands (*tierras antiguas*). Between 1979 and 1986, 1,739 communal land titles were divided into 48,346 individual tradable parcels (CVHNT 2008).[3] At the same time, the government chose to allocate the lands from the agrarian reform, originally intended to favour Mapuche communities and cooperatives, into the hands of powerful economic groups, heavily concentrating land ownership (Catalán 2007).[4,5] In the late seventies, the dictatorship also privatized the main pulp mills, built under the developmentalist economic model of the previous era. Through these efforts, new latifundio were created, which were supported largely by direct subsides via another Decree-Law, No. 701 of 1974, a mechanism that survives in contemporary Chile as a developmentalist island in the neoliberal sea.[6]

This suggests that the dictatorship saw assimilation as a precondition for the dispossession and commodification of Mapuche lands. Setting aside the fact that the forestry industry was founded using land expropriated by a socialist government, and that its development was steadily supported by government subsides, the transformation of the historic Mapuche territory into the main provider of pulp for the global market was aligned with the goals of the neoliberal project and its promotion of comparative advantages for international trade.[7]

As will be shown, the assimilationist facet of the neoliberal agenda has been recast, or perhaps hidden, by multicultural rhetoric and policies. However, neoliberal extractivism has continued without changes through decades, preventing a full deployment of multiculturalism, and providing an explanation for the persistent unrest and violence in the south of Chile.

THE NEW FAITH: THE MULTICULTURAL SHIFT

It was immediately after the end of the dictatorship when a mild form of multiculturalism was embraced in order to shape the relationship between indigenous peoples and the State. In this way, Chile was following a regional trend, namely, recasting that relationship through multiculturalism (Irigoyen 2011).[8]

This shift implies a significant departure from the assimilationist approach, which was primarily aimed at the absorption of the otherness into a homogeneous mestizo identity, which in turn underpinned the national popular movements dominating the political scene during the second half of the twentieth century.

The landmark shift was the Indigenous Development Act No. 19.253 (IDA). The bill, negotiated with indigenous communities,[9] had to pass through the peculiar transitional Congress installed following the end of the dictatorship; a body which included several senators appointed by General Pinochet, including the former dictator himself for a few months in 1998. In addition, the right-wing parties, historically reluctant to recognize ethnic diversity, were over-represented in Congress due to an election system that was tailor-made to give them an advantage.

This filter made significant changes to the proposed bill,[10] however, the act eventually passed with two distinctive features relevant to any approach attempting to be labelled multicultural: appreciation of cultural diversity and participation of the groups concerned in matters that affect them.

The former is the rubric of any version of multiculturalism, which can be inferred from the etymology of the concept. Participatory rights, in turn, are a logical consequence of cultural recognition, if recognition has any substantive meaning. Given that cultural diversity implies a certain lack of understanding between different cultures, and if authentic intercultural agreements are desired, then engaging in intercultural dialogue is imperative. In social liberalism, participatory rights play a central role in the process of citizenization,[11] and in neoliberalism, they allow the idea of "development with identity" explained hereafter (Hale 2005; Kymlicka 2010; 2012).

Recognition, Culture, and Land Restitution

In sharp contrast with Pinochet's earlier decrees, the IDA explicitly recognized the existence of indigenous ethnic groups in the country, something that had formerly been implicit in Chilean legislation since the dawn of the Republic.[12] The novelty was that for the first time the state validated those groups as an essential part of the Chilean nation. Thus, it mandated the protection of their integrity and development according to their manners and values.[13]

Recognizing indigenous culture as something valuable and worthy of protection implies accepting the special attachment of indigenous peoples to their ancestral lands. Consequently, the IDA, closely following the ILO Convention 169, made an explicit, legal recognition of land as the "main ground for their existence and culture," and mandated that society and the state protect those lands and culture. As a substantive consequence of the former, the act recognized indigenous communal possession of property, outlawed trading them, and established a special fund for land and water acquisition for indigenous people and peoples.

After making this recognition, the IDA had to give an answer to indigenous demands, especially to the Mapuche claim for land restitution. A commitment to land restitution would jeopardize the timber industry, whose main interests were in Ngulumapu, the Mapuche territory.

A compromise between multiculturalism and neoliberalism was needed, and the IDA would be an essential part of it.

The IDA states that the land's indigenousness is mainly determined by legal titles given by the state under different statutes.[14] Although the norm also included lands historically possessed, it added the requirement of actual possession, ignoring the ancestral lands (*tierras antiguas*), which are to this day the central claim of the Mapuche movement.

This limitation originated in the bill prepared by the Special Commission of Indigenous Peoples (CEPI), created in 1990 by President Aylwin (1990–1994) to advise his office. It was chaired by José Bengoa, the main scholar on the topic, who was also part of the latter National Truth and New Deal Commission (CVHNT). This commission, called by President Lagos (2000–2006) in 2001 to establish the official truth about the origins of the conflict with indigenous peoples and to give him advice on the matter, recommended identifying those land claims "exclusively originated in the loss of lands originally included in legal titles" granted by the State in order to restore them (CVHNT 2008, 577).

On the other side, Article 20 created the Fund of Lands and Waters (FTyA) aimed at remedying the loss of land via vouchers and solving land claims through direct purchase. The latter could have opened the door for restitution of ancestral lands. However, the law limited the scope of the fund to solve "land problems" to those that could be shown to have legal titles, which were mostly those granted by the state after the occupation of *Ngulumapu*. Ancestral lands were precisely those that do not have legal titles, because they were in indigenous possession prior to the invasion.[15]

The effectiveness of the fund relied on the will of the legal owner of the claimed land. This put significant pressure on land prices, opening the ground for speculation and reducing the purchasing capacity of the fund. It also gave rise to the practice of relocating communities to areas far from their ancestral territory to places where land prices were low, perpetuating the conflict, and in some cases aggravating it.[16] This design is limited by private interest, and leaves the restitution decision to third parties which are usually the timber companies. This is a key issue from the perspective of international law, which has determined this kind of mechanism to be contrary to human rights law.[17] The CVHNT (2008) even recommended that the government expropriate lands in favour of Mapuche communities when a transaction agreement is not reachable, although still limited to lands that were at one point included in legal titles.

After 20 years of operating in this way, the fund has transferred 167,910 hectares to Mapuche communities or individuals (INDH 2014, 240–2).[18] Albeit the complete size of the Mapuche land claim is not known, it is clear that this is far from enough.[19] In fact, rural violence associated with land disputes has continued, if not increased, since the fund went into operation.[20]

Development with Identity

This increase in rural violence in the south of Chile was part of a broader picture. A new kind of indigenous movement had been emerging throughout the continent in the midst of the collapse of the socialist project and just before celebrations of the official fifth centenary of the "discovery of America."[21] In Chile, the Mapuche organization Aukiñ Wallmapu Ngulam (AWNg) began in 1992 to occupy the lands claimed by the Mapuche communities. It also launched a new rhetoric, including the concepts of indigenous autonomy and self-determination that would inspire the movement in the next years, which directly confronted capitalist interests in their claimed territory (Bengoa 2007; Pairican 2014).

Thus, the sustainability of the neoliberal project in the Mapuche region required new efforts beyond the framework provided by the IDA. Multiculturalism was in hand, but neoliberalism was originally hostile to it policies. It saw them "as a prime example of unjustified intervention in the market in response to 'special interests'" (Kymlicka 2012, 107). However, this initial rejection gave way to a new approach to multiculturalism based on the concept of "development with identity," an idea fostered initially by the World Bank, and then embraced by all the large international financial institutions (Davis 2012).[22]

At the core of this version of multiculturalism is the idea that what indigenous peoples need to survive or to take advantage of globalisation is to improve their own entrepreneurial skills to pursue opportunities. Consequently, the new agenda included the strengthening of human capital, mainly by the implementation of bilingual education, the enhancement of communal forms of association as social capital to be used for economic flourishing, and the valuing of culture as tradable asset for the market.[23] Neoliberal multiculturalism also includes indigenous participation in the decisions that affect them, prior consultation and participation in benefits, and even "some degree of autonomy [. . .] in terms of their participation in local development planning and decision-making" (Davis 2012, 235). As Hale suggests (2002; 2005), the measure of that degree is determined by the interests of the long-term economic model, in this case, the heavily territorial interest of the timber industry, and by the relative position of the dominant elites in the social hierarchies, which in this case implies a deep concentration of wealth and political power.

This participatory dispositif implies cash flow from the state in the form of public investment in human and social capital and employment for indigenous leaders in state bureaucracy, and from the private sector in the form of participation in benefits. By placing resources in those communities willing and urged to receive them on the one hand, and by marginalizing, or even criminalizing, those that persist in their maximalist claims on the other, the device creates the dualism of *indio permitido* (allowed Indian)/insurrectionary Indian (Hale and Millaman, 2005). This reinforces the capacity of multiculturalism to work as catalyst for neoliberal consensus, by showing the radical Indian as isolated and dangerous.

In the midst of the upsurge in the conflict, CVHNT meeting was called by President Lagos. The Truth Commission was originally proposed by some of the main Mapuche movement organizations (Pairican 2014). Several Mapuche leaders did not participate, however, some of them eventually signed the final report (Aylwin 2007). The Commission recommended giving constitutional recognition to indigenous peoples, guaranteeing indigenous participation, including indigenous representation in electoral bodies, recognizing indigenous authorities, and creating an Indigenous People's Council for facilitating dialogue between them and state authorities. It also recommended other things, including demarcating indigenous lands, and asserted the need for land restitution, using expropriation when required.

Despite the fact that these recommendations were aligned with the basic standards of ILO convention and the World Bank operative directive 4.20, and the proposal on land restitution was limited to those claims framed by legal titles, only 10% of them were followed in the following years (Letelier 2007).[24]

Instead of following the commissions' proposals, Ricardo Lagos's government (2000–2006) deployed the "New Deal Policy" (PNT): a targeted policy designed by central authorities based on the notion of "development with identity," hoping that resource allocation would mitigate the conflict.

At the core of the new policy was the Inter-American Development Bank's sponsored programme Orígenes. Aligned with the neoliberal form of multiculturalism, it focused on strengthening indigenous organizations through investment in infrastructure, fostering productive development centered on agriculture and cattle raising, and on implementing intercultural health and education programmes. There was no land restitution component, and furthermore, following the bank's practices, the program prioritized individuals and families over communities and the basic social unity of the Mapuche society called *lof* (Letelier 2007). The programme's emphasis eventually turned to productive development, leaving behind the longer-term processes that could have enabled healthy indigenous participation. As Patricia Richards (2010:70) notes, "[e]ven the programme's motto, 'Mira el futuro desde tu origen' ('Look towards the future from your origins'), seems to encourage the indigenous to keep their traditions but forget their ancestral claims."

As several authors have noted, the whole programme was used by the political authorities as a tool for pacifying the conflict via allocation of resources (Bello 2007; Letelier 2007, Pairican 2014; Richards 2010). Meanwhile, the Government deployed an intelligence operation called Operation Patience (Operación Paciencia), aimed at breaking up the Mapuche organization CAM (Corporación Aurauco-Malleco), declared to be a terrorist group for its participation in several sabotages of the timber industry (Aylwin 2007). This operation supplied evidence for the antiterrorist trials of 2003–2004, which were declared to have violated the human rights of the defendants by the Inter-American Court of Human Rights. Consequently, the state was ordered "to nullify all the effects of [those] criminal judgements" (ICtHR 2014, par. 422).

Participation Limited

Participation of indigenous peoples in the decisions that affect them is a significant part of the multicultural programme. Thus, it was incorporated in the multicultural shift from the beginning, at least in the letter of the IDA. In fact, the act guaranteed participation of indigenous representatives at the National Council of the National Corporation for Indigenous Development (Corporación Nacional de Desarrollo Indígena, CONADI), an entity in charge of the promotion, coordination and execution of the public policies addressed to indigenous peoples.[25] In addition, the act established two indigenous councils, one in the north and one in the south, and mandated that state agencies listen to and consider the opinions of the legal indigenous organizations in matters concerning them.

The participatory momentum of the IDA was soon exhausted, however. Indigenous participation was confined to the national council of CONADI, where only 8 of 17 members were indirectly elected by registered indigenes. The model worked for a while until President Frei (1994–2000) decided to approve construction of the Ralco dam in Mapuche territory in 1997. This was despite the opposition of the National Council, who claimed that the company had misinformed community members in order to get their consent

(Bengoa 2007). President Frei had to remove two of CONADI's chairmen in a row and several of CONADI's counselors, and he also had to install the first non-indigenous chairman to force the project through (Namuncura 1999).

This episode marked the fall of CONADI as an institution of legitimate participation for the Mapuche people, turning it into a mere administrator of the FTyA. The affair is also seen as a milestone in the radicalization of the Mapuche movement (Pairican & Álvarez 2011; Piñeiro 2004).

The other components of indigenous participation included in the IDA never saw the light of day. No indigenous councils were created, nor was a consultation procedure sanctioned. The former required an executive decree to operate that was never issued, despite being announced by President Lagos in his PNT in 2004 (Gobierno de Chile 2004). The latter had to wait until 2009, when ILO Convention 169 came into effect.

Michele Bachelet's first term (2006–2010), was characterized by explicitly embracing multiculturalism as a framework for a new deal with indigenous peoples (Gobierno de Chile 2008). The culmination of this policy was the ratification in 2008 of ILO Convention No. 169 after more than 25 years of deliberation in Congress. This instrument, adopted in 1989 by the ILO Conference "with a view toward removing the assimilationist orientation of the earlier standards," represents an answer from liberal multiculturalism to the challenge of accommodating cultural diversity inside the nation-state.[26]

The treaty has more than 40 articles covering issues including public policy, land rights, labour conditions and social security, education and health. It also mandates the demarcation of indigenous land, and it even orders the establishment of "adequate procedures [. . .] to resolve land claims by the peoples concerned" (art. 14). Despite the obvious relevance of this provision, the convention's implementation in Chile and elsewhere has been focused on prior consultation. This is not by chance. It has been the ILO itself, supported by UN experts, who had qualified participation, and its preferred form, prior consultation, as the cornerstone of the instrument (CEARC 2010; ILO 2009; UN 2009). For multiculturalism, recognizing the value of cultural diversity implies acceptance of a certain lack of understanding between different cultures. Then, if authentic intercultural agreements are a desirable goal, engaging in an intercultural dialogue becomes imperative.

Indigenous prior consultation as a model of intercultural dialogue aimed at obtaining the consent of a party that has no veto powers is a perfect device for allocating resources, helping to build consensus on the foundations of the economic model, and at the same time, strengthening the idea the that those indigenes that do not want to engage in dialogue are punishable rebels.

The implementation of prior consultation has not been an easy task, however, perhaps because of a lack of understanding of its authentic nature and scope from the Chilean economic and political elites.

This can be seen in the ambiguous stance adopted by the successive governments regarding prior consultation. Ricardo Lagos promoted the approval of the convention in Congress. When the Deputies' Chamber passed the bill in 2000, a group of conservative parliamentarians asked the Constitutional Court to declare the whole treaty unconstitutional. Paradoxically, the government defended the constitutionality of prior consultation by claiming that it was just a mechanism to gather opinion, which was already present in the legal system before the adoption of the convention.[27] The court rejected both claims, asserting the constitutionality of the convention and stating that prior consultation had an essential difference with the other participation mechanism already contemplated in the legal system, to wit: its purpose in obtaining consent. Later in the same sentence, the court asserted the exact opposite, affirming that prior consultation was already included in the Environmental Act.[28] This irresolution would permeate further jurisprudence on the matter.

After the convention came into effect, the government continued to operate as before, provoking several conflicts with communities demanding prior consultation on investment projects in their territories. The decisions taken by the Supreme Court, mostly regarding development investments in indigenous territories, were initially favourable to the government's position. Despite some oscillation, this soon began to change. In general, the court has asserted that the convention's prior consultation is something different from the concept of citizen participation included in the Environmental Act, and goes further than mere information, constituting a realization of the constitutional right to equal participation (Meza-Lopehandía 2016).

Another topic of discussion has been: when a measure should be considered to affect indigenous peoples, according to article 6.1 of the Convention. This question is closely linked to the concepts of territory and habitat included in the Convention, which enhanced previous notions of indigenous land included in national legislation. The Supreme Court has been reluctant in this matter, revoking several decisions of the Courts of Appeals that adopted a broad concept of indigenous land in order to require prior consultation.[29] The Supreme Court has also required certainty of impact, instead of the just the possibility of it, and a certain magnitude of impact.[30]

This approach was followed by President Piñera's government (2010–2014), which adopted two regulations regarding prior consultation, establishing significant impact on indigenous populations and certainty of that impact as requirements for calling for a consultation.[31]

This shows a lack of understanding of the convention's multiculturalism, since uncertainty of the scope and magnitude of impacts in a multicultural society is a reason for prior consultation.

CONCLUSION

President Patricio Aylwin, who received his office from Pinochet himself, is remembered for, among other things, stating that truth and justice, regarding the victims of the dictatorship, would be achieved "to the degree that is possible" (*en la medida de lo posible*). Beyond the pointlessness of this statement—no one could expect to get anything more than what was possible—one must read a deeper meaning. It constitutes a political gesture towards the de facto powers that impose the limits of the transition to democracy in Chile. This goes beyond transitional justice and illuminates the outer bounds of Chilean multiculturalism: the State's commitment to protect the interests of powerful economic groups.

Pinochet's regime imposed neoliberalism on the whole country, and pursued an assimilation policy regarding the Mapuche people in order to support the extractivist model deployed in their territory. Perhaps predictably, he fails, just as the early attempts of European liberal imperialists at assimilation of native populations in the nineteenth century failed. Like them, which in the wake of this failure turned to indirect rule (Matena 2010), the Chilean government shifted from the assimilation program to multiculturalism in an attempt to rebuild the relationship between the Mapuche people and the State, and, at the same time, obtain a minimal consensus on the foundation of the economic model.

This chapter has attempted to show how that foundation imposes limits on the full adoption of multiculturalism, reducing it to a device for disciplining the Indian, mainly through resource allocation. Of course this analysis of the failure of multicultural strategies in Chile regarding the Mapuche people and its movement does not stand alone. It has to be read in the context of other perspectives considering racial hierarchies, especially in the local society, prejudice and exacerbated centralism, among other things.

I contend, however, that any account of the Mapuche/Chilean conflict has to bear in mind that the claim for Mapuche territory restitution stands in the way of some of the most powerful interests in the country. To start, two of the biggest corporations in the country have strategic interests in the timber industry. Land restitution according to international standards would affect them directly. It would also require the deployment of a new development strategy due to the central role that the timber industry plays in Chilean economy. Finally, the idea of an autonomous Mapuche territory would require a degree of decentralization that happens to be almost impossible to even imagine for the actual ruling class.

In any case, the days of multiculturalism seem to be over. The Mapuche movement has adopted the vocabulary of self-determination from years ago. Its claim is backed by International Law, and also by the shift from multiculturalism to plurinationalism in the region. Indigenous autonomy and land restitution should not be limited by what is possible any more, but should instead be seen as a mandate to maximize. To wit: as a constitutional principle which demands the most extensive application possible in the context of other competing constitutional principles and rules.[32]

NOTES

1. Allende's government fostered new legislation aimed at including Mapuche land claims into the agrarian reform process as indigenous land, which was based on a proposal made by Mapuche organizations themselves (Correa et al. 2005). This Act was the first to use an ethnic point of view in defining the subject it favored (Boccara and Seguel-Boccara, 1999; Correa et al., 2005). It also created the Institute for Indigenous Development to promote indigenous integration to national community while "taking into account their idiosyncrasy and respecting their customs" (art. 34). In an unprecedented manner, this new institution included the participation of indigenous representatives in its governing body. Despite the fact that this was framed by the government's own ideological point of view, it was novel both because of the way it was designed with indigenous participation, and by its pluralistic content. In some sense, this policy prefigured the multicultural shift of the nineties.

2. As early as 1859, the influential newspaper *El Mercurio* characterized the Mapuche as a horde of wild beasts ("*orda de fieras*") that had to be enchained or destroyed in the interest of humanity and the sake of civilization (Correa & Mella, 2010:42). In general, it can be said that, since the legal and military annexation of the Mapuche territory in the second half of the nineteenth century, legislation has aimed at reducing and dividing communal lands. Pinochet's legislation was the pinnacle of this policy. (Boccara & Seguel-Boccara, 1999; Correa et al., 2005; Correa & Mella, 2010).

3. Boccara & Seguel-Boccara (1999) states that between 1979 and 1990, 72,068 individual titles were delivered, affecting about 465,000 hectares. This put an end to almost all collective titles.

4. Correa et al. (2005) characterize the process as a counter reform, underscored by the fact that only the 16% of the land expropriated from the Mapuche between 1962 and 1973 remained under Mapuche ownership. This figure contrasts with the national average of 52% of the land remaining in the reformed sector after the coup (Correa et al. 2005).

5. Regarding land concentration, according to data published by the firms themselves, the two largest timber companies in the country, Arauco S.A. and CMCP directly owned 1.116.788 and 733.923 hectares respectively. For Arauco S.A., see https://goo.gl/Ov4xmH; for CMPC, see https://goo.gl/ZO5Q9V.

6. Accordingly to Carvajal (2015), between 1974 and 1998, more than the 90% of the subsides went to large and medium-sized enterprises. After 1998's legal reform, the rate changed in favour of small and medium-sized enterprises. Between 1998 and 2010 small enterprises got about the 49% of the subsides, but between 2011 and 2013, they got only the 39%. Figures from the National Forestry Corporation (CONAF) are similar (González, 2015). An older study shows similar outcomes (Catalán, 2007).

7. In this, the neoliberal project has been successful. Timber is the third largest export commodity in the country (CORMA, n.d.a.), representing about the 3% of the GNP (CORMA, n.d.b), and Chile is one of the top ten producers of pulp (CORMA, n.d.c).

8. This term comprises different approaches to the question of cultural diversity, from those that claim that cultural recognition is a requirement for authentic individual agency, to those that see it as a source of exchangeable assets for the global market, or those that give it an intrinsic value. All of them share a common feature, namely, they all see cultural diversity as a value that has to be protected and promoted. This work will center its attention on liberal multiculturalism and its variants. Illiberal communitarianism will not be addressed, since it has no significant impact in Chile's policies and legislation regarding indigenous peoples.

9. Following the precedent established by the overthrown socialist government of President Allende, the government promoted a wide process of participation, that, according to the

bill proposed to Congress by President Aylwin (1990–1994), included hundreds of indigenous communities that selected delegates for several provincial congresses, which in turn sent delegates to the National Congress of Indigenous Peoples. This group discussed the main ideas that structured the bill (BCN, 1993).

10. For a critical analysis of the contents of the bill contrasted with indigenous claims and the contents of the act in contrast with the bill, see Aylwin, J., Meza-Lopehandía, M. & Yáñez, N. (2013), specially pages 183–187.

11. The concept of *citizenization*, as James Tully understand it, refers to the "willingness to negotiate as equals the terms of belonging with the goal of reaching consent" (Kymlicka, 2012:103 n.4).

12. As early as 1813, a regulation was adopted by the Junta de Gobierno in agreement with the new Senate, which mandated the settlement of the *pueblos de indios* into *villas*, with churches, schools and town halls. In 1819, the Supreme Director of the Republic, Bernardo O'higgins, expanded citizenship to indigenous people, invoking liberalism. In 1823, during President Ramon Freire's mandate, Act No. 10 was adopted, establishing the perpetual indigenous ownership of land legally possessed by indigenous people (Jara, 1956).

13. It is worth noting that the bill drafted with indigenous participation used the concept of "indigenous peoples" to refer to them, not "ethnic groups" as the act did. The Chamber of Deputies suppressed those terms at the very beginning of the legislative procedure in favour of the concept of "indigenes of Chile" and the "main cultures of the country." Later, the Senate substituted the latter with the concept of "main ethnic groups" (see BCN, 1993, specially pages 9, 93 and 609).

14. Those were the "Títulos de Comisario," granted by the State to the *Huilliche* people after Independence, between 1824 and 1848; the "Títulos de Merced," conceded after the annexation of the autonomous Mapuche territory, between 1884 and 1929; the titles granted during the agrarian reform (1962–1973); and other titles conceded under different Indian statutes.

15. According to Zaror & Lepin (2016), at least two Mapuche communities, Temucuicui and Huañaco Millao, obtained direct purchase of land without any legal title. The authors claim, probably rightfully, that those purchases were forced because they took *de facto* control of the land. However, they omit any mention of the historical background of those claims, which is thoroughly investigated by Correa & Mella (2010). Regardless, the two cases mentioned add up to less than 3,000 hectares, a number that confirms that the law was mostly followed.

16. When purchased land is located in the claimed territory of other communities, the conflict worsens (González et al. 2007; Queupuán y Guerrero, 2004). Similar clashes occurred during the resettlement (*reducción*) of the Mapuche peoples after the Chilean invasion of Ngulumapu in the late nineteenth century (Bengoa, 2000).

17. This kind of land restitution mechanism, in which the final decision of restitution rests on the will of third parties, has been declared incompatible with the American Convention on Human rights by the Inter-American Court of Human Rights (ICtHR). See case of the Sawhoyamaxa Indigenous Community v. Paraguay, Judgment of March 29, 2006 (Merits, Reparations and Costs), specially paragraph 138. Regarding Chile, the issue has been a matter of concern for the ILO and United Nations, in particular, the Special Rapporteur on the rights of indigenous peoples and the Human Rights Committee (INDH, 2014).

18. Most of those lands were bought directly (146.585 ha) and the rest via voucher (21.325 ha) (INDH, 2014:240–2). Other mechanisms like the regularization of legal titles and transfers of State land occupied by indigenous communities have been used, but they mainly favored Likan Antay and Aymara peoples in the north of the country (INDH, 2014).

19. During the short government of Allende (1970–1973), 132.115 hectares were transferred to the *Mapuche* people (Aylwin, et al. 2013).

20. Some have argued that violence had increased *because* of the fund, since it encourages occupations to gain priority for purchase (Zaror & Lepin, 2016).

21. In 1990, the indigenous movement, lead by CONAIE, broke in Ecuador, challenging the idea of celebrating the fifth centenary of the Discovery and demanding a new constitution recognizing plurinationaliy. In Bolivia, the indigenous lead guerilla movement Tupak Katari debuted in 1991 with armed propaganda. In the 1980's, before either movement, the Miskito

people in Nicaragua struggled against the Sandinista revolutionary government demanding recognition for their lands. In 1994, the indigenous upheaval in Chiapas sealed the pan-American feature of the new *panindigenism* (Bengoa, 2007; Dávalos, 2002; Escárzaga 2012; Pairican, 2014).

22. The World Bank was the first of these institutions to take measures to protect indigenous survival by adopting the Operational Manual Statement (OMS) 2.34 in 1982. In 1991, the bank took a step further with its Operational Directive 4.20 on indigenous peoples, based on ILO Convention 169 prescriptions. It acknowledged their special attachment to their lands and sought to ensure indigenous peoples participation in the benefits of the project and to avoid or mitigate negative impacts on them. Operative policy 4.10 is currently being followed and states that the "Bank provides project financing only where free, prior, and informed consultation results in broad community support to the project by the affected Indigenous Peoples," and that "Bank-financed projects are also designed to ensure that the Indigenous Peoples receive social and economic benefits that are culturally appropriate and gender and intergenerationally inclusive" (parr. 1) (OPCS, 2011). It is worth noting that, regarding lands, the directives encourage "legal recognition of the customary or traditional land tenure systems of iIndigenous Peoples," but do not recognize any right to restitution. As Davis (2012) notes, privatization has removed from the public sector the more conventional World-Bank-financed projects (transport, energy, mining), making these standards less relevant for the protection of indigenous peoples.

23. Through the commoditization of culture, neoliberalism reduces multiculturalism from *citizenization*: from recognizing the otherness as equal for negotiating and reaching consent, to giving the individual access to the market, which is the definition of modern Chilean citizenship. For more on access to the market defining Chilean citizenship, see the seminal work of Tomás Moulian (1997), and the more recent works of Mayol (2012) and Ruiz Encina (2015).

24. ILO Convention 169 was only ratified in 2008. The Indigenous Peoples' Councils, proposed by the CVHNT, were still being discussed in Congress in 2017. Constitutional recognition is part of the broader constituent process fostered by President Bachelet. Recently, The United Nations agreed to accompany the process of indigenous participation (La Tercera, 2017). No initiative regarding land claims has been taken, except from transferring the administration of the FTAI from CONADI's Council, moving it from an organization with indigenous participation, to a new agency without indigenous participation (Burgos, et al. 2016)

25. At the end of the dictatorship, the leader of the opposition and presidential candidate Patricio Aylwin met with the main indigenous organizations of the country and reached an agreement known as the "New Imperial Agreement" ("Acuerdo de Nueva Imperial"). In the meeting the candidate pledged to push for constitutional reform and to create a new institutional framework in which indigenous peoples were represented. CONADI would become the core of the new institutional framework. In exchange, the indigenous movement committed to support the candidate and to go through institutions to reach their goals (Bengoa, 2011; Vergara, Foerster & Gundermann, 2004). It is worth to noting that Huilcaman's AWNg did not sign the agreement and denounced it as a new strategy to contain Mapuche's claims. His organization began to occupy claimed land as soon as 1991 (Pairican, 2014).

26. As I explained elsewhere, ILO Convention 169 is multicultural, since it recognizes and values cultural diversity, and is liberal, since its aim is to protect cultural diversity as a way to guarantee individual agency. The latter appears clearly in the Inter-American jurisprudence, where indigenous collective property is protected as a way to protect the individual property rights of indigenous people (Meza-Lopehandía, 2016).

27. The paradoxical stance of Bachelet's office about ILO Convention is exemplified by the tangles of its ratification. The government tried to limit the reach of the instrument by limiting the scope of article 35, which states that the application of the convention should not adversely affect rights and benefits of the peoples concerned pursuant to other international instruments, awards, custom or agreements, among other legal sources. This could give more force to United Nations Declaration on the rights of Indigenous Peoples, regarded until then, as soft law. It did so by adding an interpretative letter to the instrument of ratification. The ILO Secretariat demanded a new deposit without any addenda. More details in Silva (2009).

28. In 2013, the Constitutional Court clarified its position, affirming that ILO Conventions' prior consultation was different from IDA's opinion's gathering, that it did not imply exercis-

ing sovereign powers and that it was compatible with democratic participation (Fuenzalida, 2015; Meza-Lopehandía, 2016).

29. Oddly, the Supreme Court has adopted ILO Convention's concept of indigenous habitat in cases regarding water rights and freedom of worship of the indigenous communities of the desertic north of the country (Meza-Lopehandía, 2016).

30. The newly created Environmental Courts have ratified the requirement of impact magnitude. Regarding the certainty of the impact, opposing decisions can be found (Guerra, in press).

31. A critical analysis of these regulations can be found in Meza-Lopehandía, Yáñez & Silva (2014).

32. The Colombian Constitutional Court has elaborated on this matter. See Decision T-903/09. Available at http://www.corteconstitucional.gov.co/RELATORIA/2009/T-903–09.htm

REFERENCES

Aylwin, José. 2007. "La Política del 'Nuevo Trato': antecedentes, alcances y limitaciones." In El Gobierno de Lagos, los pueblos indígenas y el "nuevo trato." Las paradojas de la democracia chilena, edited by Nancy Yáñez and José Aylwin, 29–58. Santiago: Lom editores.

Aylwin, José., Matías Meza-Lopehandía, and Nancy Yáñez. 2013. Los pueblos indígenas y el derecho. Santiago: Lom ediciones.

BCN. 1993. Historia de la Ley No. 19.253. Establece normas sobre protección fomento y desarrollo de los indígenas y crea la Corporación Nacional de Desarrollo Indígena. [pdf]. http://bcn.cl/1znek.

Bello, Álvaro. 2007. "El Programa Orígenes y la política pública del gobierno de Lagos hacia los pueblos indígenas." In El Gobierno de Lagos, los pueblos indígenas y el "nuevo trato." Las paradojas de la democracia chilena, edited by Nancy Yáñez and José Aylwin, 193–220. Santiago: Lom editores,.

Bengoa, José. 2000. Historia del pueblo mapuche. Siglo XIX y XX. 6th edition. Santiago: Lom ediciones.

———. 2007. La emergencia indígena en América Latina. 2nd edition, Santiago: Fondo de Cultura Económica.

———. 2011. "Los Mapuches: historia, cultura y conflicto." Cahiers des Amériques latines (68), 89–107.

Boccara, Guillaume and Ingrid Seguel-Boccara. 1999. "Políticas indígenas en Chile (Silgos XIX y XX) de la asimilación al pluralismo (el caso Mapuche)." Revista de Indias 59 (217), 741–774.

Burgos, Jorge, Alejandro Micco, Nicolás Eyzaguirre, and Marcos Barraza. 2016. Mensaje de S. E. la Presidenta de la República con el que inicia un proyecto de ley que crea el Ministerio de Pueblos Indígenas. [doc]. http://www.senado.cl/appsenado/index.php?mo=tramitacion&ac=getDocto&iddocto=11108&tipodoc=mensaje_mocion

Carvajal, Víctor 2015. "Colusión del papel liquida subsidio que benefició por décadas al Grupo Matte." *CIPER*, November 10, 2015. https://ciperchile.cl/2015/11/10/colusion-del-papel-liquida-subsidio-que-beneficio-por-decadas-al-grupo-matte/

Catalán, Rodrigo. 2007. "Políticas forestales y derechos indígenas en Chile." In El Gobierno de Lagos, los pueblos indígenas y el "nuevo trato." Las paradojas de la democracia chilena, edited by Nancy Yáñez and José Aylwin, 285–301. Santiago: Lom editores.

CEARC. 2010. Indigenous and tribal peoples. Observation 2010/81. [pdf]. http://www.ilo.org/wcmsp5/groups/public/---ed_norm/---normes/documents/meetingdocument/wcms_305958.pdf

CORMA. n.d.a. "Exportaciones." Accessed October 25, 2017. http://www.corma.cl/perfil-del-sector/aportes-a-la-economia

———. n.d.b. "Aporte al PIB." Accessed October 25,2017. http://www.corma.cl/perfil-del-sector/aportes-a-la-economia/aporte-al-pib

———. n.d.c. "Chile en el mercado mundial." Accessed October 25, 2017. http://www.corma.cl/perfil-del-sector/aportes-a-la-economia/chile-en-el-mercado-mundial

Correa, Martín, Raúl Molina, and Nancy Yáñez, N. 2005. La reforma agraria y las tierras mapuches: Chile 1962–1975. Santiago: Lom ediciones.

Correa, Martín, and Eduardo Mella. 2010. Las razones del illkun/enojo. Memoria, despojo y criminalización en el territorio Mapuche de Malleco. Santiago: Lom ediciones.

CVHNT. 2008. Informe de la Comisión de Verdad Histórica y Nuevo Trato con los Pueblos Indígenas. [pdf] http://bibliotecadigital.indh.cl/bitstream/handle/123456789/268/nuevo-trato-indigena.pdf?sequence=1

Dávalos, Pablo. 2002. "Movimiento indígena ecuatoriano: construcción política y epistémica." In Estudios y otras prácticas latinoamericanas en cultura y poder, edited by Daniel Mato, 89–97. Caracas: Clacso.

Davis, Shelton H. 2002. "Indigenous peoples, poverty and participatory development: The experience of the World Bank in Latin America." In Multiculturalism in Latin America, edited by R. Sieder, 227–251. London: Palgrave Macmillan.

Escárzaga, Fabiola. 2012. "El Ejército Guerrillero Tupak Katari (EGTK), la insurgencia aymara en Bolivia." Pacarina del Sur, 11(3). http://pacarinadelsur.com/home/oleajes/441-el-ejercito-guerrillero-tupak-katari-egtk-la-insurgencia-aymara-en-bolivia

Fuenzalida, Sergio. 2015. "Desarrollo de la jurisprudencia en Chile sobre la consulta indígena: los casos del Tribunal Cconstitucional y la Corte Suprema." Rev. Quebecoise de Droit Int'l (Special Edition), 149–177.

Gobierno de Chile. 2004. Política de Nuevo Trato con los Pueblos Indígenas. Derechos Indígenas, Desarrollo con Identidad y Diversidad Cultural. [pdf]. http://www.mapuche.info/mapuint/newtreat040400.pdf

———. 2008. Re-Conocer Pacto Social por la Multiculturalidad. [pdf] http://www.intendencialaaraucania.gov.cl/filesapp/Pacto%20social.pdf

González, Francisco. 2013. "DL 701: En 40 años 70% de aportes fueron a grandes forestales." La Tercera, July 18, 2013. http://www2.latercera.com/noticia/dl-701-en-40-anos-70-de-aportes-fueron-a-grandes-forestales/

González, Karinna, Matías Meza-Lopehandía, and Rubén Sánchez. 2007. Política de tierras y derechos territoriales de los pueblos indígenas en Chile: el caso de las comunidades "Carimán Sánchez y Gonzalo Marín" y "Comunidad Manuel Contreras." Paradigmas de la negación estatal de la territorialidad Mapuche. Documento de Trabajo 6. Temuco: Observatorio de Derechos de los Pueblos Indígenas.

Guerra, Felipe. (in press). "Los Tribunales Ambientales en la implementación de los derechos indígenas durante la evaluación ambiental de proyectos de inversión en Chile." *Revista Justicia Ambiental.*

Gundermann, Hans, Jorge I. Vergara del S., and Rolf Foerster G. 2005. "Contar a los indígenas en Chile: Autoadscripción étnica en la experiencia censal de 1992 y 2002." Estudios atacameños (30), 91–113. https://scielo.conicyt.cl/scielo.php?script=sci_arttext&pid=S0718-10432005000200006

Hale, Charles. 2002. Does multiculturalism menace? Governance, cultural rights and the politics of identity in Guatemala. Journal of Latin American Studies, 34(3), 485–524.

Hale, Charles, and Rosamel Millaman. 2005. "Cultural Agency and Political Struggle in the Era of Indio Permitido." In Cultural Agency in the Americas, edited by Doris Sommer, 281–314. Durham and London: Duke University Press.

ICtHR. 2014. Case of Norín Catrimán et al. (leaders, members and activist of the Mapuche Indigenous People v. Chile. Judgement of May 29, 2014 (merits, reparations and costs): http://www.corteidh.or.cr/docs/casos/articulos/seriec_279_ing.pdf

ILO. 2009. Indigenous & Tribal Peoples' rights in practice. A guide to ILO Convention No. 169. [pdf] http://www.ilo.org/wcmsp5/groups/public/@ed_norm/@normes/documents/publication/wcms_106474.pdf(accessed 19/10/2017)

INDH. (2014). Situación de los Derechos Humanos en Chile. Informe annual 2014. [pdf] http://bibliotecadigital.indh.cl/handle/123456789/740

Jara, Álvaro. 1956. Legislacion Indigenista de Chile. México: Instituto Indigenista Interamericano.

Kymlicka, Will. 2010. "The rise and fall of multiculturalism? New debates on inclusion and accommodation in diverse societies." International social science journal, 61(199), 97–112.

———. 2012. "Neoliberal Multiculturalism?" In Social Resilience in the Neoliberal Era, edited by Peter A. Hall and Michèle Lamont, 99–126. Cambridge: Cambridge University Press.

Letelier, Eduardo. 2007. "Los derecho económicos, sociales y culturales de los pueblos originarios de Chile en el gobierno de Lagos: un enfoque de gestión pública." In El Gobierno de Lagos, los pueblos indígenas y el "nuevo trato." Las paradojas de la democracia chilena, edited by José Aylwin and Nancy Yáñez, 221–239. Santiago: Lom editores.

Lillo, Rodrigo. 1999. "La legislación como aspecto de la relación intercultural." Cultura-Hombre-Sociedad CUHSO (1), 40–48.

Matena, K. 2010. *Alibis of empire: Henry Maine and the ends of liberal imperialism*. Princeton: Princeton Universtiy Press.

Mayol, Alberto. 2012. *El derrumbe del modelo: la crisis de la economía de mercado en el Chile contemporáneo*. Santiago: LOM Ediciones.

Meza-Lopehandía, Matías. 2016. "La jurisprudencia del multiculturalismo en Chile: la consulta previa indígena ante tribunales." Revista de Ciencias Sociales (Valparaíso). 69, 13–5.

Meza-Lopehandía, M., Nancy Yáñez, and Hernando Silva. 2014. "El derecho a la consulta y su incorporación al sistema jurídico chileno." In El derecho a la consulta de los pueblos indígenas. Análisis del derecho nacional, internacional y comparado. Santiago: Embajada de Noruega/Observatorio Ciudadano/IWGIA.

Moulian, Tomás. 1997. Chile actual: anatomía de un mito. Santiago: Lom ediciones/Universidad Arcis.

Namuncura, Domingo. 1999. Ralco. ¿Represa o pobreza? Santiago: Lom Ediciones.

OIT. 2013. El trabajo decente en la industria forestal en Chile. [pdf]. http://www.ilo.org/wcmsp5/groups/public/---americas/---ro-lima/---sro-santiago/documents/publication/wcms_206093.pdf

OPCS. 2011. Implementation of the World Bank's Indigenous Peoples Policy A Learning Review (FY 2006–2008). OPCS Working Paper. [pdf] http://siteresources.worldbank.org/INTSAFEPOL/Resources/Indigenous_peoples_review_august_2011.pdf

Pairican, Fernando. 2014. Malon: la rebelión del movimiento mapuche, 1990–2013. Santiago: Pehuén editores.

Pairicán, Fernando, and Rolando Álvarez. 2011. "La Nueva Guerra de Arauco: la Coordinadora Arauco-Malleco y los nuevos movimientos de resistencia mapuche en el Chile de la Concertación (1997–2009)." Revista Izquierdas, (10), 66–84. http://www.izquierdas.cl/images/pdf/2011/09/izquierdas-10–4.pdf

Piñeiro, Diego. 2004. La acción colectiva en los conflictos agrarios de América Latina. Buenos Aires: CLACSO.

Queupuán, Prosperina, and Verónica Guerrero. 2004. "Sucesos Violentos por Reivindicaciones Territoriales en Comunidades Mapuche de San Juan de la Costa: El Caso Rukamañío." In V Congreso Chileno de Antropología. Colegio de Antropólogos de Chile A. G, San Felipe, Chile.

Richards, Patricia. 2010. "Of Indians and terrorists: how the state and local elites construct the Mapuche in neoliberal multicultural Chile." Journal of Latin American Studies, 42(01), 59–90.

Ruiz Encina, Carlos. 2015. De nuevo la sociedad. Santiago: LOM-Fundación Nodo XXI.

Silva, Hernando. 2009. "El Largo proceso de tramitación para la aprobación del Convenio No. 169 de la OIT." In Las Implicancias de la Ratificación del Convenio 169 de la OIT en Chile, edited by Matías Meza-Lopehandía. Santiago: Obsevatorio Ciudadano.

La Tercera. 2017. "Proceso Constituyente: Naciones Unidas será garante de Consulta Previa Indígena." La Tercera. September 8, 2017. http://www.latercera.com/noticia/proceso-constituyente-naciones-unidas-sera-garante-consulta-previa-indigena/

UN. 2009. Report of the Special Rapporteur on the situation of human rights and fundamental freedoms of indigenous people, James Anaya. A/HRC/12/34. July 15, 2009. [pdf] http://unsr.jamesanaya.org/docs/annual/2009_hrc_annual_report_en.pdf

Vergara, Jorge. I., Rolf Foerster, and Hans Gundermann. 2004. "Más acá de la legalidad. La CONADI, la ley indígena y el pueblo mapuche (1989–2004)." Polis. Revista Latinoamericana, (8), 1–19. http://repositorio.uchile.cl/bitstream/handle/2250/122040/Foerster_RN_040_2004.pdf?sequence=1

World Bank. 1991. The World Bank Operational Manual. Operational Directive Indigenous Peoples. OD 4.20. [pdf] http://www.ifc.org/wps/wcm/connect/835cc50048855270ab94fb6a6515bb18/OD420_IndigenousPeoples.pdf?MOD=AJPERES

Yrigoyen, Raquel. 2011. "El horizonte del constitucionalismo pluralista: del multiculturalismo a la descolonización." In El derecho en América Latina: un mapa para el pensamiento jurídico del siglo XXI, edited by Cesar R. Garavito, 139–160. Buenos Aires: Siglo Veintiuno Editores.

Zaror, Yasmin, and Juan P. Lepín. 2016. La Política de Entrega de Tierras: Análisis y Desafíos de cara a un nuevo Paradigma de la Política Indígena. Serie informe sociedad y política - Libertad y Desarrollo, 152, 1–23. http://lyd.org/wp-content/uploads/2016/05/SIP-152-La-Politica-de-Entrega-de-Tierras-Analisis-y-Desafios-de-cara-a-un-nuevo-paradigma-de-la-Politica-Indigena-Abril2016.pdf.

Chapter Eight

Immigrants

Legal Configuration of a Disadvantaged Group

Jaime Bassa and Fernanda Torres

Legislation regarding immigration purports to be based on the Universal Declaration of Human Rights, which claims: "All human beings are born free and equal in dignity and rights." This guarantee lacks a key element, however; namely, the material context that conditions the people as rights holders. That claim of universality tries to erase the structural differences that exist among the various categories of immigrants, since factors such as country of origin, socio-economic status and native language define different groups of immigrants. These circumstances make it necessary to understand migration through the concept of vulnerable groups.

The vulnerability of immigrants begins with the political, legal and social concept of an outsider, which distinguishes them from a national citizen. This otherness criteria establishes a divide between "inside" and "outside," with the outside position being disadvantaged (Mezzadra 2009, 97). The denial of citizenship allows for legal restrictions and exclusions which cannot be overcome without first denying the validity of this distinction. This suggests that membership in a political community, a basis for the juridical regulation of the immigrant's rights, cannot be determined by nationality in the current stage of globalization (Balibar 2013), characterized by a high level of migratory flows. This socio-cultural context demands that we reconsider the very notion of citizenship, given the plurality and complexity of contemporary communities. The tension between the state and the human rights of the immigrants manifested in international regulation should be decided in favor of the people. If we are serious about the equality of people as holders of rights, it is not acceptable to have a hierarchy in the exercise of those rights that creates a second-class citizenship, where the exercise of political, social and labor rights depends on the administrative status of each immigrant.

Overcoming this aporia requires being conscious about two elements that seem to be contradictory. The first is that the migrant groups do not correspond to a homogeneous category, but they differ among themselves since different significant criteria are combined. Therefore, the rights of immigrants cannot be regulated in the abstract. The second factor is that the statute of rights cannot depend on the administrative status of each immigrant. Criteria must be present that consider how the material living conditions determine the exercise of rights, and that assume the immigrant to be a person with rights, not an object of legal regulation.

In order to unveil the implications of migration laws and regulations in terms of the rights of migrants as a vulnerable group, this work will provide an empirical and normative analysis of the matter at stake. After reviewing the recent transformation of immigration in Chile from a quantitative perspective, we will analyze the legislative design of the current immigration control institutions, moving then to expose the configuration of the legal statute of immigrant in Chile, from some of its more complex categories; and finally reviewing the main characteristics of the reform proposal on migration law recently presented for a legislative discussion at the National Congress.

A NEW CONFIGURATION OF MIGRATORY FLOWS TOWARDS CHILE

Chile has been recognized as a destination for immigrants, shown by a gradual increase in immigration to the country, which has made it one of the most common destinations in Latin America. Consequently, Chile has refuted the belief that immigration pressure affects exclusively the developed world. The Migration and Remittances Report from the World Bank shows that the immigration volume among developed countries is higher than the verified volume among the OECD countries (Rathla et al 2011). Chile is part of this specific South-South type of migratory flow, a factor which could contribute to our economic and social development (Rodriguez and Busso 2009).

There has been a long-term, sustainable growth in the immigrant population. The temporary residence permits and permanent residence permits granted in Chile each increased twentyfold between 2005 and 2014, going from 41,985 temporary and 11,907 permanent residence permits granted in 2005, to 838,573 temporary and 222,475 permanent residence permits granted in 2014 (DEM 2015). With respect to the short term migrant population, there was a significant increase in visas granted between 2010 and 2016: 68,537 and 174,969 respectively (DEM 2017).

This evidence shows that net positive immigration is a growing social reality in Chile, where official figures predict a continuation of the migratory flows and, as a result, a reconfiguration of the country's social structure. The unknown number of illegal immigrants could distort the quantitative analyses, but its consideration reinforces the need to quantitatively analyze a legal system affecting hundreds of thousands of people, and the emergence of a phenomenon outside of that system (Pérez 2012). Some communities have already changed as a result of the increase in immigration. The best example is the city of Antofagasta, whose immigrant population was 6.9% in 2014 (DEM 2015). Preliminary information from 2017 census data shows that there are about 600,000 immigrants in Chile. This figure does not reflect reality, however, due to the number of people residing illegally or with temporary residence permits.

This increase in immigration shows the country to be in a stage of transition in migratory networks where the social and labor stability of the first resident immigrants motivates future immigrants (Aja 2012). The expectation of being welcomed by a familiar community facilitates labor and social integration, gradually increasing the migratory flows (Micolta 2015). This stage is followed by the phenomenon of "cumulative causation," where the root causes of immigration become diluted and give way to a culture of permanent migration (Heer 2002. Massey et al 2008).

In light of the possible transformation of social structures as a result of the consolidation of migrant networks, it is necessary to note that the Peruvian community in Santiago already has an established migratory network (Herrera 2014. Luque 2007). The expansion of these networks to other communities places Chile on the verge of a United Nations estimated average immigrant population of 3.1%. Currently, communities of Latin American immigrants are categorized by "Action Migrant Movement" group (www.mamchile.cl), which has become more important recently, making evident the need for new immigration regulation and amnesty to formalize immigrants with temporary or illegal status.

INSTITUTIONAL DESIGN

Current Immigration Law and Policy

The legislation regulating the rights of immigrants in Chile and the admission and deportation procedures comes from Decree Law (DL) 1,094, enacted in 1975 during the military dictatorship of Augusto Pinochet. Comprising most of the regulation on immigration enacted between 1973 and 1990, this law has been partially reviewed and amended since the return to democracy, but has had no significant changes. This regulation is based in theory that is inconsistent with human rights. Given the validity of the national security doctrine (Perez 2012, 23–24), immigrants are perceived as a potential threat to the internal security of the state. The dictatorship sought to control the flow of people across borders, both citizens leaving the country, whether voluntarily or not, and foreigners who entered the country. That explains the power of the administrative authority, extended by the Supreme Decree (SD) 597 of 1984, to authorize or refuse entry to foreigners, as well as to deport them even if they have committed no crimes. Both regulations remain in effect today.

There rules do not specify how the legal system guarantees immigrant rights, nor does it refer to rights linked to their material living conditions such as housing, health, education and labor, or the condition of vulnerable groups such as families, children, adolescents, and vulnerable nationalities, their integration and their cultural rights. This confirms that current legislation is still focused on national security, not human rights.

Against this backdrop, recent governments have proposed the modernization of this law through revising the country's immigration law and policy.

In 2008, the Presidential Instructions on Migratory Policy was issued. Government agencies were instructed to include international standards concerning immigrants and refugees in their programs, and to promote measures to protect their basic rights. Additionally, the Council on Migration Policy was created as an advisory body for authorities and as a link to civil society. However, these reforms did not have a significant impact. This was due to the fact that this council was only established in 2014 and has met only once to date, and that the national immigration policy did not change substantially, leaving much to the discretion of the administrative authority.

In 2013, the government presented a bill to replace DL 1,094, driven by the need to reformulate the legislation governing immigration, which is a highly dynamic and sensitive area with an effect on economic growth. In a globalized society, the economic status of Chile and other countries is a key factor in developing the conditions favorable to immigration (Sutcliffe 1998). In the opinion of the administration, the process of opening trade "has not been accompanied by the modernization of human mobility control in the context of a global market. As far as that is concerned, we still keep the protectionist and fearful gaze of the 1970s" (Legislative Bill 8,970–06).

Although the project recognized that the current legislation was developed for national security, it does not rectify certain significant failures, such as the absence of a protection for rights. In fact, the institution responsible for controlling immigration remained the Ministry of the Interior and Public Security, without even addressing the challenge of integration or discussing the possibility and further problems of transferring migratory affairs to ministries such as Foreign Affairs, Social Development or Labor. There is a lack of theoretical tools which permit addressing immigration from the point of view of integration, not only as a matter of homeland security.

Conversely, in 2015, a new Presidential Instruction was issued, establishing a new National Immigration Policy with fifteen goals. Unlike previous policies, this one assumed that emigration was a human right; a significant improvement. Unlike the document from 2008, instructions were given to the various government offices in order to create an integrated and institutionalized National Migratory Policy. Even so, that document makes a clear distinction between the legislation and the new international regulations on this matter, prompting the Human Rights Committee of United Nations to explicitly suggest that the Chilean state should "accelerate the approval of the immigration bill that guarantees in full the rights protected by the covenant" (UN 2014). Finally, the Bachelet administration (2014–2018) has submitted a bill with the aim of replacing DL 1,094 entirely, which is currently in the initial legislative stage in the national congress (Legislative Bill 11,395–06). The final section of this work will analyze the most important elements of this project.

RECENT INNOVATIONS

Due to the failure of the law to address these issues, vulnerable groups of immigrants have been facing increasingly uncertain conditions on their path into the country. Once they enter, the legal status of immigrants should reflect the policies of the country receiving them, and should guarantee their basic rights. A new social, economic and cultural reality, a result of the increase in immigration to the country, is a clear challenge to the institutions governing immigration in Chile.

The tension between the current legal system and the reality of migratory flows were discussed in the Constitutional Court. The Court stated that the DL 1,094 is a pre-constitutional and pre-conventional norm, whose regulatory scheme "admits massive violations of rights." (2273–12-INA, 2013, C.7). Also, the court concluded that, it "was issued in a period when the theory of the entry and exit rights of people were hegemonic, in the light of national security, must be compared with the constitutional text" (2273–12-INA, 2013, C.25). The Court confirmed the need to review the current legal design, which was typical of a national security paradigm in its distrust of foreigners. The sentence explicitly notes that the starting point of any analysis should be the right to emigrate from the country of origin, although it is possible for the domestic law of each state to regulate the way the immigrants are received, subject to the international standards.

In light of the tensions generated by the continued use of an outdated regulatory framework in a different social reality, some public services and regional governments have promoted actions aiming to integrate immigrants and to satisfy their basic health, education and housing needs. Measures include things such as the special action of protection of motherhood and childhood, and resolutions that facilitate access to daycare and education, as well as the public health system for children and adolescents without permanent residence permits. Other measures establish legal pathways to residency, access to the child protection network or help with issues of domestic violence. Mechanisms have been established via administrative channels that facilitate visa applications for victims of human trafficking, partners in civil unions abroad, as well as for labor effects and to guarantee access to health care. This shows how the absence of a proper legislation institutionalizing the deployment of regulatory power has left a wide space to be filled by different agencies as they see fit.[1]

Despite the fact of the outdated legislation on immigration, modifications have been introduced to meet international standards concerning asylum seekers, victims of human trafficking and the smuggling of immigrants. To this end, new laws have been enacted after the United Nations made its observations. Although they respond to different foundations and objectives, the application of these rules must be coupled to the previous regulation without institutional harmonization.

This new regulation stood on a foundation different from those of 1975, suggesting the need for a rigorous and systematic review. Based on the international standards of the 1951 Convention Relating to the Status of Refugees, Chile enacted Law 20,430 in 2010 in compliance with international commitment. This law established, in accordance with international protocols, the right to access a standardized admission process for those seeking asylum. Even though this did not recognize all applicants as refugees, it guaranteed due process when entering the country.

A specific protocol was outlined regarding human trafficking and smuggling of immigrants. Chile subscribed the United Nations Convention against Transnational Organized Crime and its Optional Protocols, to prevent, suppress and punish human trafficking, especially of women and children. Law 20,507 came into effect in 2011, defining the crime of smuggling immigrants and human trafficking and establishing rules for the prevention and more effective criminal prosecution. This legislation amends the Chilean Penal Code, creating definitions of criminality and illicit association for human trafficking and trafficking for sexual exploitation.

The Constitutional System of the Distribution of Regulatory Competences

The legal regulation of basic rights is an institutional guarantee because its regulation or restriction is verified by a public and democratic discussion in parliament (Waldron, 1999). In other words, the democratic discussion creates law; it is not merely an application of the Constitution (Zagrebelsky,

2003). The legislature alone has the competence to regulate conditions for rights to be exercised, developing the principles contained in the Constitution. This constitutional system also delimits both the Legislature's own area of competence and the other branches of the government, especially the executive branch.

Although the standard in the comparative immigrant law that is an issue reserved to primary legislation, the Chilean model departs from that standard. DL 1,094 granted ample discretionary power to the government, making them decisive in the configuration of immigrant legal status. It even granted a wide margin of discretion in important matters such as distributing or withholding visas and permanent residency permits without legal reason.

Chilean immigration law considers the discretion of the government to have two dimensions. Firstly, it delivers a wide competence to the government, allowing it to regulate immigrant rights, even crossing the limits that the legislature has provided. Secondly, it provides room for the discretion of the state official who is the direct link between the immigrant and the government whether they be border patrol, customs service or some of the national police forces. In this administrative discretion, a sort of discrimination and even institutional racism could be developed, given the practices that the system has consistently allowed. The problem is not the discretion itself, but the racist and xenophobic practices of the migration authorities that that discretion may cover.

This relationship between law and administrative regulations is contentious in Chilean immigration law when configuring the grounds for disqualifying the entry of foreigners into the country. Article 28 of SD No. 597 of 1984 exceeds the legal configuration of Articles 15 and 16 of DL 1,094, noting that "by Supreme Decree the entry of certain foreigners may be prohibited on the grounds of public interest or national security." This enabling of powers decree-to-decree infringes the constitutional principle of reserved to law as a guarantee of basic rights (Art. 19 No. 26) and exceeds the constitutional framework of the regulatory power.

There is evidently a need to establish standardized criteria for immigrant legal status. The application of legal grounds for deportation or abandonment must be compatible with protection of basic rights, in accordance with what the jurisprudence of the Inter-American Court of Human Rights (IACHR) has established (Burbano and Yves 2011). The objective is to decrease the level of discretion in the administrative decision, categorizing conducts that are punishable and identifying rights before which this regulation should concede.

TOWARDS A RECONFIGURATION OF THE LEGAL STATUS OF IMMIGRANTS

The institution of Chilean immigration law has a number of difficulties which result in lower standards of protection for immigrant rights. Among them, the following issues linked with the guarantee of equality before the law which will be explored in this section: the exercise of rights, their relation with the administrative discretion, and the deficiencies in terms of administrative procedure.

Equality in the Exercise of Basic Rights

The Chilean Constitution does not explicitly refer to immigration; however, it is possible to infer a generic guarantee of equality in the exercise of rights. Article 19 recognizes rights for all the people without distinction. There may be good justifications for legal distinctions between nationals and foreigners, for matters such as entry into the country, but the Constitution removes that possibility and protects the immigrant's rights once their stay or residence is legally authorized. In the pre-authorization limbo, a number of categories with potential for arbitrary discrimination such as race, ethnicity, language and of course citizenship converge, so any restriction in the exercise of rights must have a legal basis consistent with the constitution or with a prior constitutional authorization.

The constitutional right to equality before the law (Art. 19 No. 2) proscribes the differentiated treatment based on personal characteristics. It does not imply identical treatment between rights holders, but that the reasons given for differentiating must be compatible with the constitutional standard of the protection of basic rights. Accordingly, every regulation differentiation is not banned, but only those of an arbitrary nature.

The aphorism "to treat equals equally and treat unequals unequally," systematically used by Chilean courts, does not satisfy the standard of equality before the law. It legitimizes discriminatory treatment of groups such as immigrants. This kind of reasoning disregards the source of arbitrary discrimination: the reason behind the creation of categories of equal and different people. Nationals and immigrants can certainly be divided into different groups to the point of having different legal statutes, but it is important to evaluate whether the difference that comes from nationality justifies restricting rights.

The Constitutional Court stated that foreigners experience arbitrary discrimination and demanded that any legal differentiation should pursue constitutionally legitimate purposes (2273–12-INA, 2013, C.30). Any restriction of their basic rights should have an express constitutional authorization. At the same time, the creation of those restrictions is the responsibility of the legislature, where the requirement of equality before the law limits the government's regulatory powers. This is part of the international standard of the protection of immigrant rights, guaranteeing that all foreigners who have entered the country legally will be treated the same as nationals. "The nature and intensity of their basic rights is affected, especially if they are immigrants" required to show pretense of permanence (2273–12-INA, 2013, C.30), a requirement that affects the material conditions necessary for the exercise of their basic rights. The legal status granted to immigrants does not include basic protections to the exercise of their rights, although no significant distinction between nationals and foreigners can be invoked in this respect. Therefore, any regulatory distinction should be interpreted restrictively. In fact, the Constitutional Court has stated that any regulation that restricts the exercise of basic rights in this area of law must be justified, even in the absence of prior constitutional authorization (2273–12-INA, 2013, C.33), as it includes groups at risk of arbitrary discrimination.

Administrative Discretion and Equality before the Law

The current normative regulation also threatens the right to equality before the law in the wide margin of discretion that DL 1,094 gives to the administrative authority. Vague legal concepts, such as "utility" or "convenience," whose evaluation depend on the official who applies them, are established as grounds for deportation. Between 2010 and 2013, 4,002 people were deported, (UDP 2014, 349) and in 2014, 2,935 deportation orders were issued for illegal entry into the country (UDP 2016, 223). The same vagueness applies to the legal grounds for prohibition of entry, meaning the use of vague categories such as national security, public order or public security leaves wide margins for administrative discretion. Beyond this "utilitarian" definition of immigrant, there is an absence of legal criteria that guides the implementation of restrictions, giving the decision up to administrative discretion. Although formally there is equality in being legal subject for nationals and immigrants, this equality can be infringed upon due to the extensive powers of authority to grant and extend visas, and to grant permanent residence permits (Art. 13 DL 1,094). The constitutionality of this article was highly questioned by the Constitutional Court in 2013, the result of which is explored below.

The SD 597 of 1984 reinforced the wide margin of discretion that the migratory authority had for distributing temporary or permanent residence permits, noting "these powers will be exercised, with discretion, with special emphasis on the convenience or utility that the granting of these permits provides to the country, and on the international reciprocity prior report, where applicable, of the Investigative Police of Chile (PDI)" (Art. 13 sub.2°). If the implementation of vague legal concepts depends only on administrative discretion, the guarantee of equality before the law is at the mercy of the criteria the government chooses to apply in each particular case. The problem is that nothing stops these administrations from discriminating against certain immigrant groups. In fact, "in many cases, the technical reports of the Investigative Police are the only basis which sustains the deportation orders" (UDP 2017, 224). It therefore seems necessary for the legislature to design firm rules and criteria that are consistent with the Chilean constitution and International Law. This will set specific criteria for the judicial control of administrative decisions and more effectively protect the rights of immigrants.

This unchecked discretion is manifested in the power of the consular offices to grant and reject residence visas. Reporting generic reasons such as convenience or utility that encompass a wide margin of discretion to grant or deny resident visas. This power belongs to the Ministry of Foreign Affairs, not to the Ministry of the Interior and Public Security, creating greater uncertainty about the applicable criteria. In 2014, the Supreme Court revoked the decision of the Court of Appeals of Santiago regarding the denial of entry to a Tunisian tourist, delimiting the discretion of the respective authority and presenting criteria to be considered in such situations. Additionally, it noted

> the powers of the state agencies are conferred by law according to the purpose or object of the public service in question. The legitimate exercise of these powers requires, besides the respect for individual rights, reason in the decision of the authority [. . .]. Likewise, it is impossible to neglect that on January 6th of 2014, an individual under protection married a Chilean woman, whose certificate is duly legalized in Chile." (SC 11,521–14, C.8–9)

Through this argument, the court has reaffirmed doubts concerning the dimension "utility" which must be considered when acting in this capacity since their objective is human development. It stated that

> the elements mentioned by the authority in denying the visa application, such as "does not speak Spanish," "does not have a known workplace" or "has left the country of origin only once," should be considered unfounded reasons, clearly arbitrary discrimination, and for this reason, they cannot be included within the convenience or utility standard that the rules of immigration record for the exercise of a discretionary power from the administrative authority." (SC 11,521–14, C.11)

The same is true of entry refusals made by the Investigative Police, which has exercised its discretion on the border in a way that the Supreme Court has considered arbitrary. For instance, Article 44 of DL 1,094 states that "every tourist must have the economic means to survive during his residence in Chile; this situation must be accredited when the police authority considers it necessary." In 2013, the Supreme Court revoked a sentence of the Court of Appeals of Santiago and accepted a habeas corpus petition which was presented by a Peruvian citizen whose access was denied at the international airport. Showing the risks of police discretion, the court said that

> while it is true that provisions cited by the police and migratory authority to order the return of the woman to her country of origin empower the police to demand that she proves to have the economic means to survive, such precepts don't consider the way in which this must be specified. It is therefore subjective and discretionary, and must be carefully analyzed in a restricted manner. The legal provision does not permit distinguishing the source of the money that the foreigner brings, so if it is a gift or a loan, the police official cannot redirect it to the single qualification the rule considers: sufficiency. (SC 3,563–13, C.2)

This is a sensitive matter given the risk of discretion becoming arbitrary, so it is necessary to build more realistic parameters.

Deficiencies in Terms of Administrative Due Process

One of the important elements guaranteeing immigrant rights is a standardized administrative procedure with supplementary rules allowing gaps left by the sectorial legislation to be filled without handing them over to administrative discretion. Because regulation of administrative procedures was not a political priority at that time in Chile, the DL 1,094 did not establish a procedure in accordance with the rules of due process. It does not regulate the right to be heard, the presentation of evidence, the right to defense, and the form of notifications and legal remedies. Although there is supplementary legislation (e.g., L 19.880), its implementation has left gaps affecting immigrant rights. The presumption of innocence itself is put into question, as the immigrant is notified of this process only with the expulsion, deterring the presentation of discharges or evidence in order to combat the administrative decision. This is the general state of affairs, despite some specific initiatives, such as the informal hearing called by the municipal government of Santiago prior to expulsion (UDP 2015, 233–35).

Access to justice is also reduced, especially in a deportation process. The order for deportation of an immigrant does not have any administrative body available to appeal to. There is only one judicial process in which a special appeal must be filed to the Supreme Court within 24 hours from the deportation notification (Art. 89 DL 1,094). It is an appeal solely to the Supreme Court that does not apply against deportation measures ordered by Santiago Regional Government, even if these constitute most immigrant deportation orders, or against deportations included in official resolutions. Furthermore, if the deportation order is suspended during the procedure and appeal decision, the immigrant can be deprived of liberty and placed in a detention center. This deprivation of liberty is not ordered by a court of justice, but by an administrative authority. Between 2010 and 2014, a total of 98 appeals were submitted, 22 of which were accepted, numbers which contrast with the 2,935 deportations ordered in 2014 (Salcedo 2015, 4). Many factors undermine the effectiveness of this appeal: the need for legal assistance, the impossibility of giving testimonial evidence, or the lack of complementary services such as translation (UDP 2015, 226).

Since the immigration authority does not have an established and objective administrative process, it does not consider factors such as family ties, criminal records, vulnerability or risk an immigrant faces if forced to return to their country of origin, all of which are fundamental elements at the time of applying an administrative sanction. As none of these criteria have been included in migratory law, the decision to grant a particular permission or apply a sanction is subject to the administrative authority's will, without complying with minimum standards of due process. In fact, the Supreme Court has explicitly disregarded the effect of family ties when considering the expulsion of a Dominican mother of two children born in Chile. Hearing her claim against a deportation measure, the Court conferred responsibility for the delay in the administrative processes onto the appellant herself, including the notification of deportation and the regularization of her migratory status. In the court's view, it "shows that the delay of notification derives from her own behavior, a fact that impedes accepting the change of her individual and family circumstances that occurred during the default and irregular period in her immigration situation, as a reason to invalidate the deportation order" (SC 9,492–16, C.5).

In spite of this, in other cases, the court has used the family element to reverse a deportation order. In one case, Peruvian parents of two children born in Chile were convicted of smuggling of immigrants. Suspending the deportation order, the Court stated that

> the analysis of this court does not invalidate in reviewing the observance of the legal formalities and the subsumption of the factual hypothesis on the normative assumption invoked, but transcends and compels the court to carry out a review of considerations with respect to the personal and procedural situation of the person affected and the effects that may cause, definitely, in their family with the implementation of the measure, on one side, and the national interests sheltered by the Foreigner Act, on the other one. (SC 38,337–16, C.6)

Thus, the court granted the request of the Peruvian couple, stating that

> the reasons given by the applicants, including the older son's need to finish the school year and the difficulties to move to another country with two young children, merit the granting of the time requested which will not hinder what

> the Ministry of Internal Affairs has decided, making use of its powers, and is consistent with respect for international standards for child protection. (38,337–16, C. 8)

Both sentences were passed in 2016. The disparity in the outcome and reasoning behind the decisions shows how the absence of legal criteria generates uncertainty for the immigrant and their family, failing to protect their rights.

In conclusion, it is possible to note the absence of a legal procedure that satisfies the constitutional guarantee of due process (Garcia y Contreras 2013). The comments made to Chile in the Universal Periodic Review takes note of the situation, saying

> there are no minimum guarantees of due process for immigrants and their families according to international standards, having in multiple the cases deprived the liberty of undocumented foreigners for an indefinite in time, without judicial control or translator in the trial, based on an administrative authority's orders and executed by the police, as well as collective expulsions, without considering family unity. (UN 2009)

In this case, the absence of regulation poses a threat to the protection of immigrant rights in Chile.

The Supreme Court has directly implemented the international human rights treaties, even going against domestic legislation. In this way, it has expanded the range of protection of the rights of immigrants, not only for the immigrants, but also for their families. In 2016 the court invoked two provisions of the Convention on the Rights of the Child to suspend the effects of an expulsion order. The first was Art. 22 which requires states to guarantee that children will be protected against all forms of discrimination or punishment as a consequence of the actions of their parents. The second was Art. 91 that prevents the separation of families (38,337–16, C.8).

MAIN ELEMENTS OF THE 2017 BILL OF LAW

Definitions and General Objectives

This bill, submitted by the government recognizes the mismatch between the Chilean migratory legislation and the objectives of the national policy. In the foundations of the legislation it is noted that "the current regulatory framework focuses on the convenience and utility of the foreigner for the country and the principles of sovereignty and national security, without considering the protection and safeguarding the rights of immigrants" (Legislative Bill 11,395–06). This shows the dichotomy between theoretical foundation of current legislation since the dictatorship and the need to protect the rights of immigrants. Art. 1° of the bill states that "the state of Chile appreciates the contribution of immigrants to the development of society, in every dimension." It is a declaration that seeks to leave behind the influence of national security and recognize the contribution of immigrants.

Among the elements of the current migratory legislation and that must be resolved, they highlight two that will be especially relevant for the legislative deliberation. The first is how rigidly immigration status will be tied to the exercise of rights in order to favor legal immigration. The second is the administrative procedure that protects the rights of immigrants and allows the effective action of authorities.

One of the main innovations of this bill is an express recognition of immigrant rights. It incorporates international standards of protection with special considerations for children, stateless people, human trafficking victims and trafficking of immigrants, and applicants for refugee and asylum. A more complex legal status of the immigrant is established, not only in the interests of the state, but also the rights of individual immigrants and those immigrating to join family or a larger immigrant community.

Art. 3° sets a framework for respect for immigrant rights and duties. Art. 2° reinforces the statist perspective of the bill, focusing on regulating immigration and ensuring the exercise of state sovereignty through the establishment of control measures and a migratory policy. However, the formal procedure for foreigners still depends on Ministry of Internal Affairs and Public Security as in DL 1,094, as a "direct and immediate collaborator of president of the republic in cases of foreigners and immigration" (Art. 130).

Rights and Duties

Despite this, it can be said that this bill represents advancement in the recognition of the rights of immigrants. Unlike DL 1,094, the bill outlines a series of general principles which give content to the rules of the new statute and specify a series of rights directly related to immigration. Meanwhile, Art. 4° recognizes "the equal dignity of every human being by promoting, respecting and guaranteeing the rights and freedoms enshrined in the Constitution." The state must promote the inclusion of immigrants and respect their cultural identity (Art. 5°). Furthermore, it assigns certain duties to the state, in particular the promotion of safe (Art. 8°) and regular (Art. 7°) immigration without the criminalization of irregular immigrants (Art. 9°).

The specific rights are divided into those related to immigration status and those enshrined in the Constitution. The first category includes the freedom to enter, remain and leave the country (Art. 12) and right to family reunification (Art. 18). The second category includes equality before the law and non-discrimination (Art. 11), the right to health services (Art. 13), the right to education (Art. 14), the right to social security (Art. 15), labor rights

(Art. 16) and the right to due process (Art.17). It also writes into law what is at the discretion of administrative agencies and supreme decrees, especially concerning benefits and forms of access for the foreign population in the country.

Part of recognizing the right to equality before the law consists of establishing a punitive procedure that complies with the standards of the constitutional due process. The implementation of regulation surrounding entry and exit conditions, as well as the grounds for deportation depends on that procedure. Title VII allows challenging any administrative decision at two levels: administrative and judicial. It appeals any decision of immigration or other administrative authority to an alternative administrative agency (Art. 118) and a hierarchical appeal (Art. 19), according to Law No. 18,880 of the administrative procedure. It also allows challenging deportation by an alternate administrative agency (Art. 120), with potential for review by a hierarchical appeal (Art. 121).

It is considered a jurisdictional complaint against the deportation that is complementary to the administrative complaints. Unlike the special complaint of the current norm, the appeal is filed before the respective Court of Appeals, not the Supreme Court, within five days of notification of the measure, as opposed to 24 hours.

Entry, Exit, and Immigration Categories

The bill proposes modifications to the current legal system, but does not suggest changes to the understanding of the migratory phenomenon or the criteria for regulating the entry of immigrants into the country. Therefore, the grounds for prohibition set forth in Art. 32 are not significantly different from the current Art. 15 DL 1,094, except for Art. 15 No. 1. Consistent with the context of a military dictatorship and the validity of the doctrine of national security, this legislation prohibited the entry of political activists who could be considered a threat for social stability or state security. The bill ends without that concept, although it increases the list of crimes which impedes the entry into the country. It considers a liability exemption for children affected by these prohibitions, who "may not be subjects of migratory sanction" (Arts. 36, 69 and 100).

On the topic of immigrant categories, the great novelty of the bill is the possibility of granting temporary residence permits on humanitarian grounds for those "who must remain in the country for justified reasons which make it impossible or risky to return to their country of origin, for danger to their life, freedom, security or physical integrity" (Art. 41). This benefit also extends to the victims of the crime of human trafficking (Art. 42). It is an improvement over current norms because it makes a tangible commitment to the rights of immigrants, particularly those in vulnerable situations.

On the other hand, the agencies responsible for immigration control maintain a wide margin of discretion. This is demonstrated in the evaluation and implementation of grounds for rejection and revocation of residence permits depends on how the authority interprets the individual situations of immigrant (Art. 67 and on). The margin of discretion is too wide. Art. 70 considers three alternatives for the refusal of permit: to order the departure from the country, to grant another migratory permit or to prohibit entry. The bill does not consider parameters for the exercise of this power, creating an opportunity for discrimination and infringing the rights of the immigrant.

General Evaluation

This bill—which is just beginning the legislative procedure—is about foreigners, not immigrants. In other words, it regulates the entry and exit, permanence, permits and sanctions of a foreigner in our country, but does not consider any measure intended to improve the difficult process of integration. Cultural bias is expressed symbolically throughout the bill, whose articles refer to "foreigners" 155 times, but there is not one use of the word "immigrant."

This forms a perspective of otherness with regard to the migratory phenomenon, which is inconsistent with the integration of immigrants into the local communities. While it faces the deficiencies of current legislation, the main weakness of the bill is that it does not assume the biggest challenge of the migratory phenomenon: integration. This might explain why it maintains a wide margin of discretion for migratory authorities. As in the case of Art. 70 mentioned above, in spite of recognizing their rights, it is still considering a subject outside of community.

CONCLUSIONS

There is a very significant problem for the exercise of immigrant rights, due as much to the legislation about immigration as to the institutions regulating it. Chile needs to prepare to face the challenges of global migration. During the forty years that the Foreigner Act has been in effect, there has been a dearth of development on the topic, and the legal system has not built the tools necessary to generate a new regulatory paradigm to face the challenges of the immigration scenario successfully. The limitations of the bill under discussion demonstrate this weakness.

It is necessary to address equality before the law because the abstract subject, conceived as the owner of universal rights, erases the differences which constitute collective and subjective identities. This means determining how nationals and immigrants are equals and how it is necessary to appreciate their differences so that the legal system guarantees the right to equality before the law in a material way, not just as a formal statement. The difference between, for example, a professional, white, German man and a black, unemployed Colombian woman need to be understood so that they can be addressed in a way that makes the system work well for all people.

The way in which the legal system makes room for administrative discretion can allow for discrimination and institutional racism, given the practices which that system allows. The problem is not only the discretion, understood to be exercise of the normative powers of government, but racist and xenophobic behavior that can result from the viewpoint espoused by the administration and the language of the law itself.

NOTE

This work was developed as part of the research project No. 1180197 "Reconocimiento y protección de los derechos de las personas migrantes en Chile: desafíos y perspectivas para el Derecho Migratorio," which was funded by FONDECYT (Fondo Nacional de Ciencia y Tecnología)

1. See, regarding childhood, Official Letter 1,179 and 6,232 of 2003, between Internal Affairs and Health Ministries; likewise, by Exceptional Decree 512 of 2007, Ministry of Health formalized an agreement between the two offices; regarding education, Circular Note N° 6.232 of Ministry of Internal Affairs, 2003; regarding children's health, Exempt Resolution 1,914 of 2008, Ministry of Internal Affairs; regarding domestic violence, Exempt Resolution 80,388 of 2009, Ministry of Internal Affairs.

In 2015, the Access to Health Care for Immigrants Program was approved (Ministry of Health, Undersecretary of Health Care Networks), which aimed to ensure access to health care for all immigrants, regardless of residency status, without additional requirements. This program is very deficient especially if we consider that only 15.5% of unregistered immigrants are enrolled in the National Health Fund (FONASA) (UDP 2016, 294).

REFERENCES

Aja Fernández, E. 2012. *Inmigración y democracia*. Madrid: Alianza Editorial.

Balibar, E. 2013. *Ciudadanía*. Buenos Aires: Adriana Hidalgo editora.

Burbano, C. & Haeck, Y. 2011. "Staying the Return of Aliens from Europe through Interim Measures: The Case-law of the European Commission and the European Court of Human Rights." In *European Journal of Migration and Law* 13: 31–51.

DEM, Departamento de Extranjería y Migración. 2015. *Estadísticas Migratorias*. Retrieved from: http://www.extranjeria.gob.cl/media/2017/07/AnuarioEstadisticoNacionalDEM2015.pdf [15.07.2017].

DEM, Departamento de Extranjería y Migración. 2017. *Reportes migratorios. Población migrante en Chile*. Retrieved from: http://www.extranjeria.gob.cl/media/2017/09/RM_PoblacionMigranteChile.pdf [15.07.2017].

García, G. & Contreras, P. 2013. "El derecho a la tutela judicial y al debido proceso en la jurisprudencia del Tribunal Constitucional chileno." In *Estudios Constitucionales* 11 (2): 229–282.

Heer, D. 2002. "When Cumulative Causation Conflicts with Relative Economic Opportunity: Recent Change in the Hispanic Population of the United States." In *Migraciones Internacionales* 1 (3): 32–53.

Herrera, M. 2014. *El Mercado de La Vega Central: un estudio de caso de movilidad social ascendente en inmigrantes peruanos*. Santiago: Departamento de Sociología, Universidad de Chile.
Luque, J. 2007. "Asociaciones políticas de inmigrantes peruanos y la 'Lima Chica' en Santiago de Chile," in *Migraciones Internacionales* 4 (2): 121–150.
Massey, D., et al. 2008. "Teorías de migración internacional. Una aproximación y revisión." In *Revista de Derecho Constitucional Europeo* 10: 465–478.
Mezzadra, S. 2009. *Derecho de fuga. Migraciones, ciudadanía y globalización*. Madrid: Traficantes de Sueños, Tinta Limón.
Micolta, A. 2005. "Teorías y conceptos asociados al estudio de las migraciones internacionales." In *Revista Trabajo Social*, U. Nacional de Colombia 7: 59–76.
Pérez, C. 2012. *Migraciones irregulares y Derecho Internacional. Gestión de los flujos migratorios, devolución de extranjeros en situación administrativa irregular y Derecho Internacional de los derechos Humanos*. Valencia: Tirant lo Blanch.
Ratha, D., Mohapatra, S. & Silwal, A. 2011. *Datos sobre migración y remesas*. Banco Mundial, Unidad de Migración y Remesas. Retrieved from: www.worldbank.org/migration [15.07.2017].
Rodríguez, J. & Busso, G. 2009. *Migración interna y desarrollo en América Latina entre 1980 y 2005. Estudio comparativo con perspectiva regional basado en siete países*. Santiago: CELADE.
Salcedo, P. 2015. *Análisis de la Jurisprudencia de la Corte Suprema en Reclamos de Expulsión 2010–2014*. Santiago: Universidad Alberto Hurtado.
Sutcliffe, B. 1998. *Nacido en otra parte: Un ensayo sobre la migración internacional, el desarrollo y la equidad*. Bilbao: Facultad de Ciencias Económicas, U. del País Vasco.
UDP. 2013. *Informe anual de Derechos Humanos 2013*. Santiago: U. Diego Portales.
UDP. 2014. *Informe anual de Derechos Humanos 2014*. Santiago: U. Diego Portales.
UDP. 2015. *Informe anual de Derechos Humanos 2015*. Santiago: U. Diego Portales.
UDP. 2016. *Informe anual de Derechos Humanos 2016*. Santiago: U. Diego Portales.
United Nations. 2009. *National Periodic Review of 2009, on Chile*. United States: Human Rights Council. Available in: http://www.ohchr.org/EN/HRBodies/UPR/Pages/CLindex.aspx).
United Nations. 2014. *VI report of the Covenant on Civil and Political Rights*, Observance 23. Available in: http://tbinternet.ohchr.org/_layouts/treatybodyexternal/Download.aspx?symbolno=CCPR/C/CHL/CO/6&Lang=Sp
Waldron, J. 1999. *The Dignity of Legislation*. Cambridge: Cambridge University Press.
Zagrebelsky, G. 2003. *El derecho dúctil. Ley, derechos, justicia*. Madrid: Trotta.

Chapter Nine

Public Order and Inequality in the Streets

Paz Irarrázabal

INTRODUCTION

This chapter explores egalitarian issues that arise from policing of public order legislation in Chile, using a critical approach. Inequality unfolds in the Chilean streets as in the labor market, the education system, healthcare, housing, and any other social sphere. In public spaces, daily experiences of discrimination are shaped by the social positions individuals occupy. Throughout history, women, LGBTQ+ people, the homeless, people with disabilities, and other discriminated-against groups have struggled for access to and respect in common urban spaces. Public space is a social sphere in which power is exercised and, thus, a sphere in which the belonging and respectability of some groups of people are constantly contested. For some individuals, encounters with police officers in the streets are a primary source of serious threats of mistreatment. Exposure to police surveillance, harassment, and violence are normally in tune with the broader experiences of discrimination suffered by some groups of people. Rules banning public drunkenness, disorder, or street selling, as well as the police power to conduct identity checks, create a legal framework that not only outlaws specific behavior but also materializes power relationships in the public space.

My egalitarian assessment of public order rules is inspired by relational egalitarian ideas that demand that "the state and its institutions should not express, establish, or reinforce (certain kinds of) inegalitarian and hierarchical relationships between individuals or groups of individuals" (Fourie et al. 2014, 5). With this approach, I aim to spot institutional arrangements or structural inequalities that allow disrespectful treatment, avoiding explaining issues of discrimination as simply police malfeasance problems or individual wrongs. The egalitarian approach of this chapter stands in opposition to the traditional liberal debate developed in Chile in relation to the fairness of policing legal power and practices. This debate focuses on the individual liberties affected by policing and claims the need to strike a balance between, on the one hand, the impairment of the rights of the citizens policed and, on the other hand, the rights of law-abiding citizens or the common interest of order and security in the streets.

My analysis is empirically informed by data collected from interviews with citizens, activists, officials, and police officers conducted in Santiago in 2016. Between March and May, I conducted a total of 51 semi-structured interviews. I did 17 interviews with young people in two squares in downtown Santiago and 15 interviews with members of social organizations related to the rights of homeless people, immigrants, street-based sex workers, LGBTQ people, students, street traders, prisoners, women, and inhabitants of poor, strongly policed neighborhoods. Finally, I did 19 interviews with officials: municipal officials (4), prosecutors (3), public defenders (4), criminal law judges (2), police officers (4), and officials of the Human Rights National Institute (2).

Different reasons justify the use of quantitative methodology. First, a critical approach requires that normative analyses of rules and institutions be "historically and socially contextualized" (Young 1990, 5) in order to bring to light the power relationship embedded within them. Second, with the exception of a formalistic understanding of equality, egalitarian analyses need to take into account the impact of the application of a specific rule on different groups of people. Finally, as will be shown, policing is carried out in contexts of low visibility and accountability, primarily affecting relatively powerless groups. In fact, in Chile there is a striking lack of official data and academic research about the way police powers are used on the streets.

The chapter is divided into four sections. The first section introduces a conception of equality that will assist the subsequent normative inquiry about policing rules and practices. Based on ideas by Hellman (2008), Fraser (1999), and Young (1990), this conception suggests that we have to consider three intertwined elements to identify potential harm to equality in policing: (1) the expressive meaning of an act; (2) the power position of police; and (3) the position of vulnerability or lack of power of those individuals affected by the maintenance of public order. The following sections introduce some examples of unequal treatment in policing of public order in Chile that this conception may help to uncover. In the second section I explore the rationale of Chilean public order rules, looking at some historical milestones and current use. The third section in turn explores the power position of police officers in daily interactions in Chilean streets, focusing on specific aspects of police work that may cause humiliation and disempowerment of citizens.

Finally, the fourth section explores the powerless position of groups subjected to constant policing. Here, I focus on the experiences of street workers who deal with police officers in public spaces in downtown Santiago on a daily basis. I address problems of economic inequality and misrecognition that have exposed these groups to disrespectful treatment.

EQUAL RESPECT IN THE STREETS

Relational egalitarian theories provide a valuable approach to examining issues of equality in the policing of public space. These theories focus on hierarchies and oppressive relations that disregard the equal fundamental status of people (Fourie et al. 2015; Anderson 1999). Based on these ideas and inspired by Hellman's discrimination theory (2008), I offer here a conception of equality that aims to assist the examination of institutional arrangements that could prevent members of society from interacting with one another as peers (Fraser 1999) in the public space.

According to Hellman, "[a]n action, policy, or practice demeans if it expresses that the person or people affected are less worthy of equal concern and respect *and* if it is the action, policy, or practice of a person or entity that has the power or capacity to put the other down" (Hellman 2014a, 3045). Whether or not any particular action is able to fulfil these two requirements—the expressive dimension and the power dimension—depends on the social conditions, history, and culture of a specific society in a defined context (Hellman 2008, 38). This author has applied her theory to the practice of racial profiling in policing (Hellman 2014b, 235). According to Hellman, three features characterize the paradigmatic case of racial profiling in the United States: the profile is based on race, the practice is used to prevent crime or apprehend criminals, and the actor doing the profiling is an agent of the state. In this context, racial profiling carries a pejorative meaning and it is thus an instance of disrespect. Inspired by these ideas, I propose here the following components of a conception of equality that might guide my analysis of public order rules and police practices:

Expressive Meaning of the Rule or Practice

We need to explore whether a rule or policing practice shows disrespect for the equal moral worth of a person. In order to do so, I propose first to scrutinize the deeper meaning of a rule. While some rules connote a demeaning sense in a straightforward way, others carry a demeaning connotation even though they have a neutral appearance. An illustration of the former are rules explicitly conferring an inferior status to some groups of people, such as racial segregation laws in the United States or vagrancy laws that affect the streets in various countries. However, even after these kinds of legislation are repealed, the production of status by the state is ubiquitous in a more disguised manner, for example legislation establishing public sleeping bans or sidewalk-sitting bans.

We also need to consider how the rule or practice is interpreted and applied in a specific social context. In other words, the aim here is to explore whether an act could be "conventionally understood as denigrating" (Hellman 2008, 27), and the role of the state in creating or reinforcing these instances of disrespect. This exploration is closely intertwined with the position of authority of police officers and the way they assert their power in the streets. Finally, the stereotypes and position of vulnerability of groups affected by policing also provide elements to assess the expressive meaning of an action. These last issues will be further developed below.

Entities in Positions of Power

Hellman explains that an action has the potential to demean an individual when it comes from an agent with a "degree of power or status" (Hellman, 2008, 35). Police action in the streets possesses this feature. A shared point in the police literature highlights the unique power of police officers for the legitimate use of force, which means their intervention is always authoritative (Reiner 2010; Bitter 2005; Punch 1979). Moreover, police officers have broad discretion in the performance of their duties, which most of the time are carried out in contexts of low visibility. As Waddington (1999, 36) has put it, police officers are the authority in the street corners dispensing justice.

However, my main concern here does not focus on the existence of police power but instead on the ways that this power is asserted in specific contexts. In police literature, authors have also pointed out that police officers "communicate meaning" about power and authority in their daily work (Loader 1997, 9). In addition, police action sends specific messages of exclusion or inclusion (Bradford 2014, 22), and respectability or non-respectability among citizens (Waddington 1999, 62–63). This symbolic dimension has its roots in legal requirements and social expectations that associate police work with fighting against criminality and maintenance of order. Against this backdrop, this second element invites us to explore how different institutional arrangements and social contexts may contribute to define the power position of police as well as the communicative meaning through their acts (Loader 1997, 8–9).

Powerless Groups

A third element to consider in assessing the compliance of an action with the demands of equality is the position of the group with which the affected individual is associated. As Hellman (2008) explains, an action will more likely demean if it affects a group that has suffered discrimination in the past and retains a low social status. This is a key element in assessing the equality implications of an action or practice, and also in identifying other seemingly innocuous institutional arrangements that reinforce each other in preventing the equal standing of people in the streets.

Theories developed by Young (1990) and Fraser (1999) are helpful for identifying the institutional arrangements and social processes that may oppress groups of people, placing them in a position of vulnerability to disrespect. According to these theorists, mistreatment of some individuals is caused by both economic inequalities and misrecognition problems. As for economic inequality, the individuals' position of disadvantage comes from the lack of resources first to sustain material needs and second to be able to interact in social relationships as an equal. Young identifies the process of marginalization from the labor market or exploitation within it and the lack of authority of workers in subordinate positions as sources of economic inequality.

Injustice in the labor market as well as the unequal distribution of resources may result in deprivation and economic dependence, which force individuals to grovel before others in order to meet needs or prevent harm. Importantly, these theorists have highlighted that unequal access to economic advantages deprives the individual of equal social standing in diverse spheres, not only in terms of access to resources, but also with regards to social attributions of respectability.

The injustice of misrecognition, in turn, derives from economic structures of society and also from institutionalized patterns of cultural values. In other words, the subordinate position of some groups is the consequence of cultural values that represent their identities, options, and behaviors as worthless or deviant. These cultural values influence the way that law, policies and practices of state agents and citizens recognize or despise some identities. Therefore, as criteria for the conception of equality proposed here, this aspect of misrecognition requires exploring whether a social group has been constituted as inferior or despicable.

Finally, Young introduces the notion of violence as an oppressive process that also allows us to identify groups in a vulnerable position. The violence suffered by some individuals due to their identity at the hands of other citizens and the police reveals their lack of power and their position of vulnerability.

POLICING SUSPECT IDENTITIES

The first element of the conception I have just suggested here invites the reader to explore the contribution of seemingly neutral legislation or police practices in the production of status subordination. This section provides some clues about the rationale of Chilean public order regulation that emerge from their history and current use.

Current Public Order Rules and Clues from History

Currently, the main rules that create the legal framework for the maintenance of public order by the police are spread across several different statutes. There is no systematic regulation whose core aim is to target offensive or antisocial conduct in the streets. While the Criminal Code punishes public disorder, misdemeanors against decency, and a series of other misdemeanors related to disorderly conduct in the streets such as public drunkenness, special legislation complements this framework banning alcohol consumption in the streets and unlicensed street trading. Moreover, local governments, which are in charge of the administration and security of public spaces, have banned other forms of behavior through local regulation called "*ordenanzas*." Finally, the power to perform identity checks, a power granted to the police for the maintenance of public order, is regulated in the Criminal Procedure Code and another special piece of legislation.

These rules have complex and sometimes contradictory rationales and historical development. However, genealogical exploration reveals the recurring concerns of rule makers in relation to these public order rules. In particular, I will focus on ideas about the dangerousness of some groups that were considered in the enactment of preventive legislation.

The Criminal Code, enacted in 1875, could be regarded as the first systematic legislation that attempted to order appropriate behavior in the streets in the nascent Chilean Republic. The elite's persistent concern about the instability, laziness, and propensity to criminality of the impoverished sectors of society is shown in the punishment of "vagrants" and "beggars." The Code defined "vagrants" as those *able to* work but without a stable home or lawful occupation, and it required beggars to ask for authorization in order to beg in public spaces. The Code stated that the imprisonment or surveillance imposed on a vagrant or beggar could be revoked if the individual provided proof of good behavior and willingness to work. It seems that, for the rule makers, the condition of poverty of these individuals was a matter of lack of will or work ethic, blindingly ignoring the structural social and economic causes of destitution.

Similarly, mistrust and suspicion of some groups seemed to underpin a series of rules that imposed on citizens a permanent duty to report themselves, and to account for their actions to the authorities. For example, the Criminal Code not only contemplated the obligation to have a license to beg in the streets, but also it punished vagrants and beggars who were wearing a "disguise" or clothes unusual for them. In addition, it created the misdemean-

or of refusing to provide personal information to the authorities. Similarly, a couple of years later, the Individual Rights Act of 1884 introduced the police power to arrest under suspicion those disguising their "identity," or who were found in places, in circumstances, or at any time that could be considered sufficient evidence of "evil purposes." Additional legislation required immigrants and sex workers to carry documents providing personal information. Misgivings about marginal groups using the streets are evident in all of these pieces of legislation.

The same attitude to these groups is found in mid-twentieth-century legislation governing the use of public spaces. In tracing the different legal attempts to manage "suspicious" or "dangerous" people, the Antisocial Conditions and Security Act of 1954 could be considered a landmark of the times. Despite the debate about its scope of application, this Act illustrates the groups who were at the center of the criminality concerns of the ruling classes. The act was aimed to control the following groups: vagrants, beggars, drunkards, drug addicts, "those inducing homosexual practices," "those who disguise their personality," ex-convicts or habitual offenders, and those who habitually traded goods of dubious origin or contravened provisions relating to the conditions for selling goods. By this time, the police power to arrest on suspicion was reformed in order to include all the aforementioned conditions as grounds for arrest.

Those overtly discriminatory pieces of legislation are no longer in force in contemporary Chile. In fact, the punishment of vagrants and beggars, the Antisocial Conditions Act and the power to arrest on suspicion were abolished after the end of the Pinochet dictatorship in 1990. Arrest on suspicion was replaced by the identity check, which provided a more limited police power to request identification from any person when there was evidence of involvement in a crime. In the legislative debate, the injustice of previous rules was attacked as they punished individuals and not conduct. However, some members of congress justified the creation of a new power as a compromise between the security and freedom of law-abiding citizens, on the one hand, and the basic guarantees protecting those individuals involved in offences, on the other.[1]

The latter argument gained traction in the following years, particularly in the legislative debates in 2000, 2002, 2004, 2008 and 2016 that expanded significantly the police power to perform identity checks. Different political parties agreed on the balance of interests and costs and benefits as rationale for the regulation. For example, they maintained that carrying and showing ID upon police request amounted to a minor burden versus the increase in security and freedom to use public spaces. Preventive policing was conceived as only involving a burden for certain kind of individuals, which was expressed in what would become a mantra, that those "who do nothing, have nothing to fear."[2]

In contrast to the old punishment of vagrants in the Criminal Code and the groups mentioned in the Antisocial Conditions Act, nowadays public order rules do not target specific groups of people. The current framework of appropriate behavior in the streets ban actions that in principle anyone can perform. In that sense, they appear to be neutral. Similarly, the power to identity check creates a general duty of identification in the streets. The last reform of 2016 empowered police officers to request identification of any adult person, without need to have any grounds for suspicion. [3]

Public Order Legislation in Action

Despite the neutral wordings of current regulation of public order, interviews suggest that practices of policing still target some groups who were habitual offenders under the Antisocial Condition Act. In the understanding and application of public order rules, it is still possible to grasp the influence of the same reasons for suspicion against specific groups. In other words, even when provisions do not refer to particular identities, public order rules are still in practice, embedded with ideas of dangerousness and criminality that are associated with traditionally discriminated groups.

In downtown Santiago, homeless people, street workers, trans people, certain groups of foreigners, "habitual offenders," and young poor people—identified as "*flaites*"—were strongly policed for drinking in squares, selling goods, public disorder, outrages against morality, acting suspiciously, or hiding their "true identity." Moreover, according to local government officials and police officers, some of these groups' typical behavior are regarded as "incivilities," which need to be tackled in order to prevent feelings of insecurity among neighbors and forestall more serious forms of criminality.

To illustrate how legislation could contribute to the targeting of the "habitual" disadvantaged groups, I will examine first to the use of identity check. When the interviews were conducted, all identity check procedures were subjected to article 85 of the Code of Criminal Procedure. This provision required grounds that led a police officer to suspect that an individual had committed or attempted to commit an offense, or that he had an intention to commit the action. The police could also require identification when the individual had hooded or covered his face to hide or conceal his identity.

In the interviews, citizens and police officers reported problems in distinguishing between behavior that could be regarded as grounds for suspicion and the "suspect" people that police target in practice. For example, when I asked which behavior should be regarded as grounds for suspicion, I was told about "the *flaite* that you can recognize from afar" (Man 5, 31 years), "the criminal by face" (Man 18, Prisoners' rights activist), "the criminals known by the police" (Police Officer 1) or in general those "who are suspicious"

(Man 13, 21 years). Let me further develop this issue with the following examples, related to former convicts, sex workers, and LGBTQ people.

The first example relates to the way former offenders are targeted by identity check. Interviews conducted in Santiago reveal a belief among police officers and some citizens that prior involvement with the criminal justice system or local courts was evidence of the dangerousness of a person, that is, of being prone to committing an offence at any moment in the future. In fact, criminal justice system officers claimed that "being known by the police for being a criminal" is used as a formal ground for suspicion in police records of identity check. This was confirmed by one police officer, who reported that knowing that a person has been involved in the criminal justice system was an "objective factor" that provided legal justification to request identification and search them.

An additional reason may explain police targeting of individuals who have arrest warrants or previous criminal records. In the interviews, police officers and citizens expressed the belief that the role of identity checks was in fact to catch individuals with outstanding warrants. This understanding explains that for prisoners' rights activists, the identity check was regarded as a police power that was especially threatening for former convicts. According to them, in practice, the risk of arrest in a future identity check procedure was the second part of their sentences. As an ex-offender explained to me, proximity to any offense exposed him to being arrested, and moreover police could try to link him to any pending case in order to fulfil the demands of prosecutors.

The second example involves the policing of sex workers using provisions about concealment of identity, and misdemeanors of public disorder and outrages against decency. In the interviews, street-based sex workers did not immediately appear as a common target of police persecution. Citizens, activists not related to sex work, and criminal justice system officials do not refer to sex workers when talking about suspicious behavior and police control. However, the street-based sex workers interviewed did complain about the constant policing they suffered in everyday life. A member of a sex worker NGO described the extensive use of identity check for street-based sexual workers:

> According to my experience, around 80 per cent of the women are requested to provide identification in the streets during the year. And I think I fall short because the way that the police approach [sex worker] women in the streets is through the identity check. (Sex workers' rights activist)

The same activist added that among sex workers, ID checks are more frequent for trans people and foreign women, especially if they are black. According to him, police officers easily assume that black women have undocumented migration status. Similarly, transwomen sex workers are constantly policed, with officers requesting their IDs and accusing them of hiding their "true identity." This account coincides with the statement by an Antidiscrimination Office local official:

> The identity check is generally used in the case of trans workers. The trans workers introduce themselves by their social name [but] their IDs state the legal name [. . .] [For example] she introduces herself as Alejandra, [but] the ID says Claudio, and [then] the police officer says that the identity does not match. As a result, the workers are brought to the police station to verify the identity. Trans, in general, not only those working in prostitution, are fighting for their gender identity, to be recognized in their identity in IDs and as long as this doesn't happen, they will keep fighting to be recognized as Alejandra [but] *Carabineros*, without empathy, will keep arresting them. (Local Antidiscrimination Office official)

An additional example of the way legislation creates a framework that enables disrespectful treatment of the same discriminated groups of people regards the offense of outraging decency stated in the Criminal Code. The participants agreed that this offence is frequently used to control inappropriate sexual behavior in the streets. However, what was considered "inappropriate" or "immoral" sexual behavior was a matter of much debate, which in turn impacted on the policing practices relating to the offense. Officials of the criminal justice system explained that the Criminal Code's offence was applied in cases when people were having sex in parks, performing exhibitionism, and engaging in other sex-related conduct that was meant to be confined to private spaces. However, members of LGBTQ NGOs and the sex workers' NGO claimed that police officers make a more selective application of these rules. They explained how the offence of outraging morality was often used against sex workers who were offering their services in the streets, or against public displays of affection by same sex couples, such as holding hands or kissing in the streets.

A chief police officer noted that the lack of a clear definition and the different roles attributed to the rule were in fact a problem for police in the streets. He explained how the front-line police officer, who carries his own prejudices, needs to decide on the content of the offense in the context of divergent pressures. Widespread discrimination in society affects police officers' decisions, regardless of their intentions.

These examples reveal how the police target certain groups based on stereotypical ideas of dangerousness and deceitfulness, which can be tracked back throughout Chilean history. This seems to be an unavoidable problem when the law requires the observation of "reasonable grounds of suspicion" or "offense against decency" to enable police officer action. However, further elements need to be analyzed in order to reveal how the demeaning meaning of policing is expressed in the Chilean context.

Police Power

The second element for the equality assessment proposed here looks at the position of power of police officers. My aim now is to explore how the Chilean police force—Carabineros—affirm their authority on the streets, and how citizens' status and respectability are thus shaped.

Assertion of Power

Police officers are empowered to ask for identification in the streets or to impose fines on citizens in the case of misdemeanors. According to a police officer, the enforcement of these rules "even if they ban petty deeds" is required to prevent disorder and more serious criminality, and also to reinforce their authority and to safeguard the rule of law. Moreover, in enforcing the law, officers demand that citizens provide accounts of their behavior, and expect to receive deferential treatment. These demands have important implications for the outcomes of police procedures and the meaning of police actions.

As for the behavior expected by police officers, interviews revealed that a lack of deferential treatment to the police could be punished as disrespect to authority orders. Moreover, some forms of conduct are regarded as suspicious behavior. This includes nervous behavior in front of officers, avoidance of police officers, or the provision of unconvincing justification of behavior. Actors of the criminal justice system explained that police officers regard such conduct as grounds for suspicion that justify conducting identity check procedures. According to them, "police expertise" suggests that a person reacts nervously when they are afraid of being caught in an improper action.

These standards used by police reinforce inequalities that characterize Chilean society more generally. Self-confidence and assertiveness when facing police officers and ability to reply adequately to their demands may depend on the social position of the person controlled. A public defender explained that "in fact, in the poor neighborhoods nobody wants to come across police, and if people see police officers, they leave because police will stop them…will control them." Likewise, a citizen pointed out:

> The people who know how to behave with the police can avoid problems because you need to be like a psychologist with them [. . .] "Yes sir, yes my commander"—You need to speak to them like that and the officers will let you go. But if you make problems, they will arrest you [. . .] [Young people] are more impulsive, one can be calmer but young guys cannot. (Man 18, Prisoners' rights activist)

The respectability of citizens is not only measured in the attitude displayed in front of police officers; it can also be challenged in the eyes of fellow citizens in police procedures. In fact, among the diverse consequences that might normally follow from police control such as fines, searches, confiscation of goods, and "move on" orders, citizens highlighted the humiliation of being publicly controlled. Indeed, they associated police contact with suspiciousness and criminality.

A street seller, for instance, complained that the confiscation of products was not the worst aspect of police control but rather "the humiliation that they make you feel. . . . It is a matter of dignity." Other citizens also regarded the public display of police authority as humiliating because it caused other people to believe that the person controlled had probably done something illegal. A young woman explained it in the following terms:

> Unfortunately, the people around look at you strangely. [They wonder] why [the police] is requesting her ID? You feel ashamed because [they see that] you are with the police, so you should have done something! These things make you afraid, thus you are one day in the street and you see a police officer and maybe you will walk away because you don't want to undergo that. (Woman 10, 21 years)

Feelings of anger, powerlessness, and humiliation caused by police control are summed up by the account of a young man:

> [When police controlled me] I felt bad [. . .] I mean you feel anger because you are not doing anything and you must answer calmly and follow the orders because you are scared. Moreover, you are exposed, there are people around looking at you and you feel bad, like ashamed. (Man 7, 22 years)

Finally, police officers also perform abusive actions that define the way they assert their power in Chilean streets. Accounts about police abuse arose in the fieldwork, even though this was not the subject of the questions posed to the participants. However, several participants described experiences of police abuse as being the norm in how policing is carried out: "micro abuses" in unjustified identity checks and searches; "retentions" in police cars and police stations without intervention of prosecutors or judges; and use of violence and sexual abuse. I argue that arbitrary and violent police stops and associated humiliating procedures should be understood as mechanisms for ensuring the submissiveness and control of groups of people.

Lack of Accountability

Public order rules and identity check provide the legal framework of police work, the enforcement of which, to an important extent, is kept within the domain of the police itself. Opaque local courts have jurisdiction over the imposition of fines against the violation of street trading rules as well as alcohol consumption regulations, while generally more visible criminal courts have no involvement in the enforcement of misdemeanors. According to a Santiago prosecutor, police officers simply do not report minor cases to the prosecutors. When police do report these cases, prosecutors will use their legal powers to refrain from initiating prosecution. Only in rare occasions will they initiate a brief procedure to impose a fine.

The majority of identity checks and police instructions in the streets are known only by the people directly involved. This is also true in cases of police abuse. Officials of municipalities and of the National Institute for Human Rights (INDH), judges, and defenders acknowledged that a number of institutional shortcomings impede proper oversight of police conduct. First, they pointed to the lack of statistical information about police work. According to a lawyer of the Police Unit of INDH, in the current conditions it is impossible to know the total daily number of identity checks, to ascertain the condition under which they took place, or to determine disproportionality in controlling vulnerable groups of people. Second, no grievance machinery has been put in place. Only exceptionally do criminal law courts review the legality of an identity check when a person has been arrested for being accused of a crime. In that instance—according to a public defender—the person controlled by the police is in a weak position to complain. Moreover, according to criminal law judges and defenders, the declaration of illegality of the identity check in the first stages of the proceeding—detention control hearings—will not necessarily affect the continuation of the trial. Complaints against police misconduct could also be filed in criminal proceedings when defenders come to know of abusive events, reporting them to the Office of Criminal Prosecution. However, according to a defender, a serious investigation of the events might be hindered by the close institutional relationship between prosecutors and the police.

Some officials interviewed mentioned the Antidiscrimination Act as a potential path outside the criminal justice system for complaints against police abuse. However, an INDH lawyer and the head of the Antidiscrimination Municipal Offices claimed that the inappropriate regulation of the judicial action in the Act, which does not provide compensation to the victims, and the fact that the plaintiff could be fined if the claim is rejected, discourage citizen complaints. Finally, INDH officials acknowledge that the institute receives few complaints of police abuse and almost none of them come from vulnerable groups such as the homeless, sex workers, or street traders. Activists or young people that manage social networks make most of the complaints.

Accordingly with these institutional deficiencies, citizens and activists stated repeatedly that there was no clearly available institution for filing complaints in cases of police misconduct. They struggled to point out a competent institution apart from the police station of the officer involved. It was also mentioned that attempts to complain would be frustrated because there was no chance that authorities would deal seriously with the problem. Interviewees also mentioned the possibility of ending up in a worse position by reporting the abuse. Finally, some interviewees regarded police abuse as a common annoyance, assuming that police are the supreme unfettered authority in the streets.

The position of powerlessness of some citizens, as well as their view on police authority, can be seen in the following quotation:

> *Did you consider to complain [about intrusive identity check]?* To them? No, because you are afraid that something worse can happen. One has heard that guys complain to the cop and they end up in the police station (Man 6, 21 years). *Ok, but to another authority?* To whom are you going to complain? To the cop, it doesn't make sense. Moreover, you are afraid of the institution, the uniform represents the giant institution behind it, a powerful institution. My granddad was a cop, did you know that? [he asks to his friend, Man 6]. Yes, it is true, to whom are you going to complain? To the same cops? And what are they going to do? Nothing! Even though I consider making a complaint when they searched me, because I was angry, but I knew that it is better to behave and head down and follow the orders. (Man 7, 22 years)

The special defender of the National Office explained that people with whom he works—low-income young people, immigrants, and indigenous people—generally believe that police abuse is a normal annoyance and that at any rate complaints will never produce positive results. Likewise, the president of the indigenous street vendors union explained that unlicensed street sellers would not report police misconduct to the police station or to criminal prosecutors because of their unlicensed condition. She pointed out, "If the police mistreat us, attacks us, what is he going to say? That we tried to escape and they only followed the procedure, so we don't have any kind of protection."

The sex workers' NGO activist also emphasized the especial vulnerability of street-based sex workers. According to him, the majority of police abuse of sex workers is not reported, because women do not believe they will receive support, especially if they are undocumented immigrants. There might be some complaints from women that have been working in the field for years, but only in cases of constant and serious police harassment, such as demands for free sex services. He explained that street-based sex workers are very marginalized citizens and are subjected to intense policing. So, expectedly, they try to avoid any contact with authorities. He illustrated how these workers avoid court when they are summoned to pay fines for misdemeanors such as alcohol consumption:

> Very often women don't show up due to fear. First, because they fear facing over bigger problems. In general, they avoid any place where they may meet police or judges. On the other hand, because the social context of street-based sex work [. . .] is of poverty, of people deprived in cultural capital. We are not talking of affluent sex workers whose services are offered on the Internet by university students or people with high status. No, we are talking about people harassed by the police, and they tend to have an unstructured social attitude. They don't care. It is like the lumpen culture of the poor people. They don't even trust that we can help them. It is difficult for them to make a complaint, in the INDH or to file a legal action. They give up: "no, it is too much of a problem, it doesn´t matter." (Sex workers' rights activist)

Finally, an activist for prisoners' rights also mentioned disadvantaged people's mistrust of institutions and their acceptance of police abuse in their daily lives. According to a former offender, young people from a low-income background would never complain about police abuse because "they know they can't achieve nothing, who would care?"

To sum up, the distinctive position of power of the police in the streets might account for especially serious threats to equality. Their policing practices not only represent an assertion of their power but also provide clues to help understand their expressive meaning. Those policed have failed to prove their respectability; their interaction with the police marks them as suspicious people or criminals. In stark contrast with their grip on vulnerable citizens, police officers are not subject to proper accountability. This unfairly enhances the power of police and the related position of powerlessness of some citizens. Police work is conducted against a backdrop of poor visibility and insufficient oversight, and the affected population lack the legal and social resources to be able to assert their rights against police abuse. The lack of power of some groups of citizens to make police accountable also challenges their respectability. As Elizabeth Anderson points out, respectability relates to the entitlement of a person to have a say, be listened to, and receive a response (Anderson 2013, 14).

POWERLESSNESS AND STREET WORKERS

The third aspect of the conception of equality proposed here concerns the position of powerlessness of some social groups. The aim is to expand the analysis to other institutional arrangements that reinforce each other in undermining the standing of groups of people, which exposes them to demeaning treatment by the police. In this part I will focus on street workers in downtown Santiago. I will show how the exclusion and exploitation of the formal market pushes citizens to the informal market and puts them in a vulnerable economic position. Likewise, these groups suffer from misrecognition that arises from deficient legal protection and prejudices against street workers.

Oppressed Workers

In Chile, thousands of people work in the streets. They sell food and various other products on sidewalks, in squares, and on public transport; perform shows; provide services such as photography and shoe polishing; and look after cars parked in the streets. Municipalities regulate these activities in diverse bylaws, and special legislation prohibits unlicensed street vendors and the selling of specific products. Moreover, sex workers offer sexual services on sidewalks and streets. In this case, there is no specific legal regulation of their work.

The economy developed in the streets has historically been a source of income for those without stable jobs or access to the formal economy. Unlicensed street work was regarded by the citizens interviewed as an honest way of making a living under circumstances of economic necessity. When asked about the reasons for street work, interviewees mentioned the lack of employment opportunities, and the exclusion from the formal market of those with less education, capital, and networks ("*pitutos*"), or those with disabilities or mental health issues. It was also pointed out that this economy was the only option for former offenders and irregular immigrants.

A young man described the experience of his family as street workers in these terms:

> I don't think that police should expel the sellers because these are people who don't have the resources, not even to pay for a license. For example, my family works in a street market selling tomatoes and avocados, and we started from the very low bottom. My mom, at the beginning, we were in the *cola*[4] until we started to improve little by little, and now we have a license to be there. (Man 1, 20 years)

Likewise, a former offender explained how the street market "is the only thing left for people like us." Another interviewee elaborated on the same theme:

> The person who sells compact discs or anything in the streets is because he needs to eat, because sometimes the circumstances [. . .] and I am talking from my own experience [. . .] which has pushed me to go urgently to sell stuff in the streets because I wanted to eat that day, because I was unemployed. I had some issues in my record, and I wanted to eat that day, not tomorrow, and that is how you start doing things that can be illegal in some neighborhoods or in the country, but I feel I am not illegal because it is the only way to survive. (Man 18, Prisoners' rights activist)

The street market was defended in interviews not only based on the exclusion of some people from the formal market but also because of the exploitation and unfair labor conditions encountered in the workplace. According to one citizen, the street trading ban aims to push people "to work for someone, have a boss and being exploited, working for little money." Expressing anger at being forced to work in the formal market, he pointed out,

> My mom used to work in a street market [selling] clothes. She used to sew stuff, and had a workshop at home. . . . She was fined in *Las Rejas*, and they seized all the products. *Is she still selling?* No, because now she is working for…she went into the system, she is working for a factory, which pays her *luca*[5] each trouser, or two *lucas* and you see it in *Falabella* [shopping center] for 17 *lucas,* so then you get angry, that is wrong. (Man 16, 25 years)

Likewise, the president of the union of street vendors expressed his rejection of "*apatronado* work,"[6] in which he felt exploited and humiliated. He explained that, in spite of street work downsides—such as constant policing—the possibility of avoiding an oppressive labor relationship was an important advantage, a "matter of dignity." In his words:

> I earn my money, I don't like to be exploited, that a *patrón* can make me feel that he is doing me a favor by giving me work and that is not true [. . .] I think about the people who work in *apatronado* relationships and it is not acceptable that my work, my promotion, my salary depends on the mood of your boss that day. It is unacceptable. It is unacceptable that if you make a mistake one day they kick you out. (President street vendors union).

In the case of street-based sex workers, the interviews also revealed issues of exploitation and marginalization. According to activists, sex workers in the streets were the most vulnerable women: poor women, trans women, and undocumented immigrants excluded from or exploited in the formal labor market. A sex workers' NGO member described those offering sexual services in the streets in the following terms:

> People with less resources to associate, to rent a flat to use as workplace [. . .] are the poorest, with less capital to invest in their business. People with better appearance, education, who speak foreign languages, they work as escorts; they don't need to be exposed in the streets. This is what we argue, that the street-based sex work is for poor Chilean women, transsexuals who are rejected and suffer a high level of discrimination even to be able to work in a shop, and thirdly, the immigrant women and men, who are undocumented in Chile and can't find a job. All of them end up working in the most precarious part of the sex market, which is the street. (Sex workers' rights activist)

He explained that irregular immigrants and trans people have the worst working conditions, with the most marginal clients, and perform their services in the most hidden places. Their irregular legal status and the strong discrimination they endure prevent them from moving to different jobs. They are also more exposed to violence and abuse from police and citizens. He illustrates this with the case of trans workers:

> The trans are always trans, and sometimes, sex work is their only chance in the context of extreme marginalization in which they are in the society. They are extremely discriminated in all the fields, and their work opportunities are very limited. (Sex workers' rights activist)

Regulating and Policing Street Economy

Various pieces of legislation state the requirements to have licenses to work in the streets. The Traffic Act requires registration with tax authorities in order to sell products and perform shows in public transport. Local ordinances impose requirements for obtaining licenses and require the payment of duties to sell products or provide services in streets, squares, and parks in each neighborhood. In downtown Santiago, for instance, Ordinance 59 of the Municipality of Santiago contains a list of goods and services that can be offered in a specific place or on the move in the streets. In their applications for licenses, people need to provide reasons supporting their request, and show their national ID. In deciding whether to give a permit, the municipality will consider the applicant's place of residence, criminal record and socioeconomic situation, as well as those of his or her family members. It will also consider whether the applicant has any impediment that prevents him or her from working in a different economic activity.

According to officials of the Santiago Municipality, the provision and control of licenses for street vendors aims to manage in an effective and rational way the use of public spaces, preventing their use for "private profit." The control of street trading also aims to protect a sustainable trade and to discourage disorder and criminality. Additionally, municipality officials pointed out that the local government has an interest in providing permits to the most vulnerable individuals, that is, "people who don't have another way to earn a living," such as elderly and disabled people. In fact, in the granting of licenses, social workers interview the applicants to check on their vulnerability. This requirement to provide reasons to the authority was also mentioned by a local justice judge during the interviews. She mentioned the practice of returning the products seized by the police to vendors if they provide evidence of their economic needs. This benevolent practice demands that workers again prove their vulnerability to the state.

Finally, in sharp contrast to robust protections in other economic fields, the ordinance states that the municipality can revoke licenses without justification and compensation at any moment. A local official explained that this was justified because street trading was an undesirable work that should be transitory:

> [We do not give permanent licenses] because it is an indecent work in many senses. Because the [exposition to] the sun, the rain, the [poor] conditions, without toilets, without work contract. It is not ideal. Therefore, we prioritize those people with the worst social protection cards, disabled people [. . .] We have done several things to humanize it as far as possible, but it is still a work that does not fulfil ILO standards, or any other standards. You don't have toilets, you can't get sick. It is to make normal an unacceptable situation. You should be able to work in decent conditions. (Director of Inspection Office Santiago Municipality)

In a way that resembles the old ban of vagrants and beggars, this legislation and judicial practices express mistrust towards the "undeserving poor." They require workers to prove their poverty and inability to provide for their livelihood in any other way, and they are granted precarious entitlements, which force people to grovel to fulfil their needs.

In the case of street-based sex workers, there is no legislation banning or regulating the activity. Although the Criminal Code punishes the violation of police regulations related to the sex market, the police officers and officials interviewed could not identify the respective pieces of legislation. Sex workers and activists emphasized the need for regulating sex work just like any other economic activity in order to protect and dignify workers. They claimed that the current state of affairs exposed the most vulnerable groups among the sex workers to exploitation, violence, and constant police abuse.

Police officers perform their job of maintenance of order in this context of economic vulnerability, exploitation, marginalization, and lack of adequate state recognition of street sellers and sex workers. Street workers were not only punished for breach of the above-mentioned ordinance on street selling. The interviewed street workers complained about the constant policing they suffered in everyday life. Street traders explained that identity check was a power that allowed police officers to approach them, and they were easier targets for raised policing numbers, especially street sellers offering their products on the sidewalks. They talked about the "game of cat and mouse" or "*terceo*," and all workers talked about short "retentions," "move on" instructions, harassment, and police violence. Similarly, the lawyer of a sex workers' NGO complained that police "always claim that they are not targeting sex work but you wonder why the policing of sex workers is so strong, there is harassment to discourage this work."

In the exceptional cases when police were compelled to justify their actions by activists or the courts, they referred to the legal framework of public disorder, outrages against morality, alcohol consumption, obstruction of transit, concealment of identity, and defiance of duties to follow orders from the authority. Also, police officers and local officials claimed that it was the link between street workers and criminality that justified police control. According to them, street workers created an environment of disorder that encouraged criminal acts, or they were directly involved in criminal activities themselves, such the selling of stolen goods and drug trafficking.

In summary, groups using the streets are particularly vulnerable. Street workers develop their economic activities under conditions of exploitation, marginalization, and precariousness. They also report their desire to avoid the relationships of oppression and exploitation previously experienced in the formal labor market. But as the legal framework for these activities grants few and weak protections, in addition to their tough work in the street they also have to endure demeaning treatment by police and state officials. Stereotypes about minimal involvement constitute the grounds for the intense police harassment that many of these workers face.

CONCLUSION

The egalitarian standard guiding this chapter encourages us to examine how police power and public order offenses may create status subordination of groups in the Chilean streets. In this chapter I have provided some illustrations of mistreatment brought about by institutional arrangements and structural inequalities:

1. The brief examination of historical milestones and current use of public order legislation provides evidence suggesting that despite neutral wording of current provisions, they may still produce status subordination of some groups. As a result of policing in the streets, disadvantaged groups still bear a burden of mistrust and suspiciousness. This has a demeaning effect on these groups. In particular, identity checks are conventionally understood as a tool to tackle criminals and suspicious people.
2. Moreover, police officers are the authority in the streets dealing with criminality. In fact, the meaning that police communicate in controlling people in the streets is based on police authority and powers. Disregarding the neutral face value of rules and the possible intentions of the officers, people interpret that being subject to police control is a mark of criminality, suspiciousness, and a failure to prove respectability. Accordingly, interactions with police officers have a significant impact on the standing of citizens in terms of public shaming and stigmatization.
3. The police's position of power is reinforced by its lack of accountability and the powerlessness of people more likely to suffer from police

control in the streets. Policing in Chile involves strong mistrust of the identity and behavior of vulnerable citizens, yet minimum accountability of police officers. The lack of accountability derives, certainly, from institutional shortcomings, but it is also linked to the vulnerability of the main targets of policing: low-income young people, undocumented immigrants, unlicensed street workers, sex workers, and ex-offenders whose records will mark them for years. Among them, a learned belief is developed that nobody cares about them, and that there is no point in complaining. In a context of structural inequality, the gap between the power positions of authorities and citizens is widened, and instances of contempt and abuse are normalized.

4. Economic inequalities and social misrecognition create a situation of powerlessness that affects numerous citizens in the streets. The powerlessness of some groups is reinforced by police practices that regard being nervous in front of officers or previous involvement in the criminal system as grounds for suspicion. This powerless status is also reinforced by the neglect and disregard of lawmakers. People deprived of legal recognition of their identity—such as trans people—or their condition or activity—such as sex workers, undocumented immigrants, and unlicensed street workers—are placed in a position of vulnerability to all forms of abuse, including police mistreatment.
5. These findings raise crucial normative questions about issues of individual responsibility—"those who do nothing, have nothing to fear"—and the allure of the balancing test among the seemingly equal interests of diverse individuals in the streets. The empirical findings provide information about the structural inequality in which policing is carried out, and about the serious burdens meted out to most disadvantaged groups in this context.

NOTES

I thank Isabel Arriagada, Guillermo Jiménez, Fernando Muñoz, and Ermioni Xanthopoulou for helpful comments.

1. See Library of Congress of Chile, "History of the Act 19,567" (1998).
2. Ibid. 276, 383, 398.
3. Act 20,931.
4. This word, whose exact translation is "tail," is used to describe the unlicensed sellers who stand on the border of the street markets.
5. 1 *luca* = US$1.50.
6. The popular word *apatronado* derives from *patrón,* a term only used in highly hierarchical work conditions such as the traditional *hacienda*. Workers who get called *apatronado* are those that are perceived by their coworkers as too deferential and submissive to their employers.

REFERENCES

Anderson, Elizabeth. 2013. *The Imperative of Integration.* Princeton, Princeton University Press.

Anderson, Elizabeth. 1999. "What Is the Point of Equality?," *Ethics*, vol. 109: 287–337.

Bittner, Egon. 2005. "Florence Nightingale in Pursuit of Willie Sutton: A Theory of the Police" in Tim Newburn (ed), *Policing: Key Readings.* Cullompton, Willan.

Bradford, Ben. 2014. "Policing and Social Identity: Procedural Justice, Inclusion and Cooperation between Police and Public," *Policing & Society*, vol. 24: 22–43.

Fourie, Carina, Schuppert, Fabian and Wallimann-Helmer, Ivo. 2015. *Social Equality. On What It Means to be Equals.* New York, Oxford University Press.

Fraser, Nancy. 1999. "Social Justice in the Age of Identity Politics: Redistribution, Recognition, and Participation," in Larry Ray and Andrew Sayer (eds.), *Culture and Economy after the Cultural Turn.* New York, SAGE Publications.

Hellman, Deborah. 2008. *When Is Discrimination Wrong?* Cambridge, Harvard University Press.

Hellman, Deborah. 2014a. "Equal Protection in the Key of Respect," *Yale Law Journal*, vol. 123: 3036–3062.

Hellman, Deborah. 2014b. "Racial Profiling and the Meaning of Racial Categories," in Andrew Cohen and Christopher Wellman (eds.), *Contemporary Debates in Applied Ethics.* Chichester, Wiley.

Loader, Ian. 1997. "Policing and the Social: Questions of Symbolic Power," *British Journal of Sociology,* vol. 48: 1–18.

Reiner, Robert. 2010. *The Politics of the Police.* Oxford, Oxford University Press.

Waddington, P. A. J. 1999. *Policing Citizens: Authority and Rights.* London, UCL Press.

Young, Iris Marion. 1990. *Justice and the Politics of Difference.* Princeton, Princeton University Press.

Chapter Ten

Citizenship and Prisoners

Pablo Marshall and Carla Moscoso

Article 17 of the Constitution of Chile states that those convicted of an offense that implies an *afflictive punishment*, that is, a penalty of imprisonment of more than three years, are deprived of their citizenship. This provision has been commonly associated with disenfranchisement and has recently attracted the attention of human rights organizations who have demanded the implementation of mechanisms that allow voting for those prisoners who have not been legally disenfranchised.

However, the constitutional effect of the deprivation of citizenship due to a criminal conviction is not limited to its electoral effects. The symbolic effect of the fact that the most important norm of the Chilean legal system explicitly counterpoises the concepts of citizenship and crime, is perhaps more important. This constitutional provision expresses the idea that those who are in prison are not citizens.

Thus, as we link the concept of citizenship with the status of being a member of the political community, this clearly expresses the idea that prisoners are not part of the political community. Of course, this understanding of the relationship between crime and citizenship also has important practical consequences for the understanding of criminal and prison policy in Chile. If we link, for instance, the concept of citizenship with the status of being the bearer of certain rights, we could assume that Chile's prisons are not places where the civil, political and social rights of the inmates are generally respected.

This work is based on an interpretation of Chilean penal practice that allows us to link it with the politics of exclusion embedded in the notion of citizenship. In particular, the work seeks to find connections between, on the one hand, the relationship that exists between the prisoner and the citizen subject and, on the other, the empirical reality of the Chilean prison system.

It could be argued that at some historical moment the concept of citizenship was conceptually constructed in opposition to the legal, political and social position of the slave (Shklar 1991). As such it could be said that, at present (a time when the re-socialization project finds itself extinct and the policies of mass incarceration are on the rise) the physical, social and political exclusion suffered by those who are imprisoned defines, by opposition, our contemporary concept of citizenship.

If we understand citizenship as a status of inclusion in the community that is associated with civil, political and social rights, the reality of Chilean prisons confirms, as we seek to demonstrate in this paper, the hypothesis that those inmates are not citizens. At best they are mere human beings.

The description of prison practices around issues such as the conditions for obtaining freedom, the establishment of social ties, the performance of a job and the exercise of the right to vote, allow us to confirm the dissociation between what should be a regime of care and respect for the status of citizen of those in prison and a regime of administration of punishment that ignores any trace of citizenship.

IMPRISONMENT AND EXCLUSION FROM CITIZENSHIP

It has been argued that contemporary liberal democracy has an invisible tendency to include individuals in the political community, while at the same time embracing a dynamic that encourages their exclusion. This paradox can be explained in the following terms: those involved in the practice of a democracy must know, listen and understand each other, otherwise the practice is impossible, or a mere appearance (Taylor 1998, 143). Therefore, only a collective identity based on a strong commitment is capable of creating trust on the part of the various groups so that they can effectively be heard (145). This mutual trust is threatened when some citizens do not behave according to communal expectations, reinforcing a tendency to exclude those who do not participate in the terms defined by collective identity.

The most commonly addressed case of this tension is that of immigrants, but this phenomenon is not limited to them. In its crudest version, the exclusionary tendencies of democracy are created and directed towards those who do not conform to the admissible forms of being, and who therefore can be classified as *strangers*. However, being a stranger is not something that comes from any natural characteristic and, therefore, is neither stable nor determined. On the contrary, it is something essentially changeable and malleable (Balibar 2006).

The increasingly pronounced complexity of modern societies makes the identification of traditional cultural identities somewhat complicated. Within a social paradigm that treats people according to their behavior and merits rather than according to a predetermined social status, it could be correct to affirm that once the stranger is accepted into the community, they should be treated as a member and respected in the same way that everyone else is respected.

However, the previously mentioned exclusionary tendencies do not seem to disappear. Instead they are expressed in the informal interactions of society through racist, homophobic or xenophobic behavior, and reformulated and codified to be formally channeled through the legal system, through its devices and discourses. If the stranger is normalized and acts according to the values of the community, he will be protected by law; otherwise, both strange behavior (and the stranger themselves) will probably be *outlawed* and *criminalized.*

Criminalization is one of the fundamental ways in which contemporary nation-states express their exclusionary tendencies. Despite permitting the inclusion of the foreigner and their transformation into a citizen, it also allows the reverse process, which is what happens when those people considered citizens become strangers through the criminalization of their conduct and consequent imprisonment.

This process of *estrangement* is fundamental to understanding contemporary penal policy as a practice in which an individual is stripped of the most important rights, on account of being qualified as irremediably perverse and dangerous, that is, to be identified as *strange*. Thus Michael Foucault affirms that imprisonment implies a subjectification of the individual. From the legal perspective, which considers the convicted person as a citizen or *subject of law*, they are obliged to assume responsibility for their actions as an autonomous subject when they become the object of the criminal sentence. However, through imprisonment, this convicted person is introduced into an environment where he will be transformed into a *criminal*, someone who must be rehabilitated through the application of disciplinary techniques (Foucault 1995, 251).

The penal policies of rehabilitation and social reintegration both with good humanistic intentions and also dark technologies (governing the soul through the discipline of the body) seem to be losing the battle for the hegemony of the understanding of crime and prison. The paradoxical coexistence of the conviction of the responsible subject and the incarceration of the criminal to be reformed, influentially theorized by Foucault, seem to continue in the neoliberal prison along with new forms of treatment.

The proliferation of long-term sentences, the imprisonment of large numbers of individuals, the massive violation of many inmates' rights in detention centers, without legal authorization and with no disciplinary intent or efficacy, and with the degrading treatment to which prisoners are constantly exposed, cannot be explained anymore by the paradoxical relationship between responsibility and discipline.

The idea that best fits the penal and prison policies and practices that prevail in modern-day Chile is that of the exclusion of prisoners from the community, without hesitation, to its fullest extent. The driving force in favor of criminalization has penetrated the operation of institutions that previously operated under their own logics and with their own goals. If we follow Joshua Kleinfeld's (2016) analysis of the criminological ideas that have been developed in the United States, and of which Chile has been a prolific follower, this may be due to the fact that we have stopped thinking of the criminal act only as an illegal act of a citizen who must be therefore punished, and we have begun to consider the crime as a sign of the perversion of an individual that is foreign to our law-abiding community of citizens.

In summary: we have stopped looking at the criminal act and instead focus fundamentally on what that act says about the offender. In consequence we have stopped thinking about incarceration as a process that is aimed at both the punishment of crime and the reform of the offender. Instead, imprisonment has assumed the role of a mechanism of administration of the social risk generated by the offender. This operates primarily by keeping those who are considered dangerous under the strictest control.

This understanding allows us to establish certain premises that may justify certain punitive practices that are incompatible with treating offenders with respect, while at the same time allowing the dislocation of prison practices from the teleological discourse of rehabilitation. As mentioned previously, the latter would imply understanding crime as an incorrect act on the part of a citizen and treating those imprisoned in ways compatible with the assumption that they are still part of the community.

In contrast, considering offenders as intrinsically depraved and dangerous beings, different and worse than normal people, is what allows us to strip them of the dignity we would normally accord them, and the basic rights that we as citizens recognize for each other. It also allows the introduction of the economic calculation of risk management into the design and operation of the prison apparatus, now designed as an industry gradually disconnected from notions of human dignity and citizenship.

The discourse of exclusion both expresses and transcends the idea that there are differences between good and bad members of the community, strengthening the social validation of the punitive apparatus of the State (Drake & Henley 2014, 6). This occurs because prisoners are not completely irrelevant: their existence fulfills a function whose usefulness means alternatives like their annihilation are not considered.

The usefulness of their existence allows the presence of the stranger, who, by opposition, defines the identity of the citizen. Their superfluity as cooperating members of a community of honest citizens from which prisoners are expelled is unexpectedly transformed into something useful. However, this utility is dependent on their expulsion. They are expelled because they are a threat for the cohesion and purity of the community and this threat becomes a component part of the same cohesion and purity. The community is transformed and reinforced by the constitutive exclusion of the marginalized criminal.

This line of discourse allows the penetration of levels of violence, abuse and degradation not seen during the hegemony of the discourse of rehabilitation. However, just as prison discipline did not totally displace the discourse of legal responsibility, but rather intersected and overlapped with it, the discourse of exclusion intersects and accommodates itself within the framework of the penal and criminological discourses that preceded it. This produces an amalgamation of punitive forms and discourses that can be characterized by their great resistance to systematic criticism. Most troublingly for advocates of prison reform (those seeking to rescue the idea that citizenship remains something significant within the prison) is the fact that the reasoning and principles behind the prison apparatus are increasingly ubiquitous. The following section seeks to explore some aspects of Chilean penal practice that can be better understood through the interpretive lens of the (deliberate) exclusion of citizens.

THE EXCLUSION FROM CITIZENSHIP IN CHILEAN PRISONS

In Chile, prison life is legally ordered by the Regulations of Penitentiary Establishments (RPE), which have as their primary purpose the care, custody and assistance of prisoners (detainees, subject to preventive detention, and convicts), as well as the educational action needed for reintegration of those serving custodial or community sentences. Article 2 of these regulations explicitly states that the inmate is in a public law relationship with the State, such that his legal status is identical to that of free citizens with the specific exception of those rights lost or limited by his arrest, preventive detention or conviction.

This statement makes it clear that prisoners should remain part of the community that is confining them temporarily, and that in principle they should be treated respectfully. Hence, at least from the perspective of normative regulation, the State is set up as the guarantor of the protection and care of prisoners, supervising them and ensuring their eventual reincorporation into society.

Gendarmería de Chile is the service responsible for implementing custodial sentences and ensuring compliance with the aforementioned norms within prison premises. This means that their role in the administration of the prison is crucial for the configuration of the link between the inmates and the outside community, especially if we consider that the conditions in which their isolation is carried out can facilitate, impede or prevent the reincorporation of prisoners into the community.

In this section we review the idea that prisoners' exclusion from citizenship occurs in the Chilean case because of four aspects in which the inmate's link with the community (or loss of said link) is manifested: the possibility of enjoying freedom, the possibility of enjoying a significant intimacy and family life, the possibility of working and earning a living for themselves and their families, and the possibility of participating politically in the decision making of the community.

Although the idea of the exclusion of *citizenship* is not necessarily the predominant element in all of these exclusions, in each one we can identify practices in which different discourses are articulated such that depriving prisoners of their citizenship assumes an important role for the discipline and government of the prison population.

Liberty: Conditions and Benefits

As we have seen previously, Chilean prison system regulations state that the main objective of incarceration is rehabilitation and the subsequent reincorporation of inmates into society. This close relationship between freedom and reintegration presupposes that prison constitutes more than just the *space* for the carrying out of a conviction. It should also embrace the goal of social learning for the prisoners, which goes hand in hand with the progressive and gradual extension of greater degrees of freedom and autonomy while they are serving time. From this perspective, the granting of benefits to prisoners can be understood as the application of alternative measures (instead of confinement) thus tending to social reintegration.

The types of intra-penitentiary benefits are four: (1) Sporadic leave, which is granted if the inmate is affected by a family emergency (e.g., death, illness, serious accidents, births) or if there are urgent inquiries that require their personal appearance. It can also be granted as a prize if the head of the prison so determines, and it is always for a maximum of ten hours; (2) Sunday leave, which allows inmates to leave prison on Sundays, without guards, for a period of up to fifteen hours; (3) Weekend leave, where prisoners can leave from 6:00 p.m. on Friday until 10:00 p.m. on Sunday; and (4) Controlled release, which authorizes the inmate to leave during the week for a period not exceeding fifteen hours a day, in order to attend work or educational training establishments, social rehabilitation or personal guidance institutions, or in order to search or perform work (www.gendarmeria.gob.cl). In addition to these four types of administrative benefits there are also legal benefits, which can be given in two modalities: the presidential pardon and conditional liberty (parole).

Unfortunately, the Chilean prison system poses a series of obstacles to obtaining freedom that hinder the establishment and consolidation of links between prisoners and the community. The first is that of a *lack of clear rules* regarding the behavioral requirements necessary for obtaining the above-mentioned benefits. The request for benefits is a right of every inmate who has served two-thirds of their sentence within the prison precincts, with irreproachable conduct for at least 6 months. To be eligible they also need to have attended the prison's school, workshops, training programs, work, cultural and recreational activities, and have support or assistance from his family, prison networks or other social networks. These requirements are designed to create incentives for good behavior within the prison, making it easier to govern and facilitating the adoption of docile behavior by the prisoners, which favors their reincorporation into the community.

However, the process of review and evaluation of the applicants is perceived as a kind of *black box*, in which the reasons for obtaining or being denied benefits are not made explicit. This lack of information regarding the arguments put forward by the Technical Council, which advises the head of the prison (who ultimately makes the decision), generates high levels of frustration amongst inmates, who, along with feeling that their rights are violated, perceive that the bodies in charge of making these decisions behave in an arbitrary fashion (INDH 2013b).

Another element that contributes to the process of exclusion of prisoners is the *profound criminalization* experienced at the hands of society and the State. Evidence of this includes cases in which the Executive has taken measures against granting conditional liberty (parole). For instance, in 2014 the Ministry of Justice decided to deny *en masse* the benefit of sentence reduction contemplated in the statute which promotes the social reintegration of the convicted (Law 19,856). This decision delayed the release of hundreds of inmates who had met the requirements for obtaining this benefit (UDP 2015, 172).

In that case, the denial of the benefit not only affected the legally guaranteed possibility of the prison population to take another step in their process of social reintegration, but also stigmatized them as a *latent danger* for the community, expressly ignoring the merits associated with their good behavior during the time they had already served. This event and other similar examples expose the weaknesses of an Executive susceptible to political pressures that demand further criminalization and consequently the permanent social exclusion of prisoners. They also reveal the lack of guarantees on the part of the prison system for those convicted, who, despite compliance with the prison regulations can arbitrarily be denied the opportunity for freedom.

Finally, there is the *extreme reluctance to deliver intra-penitentiary benefits*. The process of social reintegration includes granting benefits, which are aimed at facilitating the reintegration of prisoners through greater spaces of freedom. The prison system has low levels of benefit-granting,[1] despite the low rates of recidivism of inmates who are released.[2] This fact is common in prisons where, in general, the reasons given by the heads of the Technical Area for denying the benefits to inmates who have satisfactorily complied with the requirement relates to the absence of *guarantees of success* on the part of their social environment.

Regrettably, the lack of guarantees is due to external factors, often associated with the absence of a network of family support, and the impossibility of acquiring a job (which we must remember that the inmates have suffered the loss of their links with family and community since confinement, making this particularly difficult). Therefore, the prisoner is *punished again* for not having optimal conditions for his release into a social environment that is alien to him. This is an expression of the paradox faced by the prisoners: they see their freedom limited by the lack of a link to the outside world but, at the same time, the action of the same system denies them the possibility o constructing this link. In this way the principles that give rise to the penitentiary system demonstrate their contradictions and exclusionary effects in terms of the loss of citizenship for those incarcerated.

Additionally, an important part of the prison population does not receive adequate information regarding the type of benefits for which they may apply, evidenced by a clear ignorance of their rights and the functioning of institutional mechanisms aimed at their reintegration. Likewise, corrupt practices are common on the part of some guards, who charge cash to the inmates to give good references in their application to the Technical Council (INDH 2013b).

In order to ameliorate the aforementioned problems, it is necessary to address prison treatment not only in terms of the parameters of modification of individual behavior, but also by considering the social character of the penitentiary institution in the process of punishment and reintegration of the inmate to society. Only through this recognition will social reintegration be seen as a process of recovery of rights by vulnerable people.

Moreover, from a practical perspective, along with increasing the granting of benefits such as parole, it is necessary to explain to the inmates the reasons why such benefits are sometimes denied, suspended, or revoked. The task of providing such information should be framed precisely in the context of recognizing that prison is a transitory space for the recovery of full citizenship and that the progressive return to life in society has a horizon of realization.

Affective Link: Family Visits and Venusterio

Another neglected aspect of the exclusion of prisoners from their community is the loss of family life, including daily contact with their partners. If the prison had the purpose of preparing prisoners for their re-entry into society, then, it would be necessary to reinforce their relations with the outside world, in order to counteract the isolating effects intrinsic to a custodial sentence (Espinoza and Salinero 2014, 240). In this context, obtaining freedom becomes a way of reestablishing an unrestricted link with family and friends: an incentive for the process of social reintegration.

In this context the existence of a regimen of visits by family and friends has a double purpose: maintaining the psychic integrity of the person who is separated from their community and providing adequate conditions for the protection of the family against any abusive or arbitrary action that may occur within the prison system. Additionally, it should be restated that the maintenance of a link with the outside world is a necessary condition for the delivery of benefits, hence the importance of visits by relatives and friends in the process of social reintegration of the inmate.

The *reception of visits* within prison premises is framed within a series of rules that define the terms of the link between inmates and their significant others. However, the implementation of this regulation ends up inhibiting visits and, therefore, encouraging the social and family isolation of the inmate. It is common that the process of entry into the prison takes a long time and for visitors receive degrading treatment. Family members—even women and children—must wait in long lines and then undergo a body search which is a highly invasive procedure with undressing, body contact and even genital searches in the most extreme cases (INDH 2013a, 132–133).

Another difficulty for prisoners attempting to maintain their links with broader society while confined is the absence of specially designated places for family or community visits within the prisons themselves. In an important percentage of Chilean prisons visits are received in the housing units or common living spaces such as courtyards or dining rooms. These places lack any kind of privacy. This means that the family members enter areas that are meant for the exclusive use of the prison population. This represents a risk to the safety of visitors, especially children, who roam unsupervised in an environment characterized by violence (INDH 2013a, 131).

Moreover, harassment of family members by guards is common during visits. That is, the visitors are subject to the arbitrary decisions of guards, who enforce unpredictable restrictions with respect to the entry of certain products (such as food), the limitation of visiting times, or simply the interruption of the conversations that inmates try to establish in privacy with their visitors. Thus, it has been observed that:

> The people interviewed report that they only have the right to a family visit of 15 minutes, once every 21 days. During such visits, limited to 2 people, they have to stand for the duration, in a corridor, next to the bathrooms. They have to arrive at 8:00 a.m. to be able to have the visit at 11:00 am. 15 spaces are allotted. If they do not get one, they must return in 21 more days. (LEASUR —Fundación 1367 2016, 34)

The so-called special visits are divided into family visits and intimate (conjugal) visits. The latter are known as a *beneficio de venusterio*, which is exercised in physical spaces called *venusterios* which are specially designed and equipped for the protection of the prisoners' sexual intimacy. In general, this benefit is granted if the prisoners can accredit a verifiable link with his or her affective partner (hetero- or homosexual) and also have demonstrated previous good behavior. This benefit is granted between one and two times a month at the most, to anyone who does not have internal punishments or sanctions.

In the women's prisons, the physical space destined for the *venusterios* is commonly occupied for family visits, particularly when inmates have a baby living with them inside the prison. In these cases, when a father visits it means that they are granted permission as a family to use this space. The advantage of using *venusterios* is that it allows inmates to safeguard intimacy with their partners and families. It also helps to improve the mental health of inmates, who can satisfy their sexuality with a chosen partner, instead of being exposed to the sexual violence that is generated as a consequence of abstinence and overcrowding.[3]

In spite of the advances in this matter, the reality of Chilean prisons is that there are detention centers that do not have spaces designed for these purposes. Thus intimate visits are made in the housing modules, in the gym or multipurpose hall of the prison. In these cases, inmates put up *camaros* (improvised constructions consisting of tying sheets and blankets with strings to achieve a sort of tent where they can have sex without being seen) to achieve some privacy with their partners (Cooper 2002, 506). This type of practice *de facto* resolves the absence of a space for these purposes, even if the standards established for the implementation of a sexual, affective and family life compatible with the dignity of those deprived of liberty are contravened.

In the case of the prisons with high levels of overcrowding, the available *venusterios* are not sufficient to satisfy the size of the population. This fact implies that this benefit ends up being denied, not based on the breach of any internal rules or regulations, but because of lack of time and space to meet high demand. It should also be noted that Chile is one of the Latin American countries where the prohibition of intimate visits to the prison population is most frequent for the following reasons: inadequate infrastructure, denial of the visit permit without clear explanation and not being able to afford the expenses associated with the benefit (Sánchez and Piñol 2015, 31).

The importance of maintaining links with the outside world lies in the reduction of the dissociative effect that prison has on the inmate and the rest of society. Although the granting of benefits so inmates can maintain their relationships with family and friends does not have a disciplinary goal but rather a re-socializing one, the barriers that the prison system imposes on the inmate attempting to maintain said links transform this right into an instrument of control over the individual, stripping it of its social sense.

Work: Precarious and Forced Labor

For free citizens, work—voluntary or remunerated—is a mechanism that enables both their material subsistence and their personal development as the subjects in terms of their self-determination (Sennett 2000). Penitentiary work is understood as work that is performed within the prison, under the control of the prison administration but with equivalent labor rights to those that apply to work performed in free society (Mapelli 2014, 353). Despite the restrictions inherent in the situation of confinement, the importance of work within prisons is that it constitutes a path towards the reintegration of the inmates into the social and working world, enhancing their labor skills and employability (UN 2016). Hence, the association between obtaining work and obtaining freedom is so close in the prison context. However, it is common that labor activity within the prison regime acquires characteristics that undermine the idea of freedom and self-realization ordinarily contained in this human action.

In the case of Chile, the work performed by inmates has different forms, modalities of contract, and status within the prison culture. Firstly, there are those who work as artisans in self-managed workshops within the premises of the prison. These workshops require supplies for their operation (work material, machinery and tools), which are provided mainly by relatives and sometimes by the prison administration itself. Artisanal work is the one most frequently carried out within prisons, since the possibilities of accessing paid work are very low in general (Espinoza and Viano 2008, 124).

One of the most difficult problems associated with this self-managed labor activity is the problem of confronting the barriers imposed by the administration for the provision of materials and tools by family members; a situation that worsens in the case of those who do not have support networks. Another difficulty is obtaining a permit to carry out work from the prison authority. Inmates must demonstrate good behavior if they want to be granted a space for the installation of their workshops (INDH 2013a, 120).

Secondly there are the so-called *mozos*, who—with or without a work contract—carry out tasks for the prison administration. They are mainly associated with prison maintenance, doing tasks such as: cleaning, cooking or repairing infrastructure. Being able to perform this work modality is linked with the good behavior of the inmate since, in order to be assigned it, they need to win favor with the authorities that designate those charged with this kind of work. Put simply, the granting of this benefit is at the administration's discretion and allocated in a partial and non-transparent fashion. In other words, the selection process does not have procedures or evaluation criteria that are known to the prison population. Thus this category of work reinforces the arbitrary greater hierarchy that confronts inmates seeking access to better material conditions of life and even to obtain intra-penitentiary benefits. For cases in which the work of a *mozo* receives payment, the amount received is commonly well below the minimum wage established by the State (INDH 2013a, 121–122).

Third and finally, there are prisoners who work in the Education and Labor Centers (ELC), under a contract regime for private companies or developing small businesses. The ELC buildings can be closed (they form part of the prison precinct itself, where the prison population carries out its sentence). However some are semi-open (these are centers which are part of special penitentiary facilities and have their own surveillance and security regulations—inmates thus have a specially designated and conditioned place for the fulfillment of their working day).

The ELCs function as non-profit companies which comply with all the fiscal and commercial regulations necessary to operate like any private company (Gendarmería de Chile 2014). Nevertheless, the main motivation for prisoners participating in this type of work is not the payment, which is usually very low, but the possibility of learning a skill or trade and having greater intra-penitentiary benefits (Espinoza and Viano 2008, 124). Given the associated benefits, there is a high demand to be part of the working regime of the ELCs. Hence, the main weakness of this system is the shortage of places offered at the national level.[4]

In general terms, working conditions inside prison precincts in Chile are precarious. Along with the long working hours, the absence of payment for work is common, as are threats of transfer to other penitentiary facilities if inmates do not meet the conditions that are required. It should be noted that a transfer becomes a serious threat to the inmate if it implies a physical distance from relatives or hinders a pre-established link with the outside world. This is compounded by the lack of adequate safety equipment, insurance coverage for work accidents, definition of schedules and workloads, among a number of other shortcomings that lead to abusive work conditions (INDH 2013b).

Assimilating the working conditions of the inmates as much as possible to those of the external labor market, especially regarding remuneration and safety measures at work, is still a pending task. Despite efforts to have workshops and work activities for the entire prison population, the high levels of overcrowding make it impossible to have job offers meet demand (Sánchez and Piñol 2015, 35). This fact makes work activity something for the privileged few, those who are best able to overcome the vicissitudes of administrative punishment and competition among peers. In this context, within Chilean prisons the right to work does not function as a mechanism of social integration, facilitating freedom to participate in the market and guarantee subsistence, but rather acquires characteristics that end up depriving inmates of these effects.

Political Participation: The Right to Vote

One of the characteristics of the Chilean prison population is their political marginalization. Chilean prisons are spaces in which inmates do not have the means to express their opinions and concerns or promote their interests. Thus there is no channel through which their requests can be heard by either political authorities or other citizens. Demands for improvement in their living conditions, the defense and protection of their rights by specialized and independent organizations, or the possibility of exercising in practice their rights to free association, expression and suffrage, are thus silenced (Arriagada and Rochow 2015, 205; INDH 2012, 146)

The lack of channels for participation and expression is not, however, a whim of the authorities in charge. While article 16 n° 2 of the Constitution states that the right to vote is suspended if a person is convicted of a felony or a crime categorized as terrorist, article 17 n° 2 actually states that persons sentenced to such punishment lose citizenship. These provisions seem to have a legal and political content that symbolically "irradiate" to the rest of the legal system. Part of this effect of "irradiation" is manifested in the fact that the authorities, through a practice contrary to the most basic principles of the rule of law, have failed to create an electoral mechanism to cover the case of all those inmates who have not been disenfranchised (those convicted of crimes which are not categorized as felonies). As a result, those subject to preventive detention are effectively deprived of the possibility of voting, although no regulation legitimizes this. The same applies to those who serve custodial sentences of less than three years and one day (Marshall 2010).

During the last 5 years in Chile, a series of legal initiatives aimed at questioning the electoral exclusion of prisoners have taken place, with the National Institute of Human Rights (INDH in Spanish) being one of the key actors that has shown the greatest concern on this issue. The INDH has addressed the problem of the suffrage of prisoners in their annual reports, indicating, first, that the suspension of the right to vote established in the Constitution is contrary to the presumption of innocence, as it implies a punishment without having proven the criminal responsibility of a person

(INDH 2012, 146). They also stress that the *de facto* disenfranchisement that the legally authorized voters experience within prison constitutes a general, automatic and indiscriminate violation of their rights (INDH 2013a, 50).

These arguments found their expression in the judicial actions that the INDH undertook both in 2016 and in 2017 in order to allow prisoners to exercise their right to vote. This legal process, eventually ruled on by the Supreme Court, sought to oblige the Electoral Service and the *Gendarmería de Chile* to install polling stations within penitentiary precincts. In its rulings, the Court affirmed that the Electoral Service does have the power to install polling stations inside the prisons. The Court used a series of international standards to justify its decision. On the basis of these provisions, the Court argued that the right to suffrage constitutes a citizen's right whose exercise must be guaranteed. Although this right can be limited said limitations cannot exceed what is set out in the national laws governing these rights.

As already noted, limitations on the exercise of the right to vote and citizenship are specified in articles 16 and 17 of the Constitution respectively. Based on the text of both articles, the Court found that, since neither preventative detention nor non-felony imprisonment limit the exercise of the right to vote in law, the State must guarantee its exercise.

The Court went on to argue that article 1 of the Constitution enshrines the right of the people to participate with equal opportunities in national life. In this context, the exercise of the right to suffrage constitutes one of the most important instruments of citizen participation in democracy. Thus, in short, the Court ruled favorably on the INDH petition ordering the adoption of all measures necessary so that prisoners who have not had their right to vote suspended by law can exercise it (Marshall and Rochow 2017). However, that two years and two elections after the judgment, the government has still not implemented any policy aimed at restoring the exercise of suffrage to those who have been unjustly deprived of it.

CONCLUSION: CITIZENSHIP AS DENIAL OF PRISON

While it is impossible to think of a political community that is not exclusionary in some sense, a regime of exclusion like the one described above, which allows the reinforcement of the political community at the expense of the exclusion of some of its members, must be questioned as excessive. The Chilean prison population have been incarcerated not simply because they have violated the norms adopted by the community, but also because of their poverty, that is, of their previous physical, social and political exclusion from the enjoyment of the fruits of social cooperation. In this context the prison system effectively consolidated a social regime of poverty, marginalization and helplessness that affects a certain class of subjects that have already been, probably since their birth, excluded from citizenship.

The particular *exclusion* suffered by inmates can best be understood in terms of specific exclusionary dynamics in the criminal justice system. The first and most obvious of these is the fact that deprivation of liberty isolates the inmate from society. Imprisonment is, literally, an internal exclusion, compared with, for example, transportation or exile, which are examples of external exclusions. However, it is also different from punitive mechanisms that publicly expose the criminal, in that imprisonment makes the punishment invisible to the eyes of the public. This means that the rest of us do not have to witness the regime of brutality and dehumanization that is imposed on our behalf within prison. The public, in this way, becomes immune to that suffering.

Imprisonment works by lowering the tolerance threshold to punishment (Foucault 1995, 301). In these terms, a hidden social function of the prison is to guarantee, for the outside, the invisibility of the prisoners, which constitutes the reverse aspect of the intense vigilance they face inside (Edgely 2010, 415; Mañalich 2011, 169). The conditions in which imprisonment is experienced constitute a different and often more intense punishment than the deprivation of liberty proper. These conditions are possible and acceptable only in a context where inmates are not conceived of as bearers of rights and therefore are not considered of equal dignity (the dignity that the community affords the rest of its members). That is the only explanation for the state authorization of torture, physical abuse and degrading treatment by the prison guards; of physical and sexual abuse by other prisoners and institutionalized degrading treatment by the prison administration.

However, the internal exclusion suffered by the convicted subject is not limited by the particular conditions of his imprisonment. A second aspect of the exclusionary dynamics suffered by prisoners is their permanent or temporary removal from *honest society*, a process that is usually called *invisible punishment*, resembling the old practices of *civil death* (Demleiter 2000, 775). These measures emerge silently from different governmental and private regulations, imposing themselves under the cover of darkness (Edgely 2010, 404). They are oriented towards the deepening of social exclusion. This invisible punishment includes the loss of pension benefits and housing subsidies and the prohibition of performing certain jobs. As some of the most perceptive observers of these practices claim: the full range of civil penalties and informal stigmas imposed along with a criminal conviction effectively deny individuals their citizenship rights. This denial, as has already been argued, makes it difficult to perform the tasks that society expects from the citizen (Manza & Uggen 2006, 127).

The formal denial to prisoners of all forms of political participation is the third aspect of these exclusionary dynamics. Because of this, they are excluded from the exercise of suffrage, which is the most fundamental expression of citizenship. This is crystallized by the widely accepted terminology in which public discourses about crime are framed: criminal justice is mean to protect citizens and the victims against crime and criminals. Such a distinction is codified in the very institutions of criminal law, internalized by the convicted subject, and replete with political significance, thanks to the loss of the right to suffrage.

In this way, when those who live in the most vulnerable areas of our community are criminalized, not only is their position of marginality, poverty and hopelessness confirmed, but they are also excluded from the enjoyment of civil, political and social rights. These rights, which are meant to grant them the status of free and equal member of our community, are denied to them in an effort that can only be described as an ongoing attempt at exclusion, affirming that these people are not truly citizens. The convicted prisoners are stripped of their rights as a demonstration of not being citizens, but invisible or worse, as enemies.

NOTES

This work was presented in the panel *New Studies on Citizenship in Chile: History, Actors and Theory*, in the Annual Conference of the Association of Latin American Studies (LASA), Lima, Peru, April 2017; in the seminar *Thinking about Prisons today: between the Democracy and the Market*, Universidad Austral de Chile, Valdivia, June 2017; and in the seminars *Citizenship and Disadvantaged Groups* held at the Diego Portales University (Santiago, April 2017) and the University of Valparaíso (Valparaíso, August 2017).

1. According to a survey conducted in 2012, 32. 8% of convicted inmates have applied for a benefit. Of these, only 8.7% are currently enjoying a permit. Convicted inmates have applied on average three times for benefits. However, inmates who enjoy some benefit applied more than four times on average (INDH 2013a, 141–2).

2. According to data from Gendarmería, 2,315 prisoners were released under the figure of parole in 2016. Of the total of people who obtained this benefit, 168 people have been convicted again, which represents a 7% of the total released; 131 entered to the closed system of imprisonment (prisons) and 37 entered to the open system (alternative sanctions) (Emol 2017).

3. Between the years 2010–2017, the Public Prosecutor's Office received 338 reports of rape or sexual abuse in prisons, the investigation of which was dropped in 70% of cases. In the same period, Gendarmería issued a document indicating that it had only 26 complaints, which are not part of any statistical trend, since the institution does not have a longitudinal record of this type of cases at the country level, nor does it have it disaggregated by prison. (*El Mercurio* 2017).

4. According to data from Gendarmería, up to October 31, 2015, of the total criminal population of the country (43,333 people) only 7% (3,014 people) were serving their sentences in this type of space (La Tercera 2016).

REFERENCES

Arriagada, Isabel, and Diego Rochow. 2015. "Privación de libertad en Chile: Desgobierno carcelario y afectación de derechos de la población penal." In *Informe Anual sobre Dere-*

chos Humanos en Chile 2015, edited by Centro de Derechos Humanos Universidad Diego Portales,161–207. Santiago, Ediciones Universidad Diego Portales.

Balibar, Ettiene. 2006. "Strangers as Enemies: further reflections on the aporias o transnational citizenship." Globalization working paper 06/4. Institute on Globalization and the Human Condition, McMaster University.

CIDH. 2011. *Informe sobre los derechos humanos de las personas privadas de libertad en las Américas*, 31 de diciembre 2011. Retrieved from: https://www.oas.org/es/cidh/ppl/docs/pdf/ppl2011esp.pdf [27.07.2017].

Cooper, Doris. 2002. *Criminología y delincuencia femenina*. Ed. Santiago: LOM.

Czajka, A. 2005. "Inclusive exclusion: citizenship and the American prisoner and prison," *Studies in Political Economy* 76:111–142.

Demleitner, N. 2000. "Continuing payment on one's debt to society: the German model of Felon disenfranchisement as an alternative." *Minnesota Law Review* 84:753–804.

Drake, D. H., and A. J. Henley. 2014. "'Victims' Versus 'Offenders' in British Political Discourse: The Construction of a False Dichotomy." *Howard Journal of Criminal Justice* 53, No. 2:141–157.

Edgely, M. 2010. "Criminals and (second-class) citizenship. Twenty-first century attainder?." *Griffith Law Review* 19, No. 3:403–437.

Espinoza, Olga, and Alicia Salinero. 2014. "Estudio jurídico. Chile." In *Ejecución de la pena privativa de libertad: una mirada comparada*. Madrid: Programa EUROsociAL.

Espinoza, Olga, and Carolina Viano. 2008. *El desafío de la libertad. Proceso de concesión de beneficios intrapenitenciarios para la reinserción social*. Santiago: RIL editors-CESC.

Foucault, Michel. 1995. *Discipline and Punish*. London: Penguin.

Gendarmería de Chile. 2014. *Informe de gestión 2014, Subdirección Técnica*. Santiago.

INDH. 2012. *Informe Anual de Derechos Humanos*. Santiago.

———. 2013a. *Informe Anual de Derechos Humanos*. Santiago.

———. 2013b. *Estudio de las Condiciones Carcelarias en Chile. Diagnóstico de cumplimiento de los estándares internacionales de los Derechos Humanos*, Santiago.

Kleinfeld, J. 2016. "Two cultures of punishment." *Stan. L. Rev.* 68: 933–1036.

LEASUR–Fundación 1367. 2016. *Mecanismo de prevención de la tortura sociedad civil. Informe de observación CIP San Joaquín/ CCP Colina II*. Santiago.

Manza, J., and Uggen, C. 2006. *Locked out: Felon disenfranchisement and American democracy*. New York: Oxford University Press.

Mañalich, J. P. 2011. "El derecho penitenciario entre ciudadanía y los derechos humanos." *Derecho y Humanidades* 18:163–178.

Mapelli, Borja. 2014. "Introducción." In *Ejecución de la pena privativa de libertad: una mirada comparada*. Madrid: Programa EUROsociAL.

Marshall, Pablo. 2010. "La pena y la ciudadanía: problemas constitucionales." In *Estudios Constitucionales*, edited by Cazor, Kamel, y Carolina Salas, 249–270. Santiago: Librotecnia.

Marshall, Pablo, and Diego Rochow. 2017. "El sufragio de las personas privadas de libertad. un análisis a partir de la sentencia rol n° 87743–16 de la corte suprema y sus antecedents." *Revista Chilena de Derecho* 45, No. 1: 233–54.

El Mercurio. 2017. "Las Cifras de las Violaciones en las Cárceles." *Revista Sábado*, July 15, 2017. Retrieved from: http://impresa.elmercurio.com/Pages/NewsDetail.aspx?dt=2017–07–15&dtB=20–08–2017%200:00:00&PaginaId=22&SupplementId=1&bodyid=0 [10.08.2017].

ONU. 2016. United Nations Standard Minimum Rules for the Treatment of Prisoners *(Nelson Mandela Rules)*.

Salinero, Alicia. 2007. *Los permisos de salida en la legislación chilena*. Santiago: Defensoría Nacional, Centro de Estudios y Proyectos.

Sánchez, Mauricio, and Diego Piñol. 2015. *Condiciones de vida de los centros de privación de libertad en Chile*. Santiago: Instituto de Asuntos Públicos, Universidad de Chile.

Sennett, Richard. 2000. *La corrosión del carácter. Las consecuencias personales del trabajo en el nuevo capitalismo*. Anagrama: Barcelona.

Taylor, C. 1998. "The dynamics of democratic exclusion." *Journal of Democracy* 9, no. 4:143–56.

La Tercera. 2016. "Un 7% de los reos está en centros de educación y trabajo de Gendarmería." *La Tercera*, February 3, 2016. Retrieved from: http://www2.latercera.com/noticia/un-7-de-los-reos-esta-en-centros-de-educacion-y-trabajo-de-gendarmeria/ [20.08.2017].

Chapter Eleven

The Worker by Himself

Thwarting Workers' Collective Action Through Law

José Luis Ugarte

This chapter will claim that the model entrenched in Chilean legislation to regulate labor relations has as its fundamental note the workers' collective lack of power to take part in the determination of their working conditions. This condition of total subordination, as will be explained, is substantially accounted for by the irrelevance of workers' collective actions, expressed in diverse restrictions on collective bargaining and on the right to strike.

THE POSTDICTATORIAL CONTINUITY OF THE LABOR RELATIONS MODEL OF THE DICTATORSHIP

In 1989, the platform of Patricio Aylwin, the centrist candidate who would become the first democratically elected President after 17 years of dictatorship, stated the following:

> Labor relations are an essential part of democracy. To the extent that they are fair, balanced and that they enable participation, the democratic system will be stable, finding consensual solutions for a sustained economic and social development shall be possible and there will be an effective basis for peace and reconciliation. Existing labor institutions do not satisfy these requirements of justice, equality and participation. Such institutions have placed workers in a severely vulnerable situation. They have hindered the establishment of a strong and representative trade union network, as well as the development of fair collective bargaining for labor representatives. Therefore, the social legitimacy necessary to harmonically regulate the relations between workers and employees in a future democratic regime cannot be expected to exist. (Coalición de Partidos por la Democracia 1989, p. 25)

More than 25 years later, oddly enough, the matter remains unchanged: no relevant reform has been made to modify those labor institutions that "have placed workers in a severely vulnerable position." These institutions correspond to the fundamental legal regulation imposed during the military dictatorship, the so-called 1979 Labor Plan, embodied in a set of dictatorial norms that, for obvious political reasons, did not take into account the opinion—much less the participation—of workers. These norms are Law Decree 2.756 on trade union organizations, Law Decree 2.758 on collective bargaining, and Law Decree 2.757 on business associations; after the enactment of the 1980 Constitution, these law decrees were amended by Statute 18.018 of 1981.

In a fundamental sense, therefore, the rules of the game regarding labor relations, particularly in the field of collective labor law, continue to be the same as those devised by the government of Pinochet. Although several reforms—such as the sub-contracting law or the recent labor reform—have been introduced during the years of return to democracy, they have been peripheral and do not modify the core of the labor problem: the lack of collective power of workers in Chile. From the point of view of the labor situation, this has been reflected in figures that are best appreciated with a historical perspective. In 1973, unionization rates reached their highest point in the history of Chile, reaching 34%. In 1991, right after Aylwin came to power, unionization reached a postdictatorial cap of 18%. Currently, almost 28 years after the reestablishment of democratic rule, only 14% of paid workers are affiliated to a trade union (Fundación Sol 2015, 5). And current coverage of collective bargaining barely includes 8% of workers (Fundación Sol 2015, 2). To use the terms of the electoral platform of the first democratic government itself, Chilean workers have today the same—or perhaps less?—justice, equality and participation than they had 30 years ago.

The weakness of this legal-labor model was already proven some time ago by the Organization for Economic Co-operation and Development (2009, 14) when it pointed out that "labor relations in Chile are generally confrontational and marked by lack of trust." The explanation that this organization offered to account for this high degree of conflicts in the Chilean labor model focuses on the limited coverage of trade unions and business associations; in addition to the low percentage of the workforce that is unionized, another problem is that it is concentrated in certain sectors, particularly in the mining sector where 42% of employees are unionized (Organization for Economic Co-operation and Development 2009, 14).

During her second term in office between 2014 and 2018, President Michelle Bachelet conducted the most recent attempt to try to pay the political debt with the workers, the labor reform enacted in 2016 as Statute 20.940. With the stated aim of "modernizing labor relations," it modified several rules that form part of the framework of collective labor relations. However, as we will see, such reform in no way implies significant changes to the logic of the 1979 Labor Plan, much less the creation of a labor relations model based in collective bargaining. In fact, as I will argue, the regulatory changes put forth by the government show a striking ideological continuity with the Labor Plan. Despite its moderate progress in such aspects as the elimination of the employer's right to replace workers on strike, Bachelet's labor reform did not imply a departure from the aversion to workers' collective action that inspired the Labor Plan. It merely got rid of the most embarrassing aspects from the international laws standards point of view. The Presidential Message attached to the bill that began the lawmaking process declared as one of its inspiring motivations the need to adapt our legislation to the principle of freedom of association embodied in Conventions 87 and 98 of the International Labor Organization, as well as the most important treaties on human rights. But in words of Gamonal (2016, 34), "the norms proposed in the project maintained the anti-union orientation of the Pinochet regime." The Chilean labor model, after more than two decades of governments led by center-left political parties, remains liable to the same criticisms leveled by those very same parties against the neoliberal dictatorship during the 1980s.

THE MODEL OF LABOR RELATIONS AS THE SOURCE OF THE COLLECTIVE WEAKNESS OF WORKERS

The Chilean labor model can be characterized succinctly as made out of four key aspects. In the first place, the core of labor law lies in the legal regulation of the individual work contract. Relatedly, collective bargaining and union action have no relevance in the configuration of labor relations. Securing these features, diverse restrictions to strikes and other forms of collective action prevent and punish the behavior of workers during conflicts. Finally, the protection of workers is not entrusted to the workers themselves through their union organizations, but to state apparatuses and procedures, specifically through the Labor Inspectorate.

The combination of the pieces mentioned results in a model that does not consider the participation of the workers, neither in the design nor in the execution of labor relations. Most Chilean workers do not take part in collective bargaining, with the result that their working conditions and their relation with the employer in terms of rights and duties is determined either by an abstract entity, the legislator, or by the unilateral imposition of the employer through individual contracting. Metaphorically speaking, workers find themselves dramatically on their own.

In order to adapt the existing model of labor relations to acceptable standards of protection of their dignity as persons and citizens, some basic conditions would have to be considered. Several labor rights defined in constitutional rules and in the international treaties in the field would have to be formally recognized and guaranteed. This is particularly true in the case of basic collective labor rights, such as collective bargaining and the right to strike. As we will see, the Chilean labor model does not adequately recognize these rights; rather, it thwarts the collective rights of the workers. As a result, a heteronomous, top-down, and legalistic labor model that restrains the participation of the workers themselves in the protection of their rights is established, hindering the progress of a balanced and democratic labor relations model.

THE MODEL OF LABOR RELATIONS AND THE RIGHTS OF WORKERS: RESTRICTIONS TO COLLECTIVE BARGAINING

What is the relevance of workers' collective action in the labor model enshrined in Chilean law?

Data leaves little room for doubts: regarding the coverage of collective bargaining, the highest point of attainment was registered in 1992 with 12% of coverage for paid workers. In 2013 it reached only 8.4% and in four regions of the country it is not over 5 % (Fundación Sol 2016, 7). At the beginning of democracy (1991) the figure was 11.7%. In other words, in the decades following the end of the military dictatorship and the return of democracy, the situation of workers organized collectively not only did not improve, but it got worse. In fact, compared to the other countries of the Organization for Economic Co-operation and Development (OECD), whose coverage rate of collective bargaining is around 60%, Chile appears as the one country among its members with the least number of workers supporting a collective instrument. It is worth mentioning that Chile is the only country in the OECD that set its collective bargaining norms and criteria during a dictatorship (Fundación Sol 2011).

The figures also show a pressing trade union weakness. Nationally, in 81.8% of the companies with 10 or more workers there has never been a union. This figure grows in the retail industry, where 90% of the companies with 10 or more workers never had a union (Fundación Sol 2016, 7). This weak capacity for collective action is not a strange piece in the labor model established by the Chilean laws. It is consistent with the labor relations model we have explained herein. And as we anticipated, this model is established on a strong aversion towards the normal repertory of workers' collective action; its fundamental commitment seems to be to stifle collective bargaining, freedom of association, and the right to strike.

At this point it is necessary to highlight the special meaning of collective bargaining, in that it establishes a basic right of workers included both in the Political Constitution of the Republic of 1980 (article 19 No. 16, section 5),

as well as in multiple international instruments ratified by Chile, such as the International Covenant on Economic, Social and Cultural Rights (article 7). At the same time, at the supranational level and in the strictly labor sphere, collective bargaining, particularly, and freedom of association, in general, have gained the value of internationally recognized fundamental rights, as clearly shown by the conventions of the International Labor Organization, numbers 87 on Freedom of Association (article 3) and 98 on Collective Bargaining (article 4). The right to strike, in turn, is an essential demonstration of freedom of association and is expressly acknowledged in article 8.1 letter d. of the International Covenant on Economic, Social and Cultural Rights (1976).

Well, as we will see, these rights—of collective bargaining and to strike—are subject to strong regulatory restrictions deriving from the legal regulations to which the Labor Plan subjected and continues to subject them nowadays.

The belief that underlies our labor model is simple: collective actions of workers must be minimized as an expression of conflict at work since it is considered a demonstration of class struggle. The words of the historical writer of the Labor Plan, José Piñera, Labor Minister of Augusto Pinochet, leave no room for doubts:

> the competition called by free economy is among companies, and in each company the employer and the worker share the same challenge. The new labor legislation hinders the attempts of the Marxist scheme of class struggle by refraining from dividing the productive structure of the country between those who are up above and those who are down below. In a social market economy the company must not be the stage for class struggle; the company is and should be a body of social integration. (Piñera 1990, 66)

The result was the establishment of a regulation of the collective labor phenomenon whose express aim was, and continues to be, the loss of centrality of union actions and the hindering of any chance of amassing collective power for workers. In order to achieve that objective, the Labor Plan used as its fundamental pillar the decentralization and over-regulation of collective bargaining assisted by a supporting pillar: taking away from workers the right to strike. On the basis of this narrow and biased notion of collective bargaining, and the evident minimization thereof as basic right, the legal model of labor relations constitutes a framework of strong restrictions to the collective self-protection of labor rights. In contrast with the fundamental place that collective bargaining receives as a basic right in a large number of democratic countries, the model of the Labor Plan assigned it a peripheral role in the regulation of working conditions.

In this way, workers are in no condition to challenge the rules that come from the legislator, and cannot supersede the individual autonomy of the parties which often reveals itself as nothing but the supremacy of the corporate will. The reason for this is simple: neither labor laws nor the individual contract have any intent on balancing capital and labor, but they merely aim at setting minimum working conditions that avoid socially unacceptable situations of exploitation. Collective bargaining alone has the intention of creating equality in labor relations, because it implies acknowledging collective conflict at work as a physiological—and not a pathological—fact of work relations. Collective bargaining is the crystallization of the power that arises from that collective conflict for workers. Hence, the Labor Plan sought to promote legislation and the individual work contract as the primary material sources of labor law while minimizing and discouraging the collective actions of workers.

The current Labor Code turns collective bargaining irrelevant in two ways. Firstly, it makes it inaccessible for most of the workers by setting it at the company level. Secondly, it subjects it to an over-regulation aimed at limiting both its development as well as its effects.

Level of Collective Bargaining

Comparative labor law offers no examples of countries where collective bargaining plays a relevant role and bargaining is centered in the company, the lowest level of the productive structure. Fully aware of this fact, the 1979 Labor Plan established a model of decentralized collective bargaining where the company is the only level of legal bargaining and there is no industry-wide bargaining. In fact, in its original version, collective bargaining above the level of the company was prohibited; Law 19.759 (2001) made it legal, but not compulsory for companies.

There is no doubt that constraining the scope of collective bargaining is the basic pillar upon which the Labor Plan was established. The result of such legal regulation is simply devastating for workers' collective rights: it results in the exclusion from collective bargaining of most of the paid workers in Chile, who work at companies of smaller sizes in which the legal chance to form a trade union does not even exist, since the law requires at least 8 workers from the company (article 227 of the Labor Code). Then, what does the basic right of collective bargaining, constitutionally acknowledged, mean to a significant part of Chilean workers? Nothing. No chance whatsoever exists for them to access its collective protection because they cannot even legally form a union, the only subject authorized to compel employers to collectively bargain in our legislation.

Regulation of Collective Bargaining: Procedure Restriction

An important pillar of the labor model is the obsessive and detailed regulation of collective bargaining with the evident purpose of suffocating regular labor relations. Therefore, the Labor Plan explicitly restricted the matters that may be subjects of collective bargaining; in this way, the legislator has placed aforehand a restriction to the social players, making it impossible for them to establish other matters of interest in the negotiation through their collective autonomy.

Although article 306 of the Labor Code was modified with the recent labor reform of Law No. 20.940, the legislation kept the most serious restriction regarding what can be collectively bargained. This article, as it currently stands, states that "those matters that are of common interest to the parties and that affect mutual relations between the workers and employers, especially those referred to the remuneration or other benefits in kind or money and, in general, all common working conditions, are matters of collective bargaining." However, it adds that "those matters that restrict or limit the power of the employer to organize, manage and administer the company and those external thereto shall not be object of collective bargaining."

As can be seen, Chilean law is concerned over the manner in which workers may try to participate in the government of work relations, setting management powers derived from property rights as an insurmountable barrier to the actions and the will of workers. This naturally compromises their freedom of association, as the Committee of Freedom of Association of the International Labor Organization (ILO) has repeatedly acknowledged, stating that the measures that are unilaterally applied by the authorities to restrict the range of issues that may be subject to bargaining are not compatible with Convention 98 on Collective Bargaining of the ILO that guarantees the breadth and autonomy of collective representatives in the matter. (International Labor Organization 2006, paragraph 912).

On the other hand, together with restricting the matters that can be the subject of collective bargaining, the Labor Plan sought to over-regulate workers' collective actions by establishing a rigid procedure in what is usually called *regulated collective bargaining*. The Labor Code continues up to this day to enclose collective bargaining through this *procedural corset*, to the point that it sets it as the *official* model of bargaining in two ways. Firstly, it is the only procedure for collective bargaining in Chilean legislation that is compulsory for the company. Secondly, it is the only way of collective bargaining that assigned warranties for the workers involved, particularly jurisdiction and strike.

What is the purpose of the procedural corset that constrains collective bargaining in the current Labor Code? Its sense is basically ideological. As we noted at the beginning, the underlying idea in this regulation is frontal aversion to conflict in labor relations, which accounts for its disciplining through a rigid procedure that ensures that conflict can be controlled either by the state or the employer himself.

The labor reform maintains the procedural over-regulation of collective bargaining. It could even be argued that it worsens it: new proceedings and stages that are densely regulated are created which make the already exaggerated regulation of the current Labor Code more complex. It is the case, for example, of the fixation of "minimum services" (article 360 of the Labor Code), which translates in the union duty of providing personnel during a bargaining procedure for the performance of certain basic functions in the firm that have been determined aforehand.

The Labor Model and the Restrictions on the Right to Strike

It is worth recalling that our own Constitution guarantees union autonomy (article 19 number 19). At the same time, Convention No. 87 of the ILO, in its article 3, guarantees that all trade union organizations have "the right to draw up their bylaws and administrative regulations, to choose freely their representatives, to organize their administration and their activities and to elaborate their action programs," adding that "the authorities must refrain from any intervention that might limit this right or that hinders its legal exercise." The logic of the Chilean labor relations model impinges on the exercise of these fundamental labor rights.

Firstly, the right to strike is an essential demonstration of freedom of association, amply acknowledged by the constitutional text, both in article 19 number 16 of the Constitution—that acknowledges the right to collectively bargain—and number 19—that embodies collective autonomy. Considering the international treaties subscribed and in force in Chile reinforces the foregoing since the right to strike is expressly acknowledged in article 8.1 letter d. of the International Covenant of Economic, Social and Cultural Rights (1979).

On the other hand, it must also be taken into consideration that the right to strike is an essential demonstration of freedom of association included in convention 87 of the ILO, international treaty of basic rights in force in Chile since 2000. Based on the foregoing, the Committee of Freedom of Association of the ILO has resolved that "the right to strike is one of the essential elements of union rights" (International Labor Organization 2006, 31).

The efficacy of the other labor rights largely depends on its efficacy. Therefore, in a recent decision, the Supreme Court affirms without hesitation that strikes are a fundamental right—of implicit acknowledgment in the Constitution and grounded in freedom of association—and attributed it a basic significance, as occurs in a large number of modern societies: "The dependents lack another pacific tool that can counterbalance the autonomy and power of property" (Judgment Role 3514/2014).

But this has not mattered at the time of setting legal rules on the matter. As the right to strike is considered the maximum demonstration of class conflict inside companies, the legislation of the dictatorship wanted to turn strikes into a completely inconsequential demonstration. Despite it being a basic right of workers, its legal regulation is more proper of an action that is considered unwelcome by the legislator, forcing workers to use it as the last resource within the framework of collective actions.

Our legal model of strikes shows an evident and poorly concealed aggressiveness towards the autonomy and self-protection of workers. This is why the strike is considered in the Chilean legal framework as nothing other than a stage within the regulated collective bargaining procedure, not as a fully fledged right. Labor law only legalizes strikes in the stage after direct bargaining among the parties has faltered and as a measure that can be taken only and exclusively in relation to a negotiation or renegotiation of a collective contract. And although the recent labor reform derogates one of the most aggressive rules against the right to strike originally included in labor laws of the dictatorship, the corporate power to replace workers during a strike, the result does not end up being a relevant progress. In fact, said progress—the prohibition to replace strikers (article 345 of the Labor Code)—is undermined by the insertion of several restrictions that undermine its effectiveness as basic right and that embody an approach that is ideologically hostile towards collective actions of workers.

Procedural Restrictions upon the Right to Strike

As with collective bargaining, one of the preferred ways to limit strikes is to submit them to a strict procedure. Our labor model sets an *over-regulation* of the exercise of the right to strike whose purpose is to exercise an obsessive control upon the itinerary of the strike aiming at reducing its disruptive potential. Such characteristic was fully kept in the recent labor reform, that continues with the characteristic of *proceduralization* of the decision to strike in the context of collective bargaining, subjecting it to a strict calendar set by law that determines the day when a vote on the strike must be called, the day when voting must be carried out and even the day when the strike must be made effective. In fact, not only is this procedure maintained, but also, new stages are added, such as the fixation of minimum services, forced mediation, and arbitration in cases were the strike does not obtain absolute majority among the workers.

With regard to the procedure that workers have to go through in order to strike, the following rules are especially restrictive upon the exercise of the right to strike:

Absolute Majority as Quorum to Approve the Strike

Article 350 Labor Code now requires an absolute majority among union members to approve the strike. In this regard, the ILO Committee of Freedom of Association has established that it may be difficult to reach an absolute majority in a declaration of a strike from the workers, particularly in those unions that group a large number of affiliates; therefore, provisions of this kind entail a significant risk of limitation to the right to strike (Gamonal 2011, 392).

The Term of Execution of a Strike

The law sets a waiting period of five days between the declaration of strike and the possibility of making the strike effective. It is a term that has no reasonable justification and that undermines the idea of the strike as a demonstration of the autonomy of the workers, that includes the fact of deciding when the strike will become effective.

Forced Mediation of the Labor Inspectorate

In the recent labor reform, the administrative process called "good offices" changed its name to "forced mediation." Any of the parties, within the term of four days following the approval of the strike, may compel the other to be subjected to mediation by the Labor Inspectorate, which compulsorily lasts 5 days. During this period, the strike is suspended. It is a rule that affects union autonomy since the workers have already decided to go on strike, and the laws allow the employer to suspend its implementation for 5 days unilaterally. Why can the exercise of a basic right of workers be suspended by the sole will of the employer? Why do workers have to involuntarily wait for over nine days, between the days set to make the strike effective and the forced mediation, to exercise a basic right? That total period represents a significant delay of the effects of a decision to exercise the right to strike and allows the employer to adopt retaliation and manage the loss of economic efficacy that the strike implies.

Needless to say, such long forced wait to exercise the right to strike does not abide by the international criteria set by the ILO with respect to settlement and mediation, procedures that must have "the sole purpose of facilitating bargaining" and thus "should not be so complex or slow that a lawful strike becomes impossible in practice or loses its effectiveness" (Gernigon et al. 2000, 26).

Restrictions upon the Right to Strike by Way of "Universal Minimum Services"

The recent labor reform has incorporated a new limitation to the right to strike:

> the union bargaining commission is bound to provide the necessary personnel during the strike in order to comply with the minimum services needed by the company that allow caring for its essential operations to avoid effective and irreversible damages to material property, the facilities or infrastructure thereof or that cause severe damage to the environment or a health damage to the users of an assistance or health establishment. (Labor Code, article 361)

As a starting point, this rule results in a relevant concept confusion. In comparative labor law, minimum services constitute a legitimate limitation to the right to strike only to the extent that the right to strike conflicts with basic rights of third parties, i.e., the public. In these exceptional circumstances, the solution is to maintain a certain degree of performance of work so as not to affect fundamental rights that do not belong to the employer. Minimum services are a limiting technique to the right to strike that seeks to resolve conflicts between the strike and the basic rights of third parties and whose basic characteristic is to operate a priori—before the strike occurs—and in abstract—restricting all strikes. The recent labor reform to the Chilean laws does not follow this model; it applies the technique of minimum services to compensate the *excess damage* that the strike can cause on the economic interests of the employer, that is, a problem that requires a specific solution—for certain strikes—and a posteriori, when the strike has become effective, establishing a preference of the right of property based on some sort of *speculative damage*. How can the effective and irreversible damage caused by the strike on *tangible property* of the company be known beforehand and with certainty?

Unlike what is proposed by the new legal rule, the situation of a strike that produces a damage that is considered illegal on the property or the facilities of the employer must be resolved through the application of civil or criminal rules of responsibility, not through a labor rule that gives a preference in the abstract and aprioristically to the right of property over the right to strike.

It could always be argued that the labor reform establishes express causes to determine the grounds for establishing *minimum services* and therefore that their use by the companies will be restricted. In this regard, it is possible to point out that the relevant clauses are quite ample and lend themselves to an expansive interpretation: they protect the "material property, facilities or infrastructure" of the company, damages "to the environment" or the "health of the users." In this sense, the use of this limitation to strike is potentially universal: any company may request it, with no exclusion whatsoever, whether it performs an essential productive activity for the protection of the rights of third parties or not. In the cases where minimum services set by the authority are used, the strike will not be the autonomous exercise of an effective basic right, but of a right decreased in favor of the positions of the employer. In those cases, it is not preposterous to say that the replacement of strikers is still in force, but now under the name of minimum services.

Needless to say, the rule proposed violates the doctrine of the ILO on minimum services. According to the ILO, "the establishment of such minimum services in case of a strike should only be possible when the interruption of those services may put at risk the life, security or health of the person in the entire or part of the population (*essential services* in the strict sense of the term); when the strike among non-essential services, in its strict sense, are of such extension and duration so as to provoke a situation of *acute national crisis* where the normal conditions of existence of the population may be compromised, and they are *public services of paramount importance"* (Gernigon et al. 2000, 31).

Restriction upon the Right to Strike by Way of Resumption of Works

As if the foregoing limitation was not enough, in an inexplicable decision, the labor reform of Statute No. 20.940 modifies a rule of the current Labor Code that had not been applied since the return to democracy. Article 364, as amended, establishes that "in case a strike or lockout that, given its characteristics, timing or duration, causes severe damage to public health, the provision of goods or services to the population, the country's economy or national security, the respective Labor Court may decree the resumption of works, prior request by the party."

With this rule, the application of the so-called "resumption of works" is given actual efficacy, which translates into a new and significant limitation to the right to strike. The way chosen to make this rule operative is to transfer its application from the jurisdiction of the President of the Republic to that of lower labor courts. As it is easy to see, it seems reasonable to reserve such a relevant decision to the highest political authority, since it entails a global evaluation of damage to the population, sole reason that would justify such a severe limitation to the right to strike. Now, a decision of the highest political responsibility—such as that of the resumption of works by political reasons—is transferred to labor judges without a relevant justification. And at the same time, procedural action to request it is granted to the employer himself.

A perfect circle against strikes is closed: it can be limited by the request of the company, and since the President of the Republic has been removed from the decision to suppress the strike, nobody remains accountable politically for such severe damage to the right to strike. Additionally, the fact that the causes that would enable "resumption of works" are especially vague, such as "severe damage to the services of the population" or to the "country's economy" or "to national security," this will lead to litigation to a number of relevant strikes, especially those of national scope, leaving the unions subjected to such vague and controversial causes.

Restriction to the Right to Strike Through the Sanction of "Abuse"

The recent labor reform establishes as an anti-union practice to use union rights or the litigation procedures of the Code "in bad faith or in abuse of right" (article 290 letter f).

Strikes are a union right, under the terms regularly used in labor law. In this way, it can be deemed that its abuse constitutes an illegal conduct, which would turn this rule into a new limitation to the right to strike. It is obvious that the idea of abuse of the right to strike does not only imply subjecting the collective action of workers to an open and essentially vague criterion. The law gives no indication of how this broad concept should be interpreted, but it will generate another space of judicializing the collective action of workers.

In case the strike is considered an "abusive strike," the consequences for the workers might be significant: the strike would become illegal and, therefore, its immediate end must be ordered, the fines provided for due to unfair practices of collective bargaining notwithstanding. Furthermore, it may also constitute a crime as the model of "collective interruption or suspension, stoppage or strike" is criminalized, included in law 12.957 dated 1958, on National Security of the State (Rojas 2007, p. 208). In this respect, the Commission of Experts of the ILO has pointed out to the Government of Chile that "workers and their organizations must be able to demonstrate with ample scope, if necessary, their possible discontent on economic and social matters related to the interests of their members" (ILO, 2006, p. 117). And adds that "the prohibition of any strike not related to a collective conflict in which the workers or the union is a part, contradicts the principles of freedom of association" (ILO, 2006, p.118).

A Model of Democratic Labor Relations Looking into the Future: Collective Bargaining

Lastly, it is worth mentioning shortly, the political and social sense of a transformation in the future Chilean labor model and the relevance of it being elaborated from collective bargaining.

In collective bargaining, convening diverse traditions of social thought is possible. This makes possible to justify it as the ideal way to order labor relations in modern societies. The most classical one, and in this sense the most obvious one, is the one established from legal labor theory: collective bargaining strengthens the exercise of labor rights through the self-protection of workers themselves. Less obvious is the ethical basis that stems from social theory: collective bargaining is part of distributive justice efforts made by capitalist societies in the form of economic and social rights. And lastly, the strictly political grounds: the collective labor phenomenon significantly improves participation and debate in a democratic society.

In this sense, there are good egalitarian reasons to sustain a closed defense of collective bargaining as a model of labor relations: it is a powerful instrument, not only to materialize legal equality (overcoming the weakness of the individual worker), but also for material equality (it helps distribute more equally the minimum property for a decent existence, socially speaking), and specially, for political equality (endowing a sector that is specially weak inside the democratic political system with complexity and political visibility).

Finally, the weakness of the worker is therefore expressed in an inequality in several dimensions: as contractor, as social subject and as a citizen. The reasons that justify collective bargaining as founding principle of an alternative labor model for Chilean laws precisely answer all those dimensions of inequality affecting workers.

REFERENCES

Coalición de Partidos por la Democracia. 1989. *Programa de gobierno de Patricio Aylwin*. Santiago, Editorial Publiley.

Fundación Sol. 2011. Negociación colectiva de alta cobertura: una herramienta poderosa contra la desigualdad. Santiago.

Fundación Sol. 2015. Sindicatos y negociación colectiva. Santiago.

Fundación Sol. 2016. Sindicatos Pulverizados. Panorama Actual y Reflexiones para la Transformación. Santiago.

Gamonal, Sergio. 2011. *Derecho Colectivo del Trabajo*. Santiago, Legal Publishing.

Gamonal, Sergio. 2016. "La reforma laboral, la Constitución y la libertad sindical," in *Reforma al Derecho Colectivo del Trabajo*. Thomson Reuters, Santiago.

Gernigon, Bernard, Alberto Odero and Horacio Guido. 2000. ILO Principles concerning the Right to Strike. International Labor Office, Geneva.

International Labor Organization. 2006. La libertad sindical Recopilación de decisiones y principios del Comité de Libertad Sindical del Consejo de Administración de la OIT. Geneva.

Organisation for Economic Co-operation and Development. 2009. Evaluaciones y Recomendaciones. Paris.

Piñera, José. 1990. *Revolución Laboral*. Zig-Zag, Santiago.

Rojas, Irene. 2007. "Las reformas laborales al modelo normativo de negociación colectiva del plan laboral." *Ius et Praxis*, vol. 13, pp. 195–221.

Index

About the Editor

Pablo Marshall is associate professor of law at Universidad Austral de Chile. He holds a PhD in Law from the University of Glasgow. He is also Chief Editor of the journal *Derecho y Crítica Social*. His scholarly interests focus around political participation, critical constitutional theory, human rights, social inclusion and mental disability. He has authored *Derecho Constitucional* with Fernando Muñoz (2015) and articles on issues such in political theory, constitutional theory and human rights.

About the Contributors

Jaime Bassa is Professor of Law at the Universidad de Valparaíso, Chile. He holds a PhD in Law from the University of Barcelona and Masters on Public Law from Universidad de Chile and on Philosophy from Universidad de Valparaíso. He has authored *Elementos para una teoría constitucional democrática* (2014), edited *La Constitución chilena. Una revisión crítica a su práctica política* (2015), and published several articles on fundamental rights and constitutional theory. He is researcher of the *Interdisciplinary Centre of Social Theory and Subjectivity* at Universidad de Valparaíso.

Paula Hollstein is MSc in Philosophy and Public Policy, University of London (London School of Economics & Political Science) and LLM candidate with specialization in Human Rights, University of London (University College). Her interests focus on gender legal theory, violence, memory, and human rights.

Paz Irarrázabal is a PhD candidate in Law at the University of London (King's College). She holds a LLM from University of London (London School of Economics & Political Science). Her research interests are related to political theory and criminology.

Pablo Marshall is Associate Professor of Law at Universidad Austral de Chile. He holds a PhD in Law from the University of Glasgow. He is also Chief Editor of the journal *Derecho y Crítica Social*. His scholarly interests focus around political participation, critical constitutional theory, human rights, social inclusion and mental disability. He has authored *Derecho Constitucional* with Fernando Muñoz (2015) and authored articles on issues such as political theory, constitutional theory and human rights.

Matías Meza-Lopehandía is Researcher at Library of National Congress (Chile). He is also Lecturer at Pontificia Universidad Católica of Valparaíso. He holds a MSc in Human Rights from the University of London (London School of Economics & Political Science). He co-authored *Los pueblos indígenas y el derecho* (2013). His research interests focus mainly on indigenous people's rights, human rights law and Third World Approaches to International Law (TWAIL).

Carla Moscoso holds an MPhil in Modern Societies and Global Transformations from the University of Cambridge and is a PhD Candidate in Sociology in the same university. Her research interests related to political theory, media and democracy, and human rights. Her academic specialization focus on the social impact of the media and their effects in the constitution of democracy and citizenship in developing countries, with a special focus on Latin America.

Fernando Muñoz is Associate Professor of Law at Universidad Austral de Chile. He holds a JSD from Yale Law School and is a PhD Candidate in History at Universidad de Chile. He has published articles on constitutional theory, legal history, and discrimination law, and is the author of *Hegemonía y Nueva Constitución* (2016). His current research deals with the history of the constitutional state from the perspective of ideological and political conflict between workers and capitalists.

Paula Nuño is Instructor of Law at the Universidad de Chile. She holds a LLM from University of London (University College)

Fernanda Torres is a PhD Student in Law at the Universidad de Valparaíso. She holds a Master of Public Litigation and public politics in Chile. She was Head of Nationalitiy of Inmigration Departarment and regional head of Human Rights Institute in Antofagasta, Chile. Her interests focus on migration, refugges, stateless people, human trafficking and smuggling people.

José Luis Ugarte is Professor of Law at the Universidad Diego Portales. He holds a PhD in Law from the Universidad de Salamanca. He has authored *Derecho del Trabajo: invención, teoría y crítica* (2015). He has published articles on fundamental rights, labor law and strike.

Ximena Valencia is an MSc candidate in Gender, Development and Globalisation at the University of London (London School of Economics & Political Science). Her interests focus on feminist legal theory, postcolonial theory, queer theory and Labour law.

Luis Villavicencio is Professor of Law at the Universidad de Valparaíso. He holds a PhD in Law from the Universidad Autónoma de Madrid. He is Chief Editor of the journal *Anuario de Filosofía Jurídica y Social.* His research interests are the communitarian, multiculturalism and feminist critiques of the liberal conception of citizenship. He has authored *Las críticas comunitaristas al liberalismo igualitario. Un balance* (2014) and published articles on political philosophy, constitutional theory and human rights.

Lieta Vivaldi is a PhD Candidate in Sociology at the University of London (Goldsmiths). Her research interests include: feminist theory, social movements, human rights, critical theory, queer theory and gender. She has published different articles related with these issues, mainly about reproductive rights, activism and abortion. The title of her PhD thesis is "Abortion in Chile: Bio-politics and Contemporary Feminist Resistance."

Yanira Zúñiga is Associate Professor of Law at the Universidad Austral de Chile. She holds a PhD in Human Rights from the Universidad Carlos III (Madrid). She has published extensively on gender and human rights, including work on women's political participation and sexual and reproductive rights.

www.ingramcontent.com/pod-product-compliance
Ingram Content Group UK Ltd.
Pitfield, Milton Keynes, MK11 3LW, UK
UKHW041630031026
15587UKWH00001B/186

9 781498 563147